Hollywood and the Box Office, 1895–1986

John Izod

Head, Department of Film and Media Studies
University of Stirling

MACMILLAN

First published 1988

Published by
THE MACMILLAN PRESS LTD
Houndmills, Basingstoke, Hampshire RG21 2XS
and London
Companies and representatives
throughout the world

Typeset by
Wessex Typesetters
(Division of The Eastern Press Ltd)
Frome, Somerset

British Library Cataloguing in Publication Data
Izod, John
Hollywood and the box office, 1895–1986.
1. Moving-picture industry—California
—Los Angeles—History 2. Hollywood
(Los Angeles, Calif.)—Industries—
History 3. Los Angeles (Calif.)—
Industries—History
I. Title
384'.8'0979494   PN1993.5.U65
ISBN 0–333–38466–0 (hardcover)
ISBN 0–333–46123–1 (paperback)

Printed and bound 1994
in Great Britain by
Antony Rowe Ltd, Chippenham, Wiltshire

For my parents
Alan and Olive Izod,
honour and love

Contents

Acknowledgement

An extract from Chapter 12 has been published as 'Walt Disney Innovates the Television Showcase', in *The AMES Journal*, 2 (1985). The author and publishers are grateful to *The AMES Journal* for permission to reprint here.

Introduction

Profits have always, from the earliest days, been the primary objective of the American film industry. However it may appear from outside, Hollywood has always been first and foremost a business; and although occasional exceptions have been made for movies that were thought likely to enhance a studio's corporate image, few films are released in the certain knowledge that they will lose money. This is not to say that all American features do make profit – but almost all are intended to do so.

This fact has consequences. Broadly it means that production companies cannot simply make the films their writers, directors and producers want to, without regard for the market into which they will be released. They have to try to produce features that large numbers of people either already want to see, or can be tempted to see. As every hopeful scriptwriter knows, this is a double constraint. Not only are there limits at any given time to the popular desires of the movie-going public, but in their interpretation of what those desires may be, executives in charge of production are likely to err towards caution. In general they prefer, rather than new, untested ideas, to approve for production a movie that resembles others for which the public has already shown a liking.

Nonetheless innovation does take place, and sometimes it is led by a single film. For example, a proposed movie may develop a style, an idea or a plot which is at least partly unfamiliar, and which marketing agents believe they can sell to audiences. Paramount's enthusiastic promotion of *The Godfather* (1971) illustrates such a case. The film broke new narrative ground both by portraying its gangster heroes as sympathetic figures, and by making their history a part of the epic of modern America's founding. But it is worth noting that the movie was also in line with certain developments in the movie business, in that it extended the concept of the blockbuster to new dimensions. It cost a fortune, ran for three hours, and was sold as something more than a feature film: it was an event.

It is on this kind of business-led innovation that this book concentrates. Often such innovation comes about not through a single film but through an attempt to reorganise the market. Typically in such a case, one or a number of companies in the industry try to increase their share of business by promoting an idea or a technique which their rivals do not use. This can be done by launching a new kind of film (the feature was introduced to the North American market by only one sector of the industry in the 1910s). Alternatively the innovation of new technology may give smaller companies the means to challenge larger ones for a share in control of the market (as happened when two medium-sized companies introduced the sound film). Such innovations not infrequently contribute (on occasion lead directly) to changes in the films which the industry routinely releases. As we shall see, there has been a surprising number of such developments. Hardly a decade has passed since the foundation of the film business in which it has not undergone upheaval. Much of that disturbance has its roots in competition to take greater profits from one or a number of arms of the entertainment industry.

This study takes a general approach to the changes brought to American films by commercial circumstances, and it does so for a number of reasons. In the first place, even granted their weighty influence, business considerations comprise only one determinant among many upon the individual film. That influence can often be more clearly identified in a cycle of films than in a single instance.

Secondly, the nature of the statistical evidence admitted by the industry makes it unreliable. Because of this the quotation of figures has been limited as far as possible to illustrating changes or trends. To take just one example of unreliability: one source quotes the year's total domestic admissions for 1960 as 1304 million people, declining to 1024 million in 1964. Gross takings are said to have declined from $948 million in 1960 to $874 million in 1962 before returning to their former level at $947 million in 1964. However, a second source gives weekly admissions of 40 million people in 1960, rising to 44 million by 1964. That implies an audience of 2 billion rising to more than 2¼ billion. But this same source shows takings as having declined from 1960 ($951 million) to 1964 ($913 million). The logic of these figures is that in 1964 people in the audience reported by the first writer paid on average 90 cents for admission, while those described by the second paid no more than 40 cents. Yet this same historian quotes an average ticket price of 92 cents for that year.

The point is that a disparity of this kind arises from more than the plain carelessness of the second writer. Many of the reported figures are suspect. In some cases, as with the weekly admissions figures quoted above, although they are said to come from the US Bureau of Census, they appear simply to be wrong. Then too, certain practices have allegedly long been widespread in Hollywood. For example, much 'creative accounting' is said to take place. One temptation for members of the industry is that in some circumstances showing business as better than it really is may boost the confidence of shareholders or trading partners. On other occasions, particularly when it comes to dividing profits with those who have a right to share in them, there will be advantage in showing reduced income and enhanced overheads.

The final reason for making this a generalised study is that it is a survey history. As such it does not refer directly to the primary evidence – company records, legal documents, publicity material, the records and reports of participants and immediate observers – from which are constructed accounts argued in fine detail concerning particular aspects of the industry (for example, the innovation of a new technique, the operations of a single company, or the impact of specific circumstances in society). The survey history makes use where they exist of these detailed studies as a substantial part of its evidence. It has, however, to sacrifice their attention to minute evidence in order to make space for a long view of the ninety years of business activity within the industry.

During the past fifteen years scholars of the American film business have rewritten significant sections of its industrial history, bringing into play both new evidence and more reliable methods than their predecessors used. But these new writings have, with few exceptions, not been absorbed into the wider context of a survey history. The main use of such a history is to introduce an unfamiliar subject. Since the concept that movies are produced by a highly organised and sophisticated industry is still barely more than half-formed both among general readers and students enrolled in formal courses, that is what this book seeks to do.

A word of caution about the nature of the survey history may be helpful. Because it covers a wide span of time, such a history can appear to claim both completeness and objectivity. In actuality (although the responsible historian will want to make the work as accurate as possible) modern historiography teaches that it can have neither of these qualities in any simple sense. The survey history is by its nature highly selective. It presents arguments and data in summary form, often chosen because they seem to the writer to indicate large-scale changes. It does this at the necessary expense of omitting or glossing over a great deal of detailed material. In this, however, it is not radically different from the work of other historians, all of whom must evaluate and interpret the information they obtain. All history is in part subjective, being shaped by the values of both the writer and the anticipated reader. The survey history, which extrapolates its information from the work of other historians rather than from original data, is doubly subjective.

JOHN IZOD

1 Inventions and Patents, 1895–99

Traditionally a good deal of writing on the early history of cinema devoted itself to the search for the individual who first managed to screen films. Such a quest for the source of cinema is delusory, not so much because it is impossible to come up with names and dates as because the romantic search for the one true originator of the movies leads us to think of the new industry in the wrong way. For the significant factor about the beginning of the industry is that it developed from competitive industrial technology rather than the inspiration of a genius.

From about 1890, inventors in at least four countries – America, Britain, France and Germany – were competing in the effort to make the first motion picture cameras and projectors.[1] Furthermore they knew that they were in competition, and that they intended to make money from the equipment they hoped to develop. The evidence for their shrewdness in business matters lies in the promptness with which most of the successful inventors patented their discoveries, and scrutinised each others' patents for possible loopholes. For example, Edison's uncharacteristic indifference to patenting his Kinetoscope internationally allowed Robert W. Paul to duplicate it in London.[2]

Contrary to myth, the work of invention was not carried out by lonely geniuses. Although Thomas Edison is credited with the development of both the motion picture camera and projector in America, in fact he did very little work on either machine, delegating much of it to employees, and buying up the rights to other inventions as he needed them. In short he concerned himself with the business exploitation of the inventions. For example in 1891 an Edison employee, William Dickson, discovered a means of recording a succession of pictures on a strip of celluloid, and of moving the strip through the camera so that it stopped intermittently behind the lens for the registering of the images. Edison's contribution seems to have been confined to applying for the patents on these devices (which were granted in 1893).[3] A couple of years later he managed to persuade another inventor, Thomas Armat, who had developed an operable projector with a satisfactory stop-motion mechanism,

1

that it should be marketed under the Edison name – and in this instance too Edison secured both the patents and the profits.[4] Thus the actual inventors allowed their rights to accrue to their employer, who was to benefit massively from them. The question arises of course whether the inventors themselves would have known how to exploit what they had created without Edison's business sense to guide the project. The energy with which he set about exploiting the motion picture equipment that he began to market in 1896 is confirmed by his initiation as early as 1897 of a series of lawsuits to protect his patents in the camera.[5] Ironically he had initially been slow to appreciate the market potential of the moving picture. Once he realised just how great it was, he worked at securing the best returns he could get from it. Such pooling of inventive skills and of marketing techniques is typical of a certain kind of small nineteenth-century business operation innovating industrial technology.

To concentrate for a moment at the beginning of our history on the equipment rather than on the films themselves is more appropriate than it might at first seem. For this is what the manufacturers themselves did. They entered the business to sell equipment because it appeared to them that profits lay in that side of the motion picture business. They moved into production of films only in order to supply their customers with something to show on the equipment they had purchased; but this was not their first interest. A few years later this would have seemed a strange attitude, when fortunes were being made from the films themselves, but it has to be remembered that cinema did not spring fully perfected into being at the completion of a single invention. It was achieved as a consequence of a whole string of developments essential to its establishment, and it had been immediately preceded by the Kinetoscope.

The Kinetoscope, which Dickson had developed for Edison, had all the characteristics of the earliest cinema except one. It had a photographically registered moving image, but no device for stopping the movement of the film long enough for light to be shone through it on to a screen. Consequently the Kinetoscope was limited to playing to one individual at a time, the viewer peering into an eyepiece in a large standing box. This arrangement meant that every customer had to look into a separate machine to see the moving image; and as a consequence operators of the amusement arcades for which they were intended had to run a number of machines to satisfy demand. The idea that provision of equipment would be an endlessly profitable business seems to have originated here, and to have stuck.

It is convenient to date the arrival of the cinema from the perfection of the projection process, which of course made it possible to show images on a large screen to a room full of people. Credit for winning that race, though the result is still disputed, usually goes to the Lumière brothers for their Paris screening in December 1895. Whoever got there first, Edison joined their number in April 1896. Nobody missed the point that the screen changed the nature of the business entirely because it enabled the operator to admit considerable numbers of people to each screening, using just one machine. This opened the way for the exhibitor to increase his revenue substantially, and a number of entrepreneurs at once began to work out how best to do so: from its earliest days the motion picture industry in America was in the hands of businessmen and corporations whose survival depended on the making of profit.

Following the first demonstration in April 1896 to a music hall audience of the machine Edison called his Vitascope, a vaudeville theatre chain, the Keith Theatre Circuit, decided to install moving picture projectors to provide one of the attractions in their houses. This was an event of major significance for the motion picture in America. The circuit was well respected in the entertainment industry, and other vaudeville managers quickly recognised that to compete they too would need to include moving pictures as part of their programmes.[6] Their decision brought films to the attention of a far wider audience than they might otherwise have had if screenings had been confined to amusement arcades. As Allen says, movies soon proved to be the single most popular act in vaudeville. In return vaudeville provided movies with a weekly audience of a million or more entertainment seekers. Equally important, it offered a tradition from which films lifted several generic forms, including such visual novelties as living pictures, magical illusions and magic lantern shows.[7]

Another aspect of the Keith Theatre decision needs to be remarked on. They chose to install the French projector manufactured by the Lumière company because, unlike Edison's machine, it could operate independently of local municipal power supplies, which were not as yet standardised. Thus the Lumière machine could be readily toured as a vaudeville act. The Keith Theatre choice thus signalled the beginnings of bitter rivalry between equipment manufacturers because the projectors marketed by the various firms were, in the first years of the industry, incompatible and unable to take film supplied for other companies' projectors. This state of affairs arose not by accident but partly as a means of avoiding the infringement of other firms' patents, and partly, as still happens today, as a means of tying the customer to the company from whom he bought his first piece of equipment.[8] For this is what occurred. Willing to sell as many projectors as they could, manufacturers attempted for a while to prevent altogether the sale of cameras so that each new exhibitor had to turn to them for material to screen. Thus manufacturers looked for continuing profit after the sale of a projector from the regular sale of films, over the production of which they attempted to keep a monopolistic control. Small wonder that from the start the inventing companies went repeatedly to law to protect their rights on patents to cameras. Edison (the most litigious company of all) began to pursue with vigour from December 1897 almost every firm or individual that had entered the business of film production.[9] Exhibitors for their part had in the early years very little choice but to screen the films with which the manufacturer supplied them. They had to buy prints, and then had the right to screen them as often as they could before wear and tear rendered them indecipherable. The requirement to purchase prints continued even after the equipment of competing manufacturers was made compatible.

Faced with such complications, many vaudeville houses contracted with outside firms to supply as an act a complete package with films, projector and projectionist. The house merely paid the act's salary, and did not have to trouble itself with the ordering of fresh programmes. The contracting firm cycled films among its clients and thus amortised its investment in them. And the vaudeville house was protected from having to write off an expensive capital investment if its audiences lost interest in the photoplay.[10]

During the first years of production, films were simply as long as the piece of celluloid upon which they were photographed – about 50 feet. Ten or twelve of these films would be shown as a vaudeville turn lasting about 15 minutes.[11] But what were the films themselves like? They were, quite simply, marvels. Or at least that is the way they appeared to their audiences, and their willingness to admire them as such explains a great deal about the lackadaisical attitude of producers. At a time when audiences would pay to think wonderful anything that reached the screen, simply because it moved, it was hardly necessary for a producer to trouble about the film's quality.

Since the important thing to audiences was that films succeeded in capturing the moving image, actualities were popular as subjects. Trains arriving at stations, pictures of the sea, people at work, all seemed marvellous at first. However, after the first pleasures of novelty had worn off, audiences found it more exciting to experience that with which they were not familiar. Then scenes of exotic places, minute dramatic incidents, and scenes from other forms of entertainment – of dancers and acrobats in particular – became attractive.[12]

In its first years in America the new medium continued to exist for the most part as a kind of parasite upon the older vaudeville theatre, whose prestige and audiences it needed for its launch. Kristin Thompson remarks that the economic dependence of the early film on vaudeville helped determine its formal norms and genres. These necessarily short films were modelled largely on types of stage acts: the variety, the fictional narrative, the scenic (views of interesting locales), the topical and the trick piece all became films.[13] Producers believed they could entertain audiences with such films after enthusiasm for the novelty of movement had worn off. All were designed to meet proven appetites of the vaudeville audience; and their advertising emphasised their subject-matter.[14]

In particular the 1898 declaration of war against Spain over Cuba precipitated the motion picture into new prominence in the ensuing war fever. Robert Allen argues that both the Cuban and the Philippine campaigns had immediate visual appeal. The movies appeared (some of them were notorious cheats) to give patrons a picture of action in these exotic locations, something newspapers could not do; and war films became a big attraction. In more peaceful times actuality films appealed greatly, with footage of disasters competing with films of local events in which members of the audience could hope to see themselves on screen.[15]

All the same it could not have seemed to vaudeville managers that films, limited by very tight technical constraints on length, could prove any kind of threat to their livelihood. This was simply a new kind of variety turn. But although vaudeville gave the American cinema its first home, it also tended to select – by the cost of admission and the length of its programmes – the cinema's earliest audiences. According to Sklar tickets cost around 25 cents apiece. This was too much, when added to the price of transport to the city centre, for the working man to be able regularly to treat his family to this kind of entertainment. In addition programmes were long and meant an unacceptable loss of sleep to working people who, about the turn of the century, had to put in an 11 or 12 hour day at their employment. For these reasons vaudeville was largely patronised by the middle classes.[16] There were some amusement arcades that screened films, and these would have been more accessible to working people. They were not, however, sufficient in number for it to be possible to describe film-going as a mass entertainment in the years from its inception to about 1903.

This position was the more pronounced in that small towns and rural areas tended to have none of these facilities. People there had to await the travelling picture showman. His visits, since he brought the only moving pictures these places saw in the early years, made him such a magical figure that he, rather than the films or their producers, featured largest in the touring show bills.[17] Only the advent of the nickelodeon brought permanent movie houses to rural America.

2 Nickelodeons and Narrative, 1900–8

By the year 1900 the best films screened in the United States were not made by an American at all, though many in the audience would probably not have known it. Georges Méliès's films were so popular that the exhibitor who wanted to attract a large audience inevitably wished to screen them. Demand was so great that it led, for the first time in the fledgling industry, to massive piracy. American manufacturers eager to get in on the profits simply bought copies of his films, duplicated them illicitly, and sold them under new titles as their own.[1] The merciless leeching of his profits was so severe that ultimately, combined with Méliès's reluctance to adapt to changing patterns of film-making, it brought a remarkable career to a painfully early end.

When his films are compared with the work of his contemporaries, their popularity can readily be understood. Other films still relied on methods that had been devised five years earlier for recording a subject: the camera was placed in front of a scene, or a small event was choreographed to happen in front of the lens. The camera was cranked until the film ran out, and that was it. The main change was that from 1900 the length of films began to increase fairly rapidly from the very tight limits within which they had previously been confined. By 1903–4, while Méliès's output and craft were still at their peak, longer films ran for about 10 minutes (or one reel). This became standard for most of the next decade, and it made possible the telling of short narratives, something that had been very hard to do in only a minute or two. Méliès took advantage of this new freedom, and his story films string together a succession of static scenes each of which might run as long as an entire film had done a few years earlier.

From the beginning Méliès occupied himself, suitably for a man who was a magician, with inventing trickery: his films were full of witty invention. People appear and vanish magically; objects move with a will of their own, persecuting people; fantastic creatures parade before the lens. While in his first films the elements of fantasy were simple items (for example notes of music on a page which come to life and sing as human heads), in time they grew to

7

illustrate entire tales; for from about 1900 his films become the first that can be identified as consistently built around plots. Although it is reasonable to say as Jacobs does that Méliès would illustrate rather than tell the tale, his plots were either based on popular themes (*Cinderella*, *The Seven Deadly Sins*, *Bluebeard*, *Red Riding Hood*), or their titles revealed the essentials and the audience could work out the rest from what it observed (*A Trip to the Moon*, *The Impossible Voyage*).[2] Given that these films provided spectators with something dramatically different from the actuality films with which they were familiar, there is little doubt that what they particularly admired was both their trickery and the beginnings of storytelling.

The powerful attraction exerted by narrative on the screen was confirmed in 1903 when the Edison company issued two story films made by Edwin Porter. *The Life of an American Fireman* and more especially *The Great Train Robbery* crystallised certain developments in the telling of narrative, and they featured specifically American themes, train robberies being a topical subject of the day. Above all they combined stories with action, and this is at its clearest in *The Great Train Robbery*, in which the things characters do tell the story. Here there is no illustration, in the manner of Méliès, of a pre-existing story. And whereas Méliès's scenes ran in a leisurely way, longer than necessary to the making of the narrative point, in Porter's films a tendency begins to develop in which the scene is cut no longer than the length required for the making of its dramatic point. In Méliès's films each shot usually ran as long as the entire scene lasted: a number of people prepare a rocket for the moon and embark. In Porter's *Train Robbery* that pattern is eroding, and some shots tell only a portion of the action and would be inexplicable without the context of the shots that come before and after. The camera begins both to follow and to highlight the action – developments which furnish the story film with a new excitement and a previously unknown narrative drive. The impact of the new action film on audiences was such that huge numbers of people saw Porter's two films. Inevitably they were so profitable that they became a model which other film-makers, and even Porter himself, followed rather mechanically for some years. Those film-makers like Méliès who did not adapt to the new style found their pictures soon lost their box-office appeal.

Moving pictures seem at the turn of the century to have done better business in the amusement arcades than in vaudeville theatres, which suggests they appealed more consistently to a working-class than a middle-class audience. It was this working-class audience that responded to the advent of the action storytelling film with obvious increases in the numbers of people paying to go through the turnstiles. Narrative films were thrust into prominence almost from their inception, in part because a number of amusement arcade operators noticed they had made the moving picture once again the most popular entertainment in the penny arcades.[3] A few began to convert their halls so that in future they would only show films.

One of the first to make the change, in 1902, was Thomas L. Tally, who operated a Los Angeles city-centre amusement arcade. According to Jacobs the early success of his venture, The Electric Theatre, was limited until he added to its name the explanatory subtitle 'A Vaudeville of Motion Pictures', after which he attracted good numbers of people. His choice of both this marketing tag and something like the vaudeville format of film programmes were central elements in the changing pattern of film exhibition that now developed. For, encouraged by response to the story film, hundreds of businessmen risked similar ventures shortly after Tally; and by 1905 the craze for the new form of entertainment had reached right across the United States.[4] In that year somebody coined the name that stuck – nickelodeon. It signalled as clearly as Mr Tally's establishment the twin promise of this new kind of theatre: cheap entry and reliable entertainment.

Although the cost of entry settled fairly quickly not at a nickel but at a dime, this was a ticket price which the working-class audience could afford. And there were other features besides cost of admission which attracted them. Nickelodeons began to open in the right places as, until 1907, preferred sites for them were in populous working-class residential or shopping locales. Here, with their barkers shouting their wares and their box offices almost in the street, they could catch people as they went about their business. The housewife could drop in when she was out shopping; her husband could catch the day's programme on his way home from work. Equally important, their programmes combined entertainment with brevity. At between 15 and 20 minutes duration they could be fitted into working days which left little free time for leisure.[5]

From the standpoint of nickelodeon owners, the quick turnover of custom was an essential ingredient of profitability since their halls were usually small. (This was partly because the auditorium that sat more than 200 people became liable for a costly theatrical licence.) With their cheap tickets, nickelodeons had to take considerable

numbers of people through the turnstiles to make money: Brownlow
estimates that about 4000 people per week would typically enable
them to break even on overheads of about $200.[6] In fact they
opened long hours, most of them starting at noon and running late
into the evening – and they did very well.[7] By 1907 upwards of 3000
nickelodeons had opened right across the States, and some 2 million
people visited them each day.[8]

The promise of classy entertainment implied by the name
'nickelodeon' was often reinforced by their exterior appearance.
Typically they resembled miniature theatres decked, as May records,
in plebian splendour of gilt and white. Not uncommonly they
imitated the neo-classical architecture of traditional theatres;
sometimes they adopted more exotic lines.[9] This was one means of
associating them with the glamour of the big vaudeville theatres
and, equally important, of reassuring audiences that their programmes
would have the propriety of vaudeville. Some of the amusement
arcades had at times shown films, however coy by today's standards,
somewhat too salacious for the taste of large sections of the
Victorian audience. The nickelodeons wanted to appeal to audiences
of women and children as well as men, and to assure them they
would be comfortable in every way.[10] Actually in many cases their
interiors betrayed that reassurance, the roughest being overcrowded
and dirty. The best, however, were clearly of a different calibre and,
besides cleanliness, at their most enterprising offered a lot more
than movies. In such houses the show might start with a sing-along
illustrated by lantern slides; it might continue with a movie or an
inexpensive vaudeville act; and on occasion an illustrated lecture, an
account of exotic travels perhaps, would be slotted in between the
films.[11]

The film programmes themselves did not by any means comprise
an unchanging diet of action movies, though it seems likely these
were the centrepiece of the schedule. Sklar notes that together with
comedy films, trick, and fantasy pieces, action movies made up the
bulk of the programmes; and in some halls, in absolute negation of
the implied promise of decency, *risqué* pictures of women undressing
were still screened. The action films comprised Westerns, crime and
romance movies in increasing numbers. Thus, says Sklar, from
about 1905 the movies entered vigorously a familiar sector of
American culture, taking their ideas from some of the bestselling
genres of published fiction – Westerns and realistic novels dealing
with city life. The popularity of these films and the explosive

increase in their production over the next couple of years helped American producers challenge the earlier dominance of the European photoplay with its staged drama. The content of the films rarely differed much from the accepted subjects of other popular forms of entertainment – the vaudeville, stage melodrama, burlesque, and dime novels – but the nickelodeon had the advantage over the older media in offering an immediate visual experience to an audience that needed neither literacy nor even spoken English to enjoy it.[12]

It is generally agreed that many members of the working-class audience sought, albeit unconsciously, to pick up and reinforce American values. Jowett, for instance, records how rapidly American society had changed before the introduction of the movies. An aspect of that change was the rapid industrialisation of the nation, and the movement – which formed part of that process – of great numbers of people into the cities. Equally, heavy immigration from Europe had brought to the industrial centres large numbers of labourers who wanted to find a sense of belonging in their new home. The movies, together with the popular press, helped bring about a sense of community. They built large audiences, which though heterogenous in ethnic composition, shared the desire to build a set of common values.[13] This was not, however, something which the movies set out deliberately to foster. Their main attraction was then – as now – that they entertained. May, for example, cites a survey carried out in New York City in 1908 which showed that those labourers who raised their income above subsistence level spent much of the surplus on leisure activities; and indeed the long hours of monotonous, unrelenting work in the new industries would build a strong need for relaxation. Amusement arcades and movie houses were not the only places to attract massive business: from the 1890s saloons and bars had also proliferated.[14]

While the needs of many people in the working-class audience were primarily for entertainment, it seems likely, then, that the desire to orient themselves towards contemporary American culture also motivated their movie-going. While middle-class audiences, who attended in ever larger numbers after 1907, also sought entertainment, their ideological orientation towards moving pictures is likely to have been different.

It is not irrelevant at this point to remark that the interior of a nickelodeon differed from that of the vaudeville and legitimate theatres, where the classes sat in divided seating areas. For in the nickelodeon the standard price admitted everybody to

undifferentiated   seating   accommodation.[15]   Aspects   of   this
arrangement can be seen to have been deeply attractive to middle-
class audiences, however paradoxical it may seem.

May sees the response of the American middle classes to films as
determined by their inherited morality. He argues that at the turn of
the century film-makers were thwarted in their desire to open up the
middle-class market by the continuing strength of Victorian
assumptions about amusements. They were held to be dangerous,
tending to attract people to vice, a notion confirmed by the apparent
opposition between leisure and the Protestant ethic since amusement
must detract from the sanctity of the work ideal.[16] However, rising
living standards gradually encroached on the ethics of self-denial,
and the prosperity of the legitimate theatre in New York at the turn
of the century indicated the growing attraction of entertainment.[17]
By about 1908 motion picture producers were beginning to recognise
that films might appeal to substantial elements of the middle classes
by offering them pleasures denied by the old morality. The
excitement of entertainment vividly presented was complemented by
the assertion of values that Victorianism did not countenance, and
the democratic arrangement of the auditoria themselves. The cinema
opened up the possibility of conversation with someone in the next
seat who might come from an entirely different background from
oneself.[18] Thus where working people seem to have sought
confirmation through the movies of the ideology of the new order
into which they had been gathered by industrialisation, elements of
the growing middle-class audience seem to have sought a change
from old, oppressive ideologies.

There is no question but that the owners of nickelodeons were
eager to attract this new audience. Actually it does not seem to have
occurred to them at first that they might be able to take more cash
from middle-class customers by raising the price of admission –
though they would have welcomed increased numbers through the
turnstiles. Rather they seem to have wanted to identify their new
business with respectability, which in those early years the movies
emphatically lacked. Nickelodeon owners, just as much as equipment
manufacturers, wanted to confirm their right to a place in the middle
classes, and they now set out to woo them. From about 1907 they
began for the first time to build in the better-off residential areas.
They realised that these clients would be happier in cleaner, more
comfortable theatres, and they attempted to provide such
surroundings.[19] Once again they emphasised their desire to draw the

family audience, and to enhance their image they sought in particular to gain acceptance by women, the hallmark of respectability.[20] After 1908 new means of reassuring this audience were deployed, as films for the first time came under censorship, and film production turned by degrees towards subjects with a safer, middle-class orientation – developments we shall follow later.

For the moment, however, we must recognise that all these changes in film exhibition had put massive strain on the burgeoning industry's production and supply lines. Symptomatic of that strain was the appearance in 1906 of the first trade publication *Views and Film Index*, soon followed by two rival journals. Their object was to make it possible to deal with the growing complexity of the film trade by furnishing professional information.[21]

That growing complexity derived from the opening of hundreds of new nickelodeons in the years since 1903, and their hunger for new films. With their cheap entry and short programmes they needed to entice customers to return regularly. To this end they quickly learned to change their programmes frequently so as to offer perhaps three different programmes each week. The demand for new films was so intense that it has been speculated that it stultified the aesthetic development of cinema: that after Porter and his contemporaries discovered a basic machinery for creating narrative through action, film-makers were so inundated with work they had neither time nor energy to experiment with further development of his model, which they merely duplicated time after time.[22] Though this analysis leaves problematic the question how for instance Griffith managed under equal pressure to sophisticate the storytelling routine of cinema, it does suggest that for many production companies getting films made in volume was their main objective. The great shift to narrative that occurred about 1907–8 pleased producers not only because these films were popular but also because they could be made at a low, predictable cost per foot at a central studio facility, and then released on a regular schedule. Thus they were both cheaper and more certain than films of topical events or scenic films, the production of which kept cameramen idle while travelling or awaiting an event, at cost to the production.[23]

A further pointer to the pressure of demand upon production facilities is found in the fact that some companies began for the first time from 1906 to use electric light. They intended simply to avoid delays caused by bad weather and the short hours of daylight in winter. Artificial light was thus used for business reasons only and not to gain expressive ends, for operators made no attempt to mould the details of actors' faces and tried to achieve a flat, bright level of illumination. This is confirmed by the fact that electricity was used in some of the more modern glass studios where production on interior scenes could go ahead at any time using mixed sources of natural and artificial lighting to obtain a shadowless image.[24] Film was still a simple commodity to the producer; its power to communicate anything other than the most rudimentary entertainment seems not at this time to have interested more than a handful of American film-makers.

If the pressure of demand showed itself in the conditions of production, where many companies required their crews to complete two or three single reel films each week, those pressures manifested themselves even more clearly in the changes which came about to the supply line.

Firstly, film was standardised to a single gauge when Biograph, one of the three big producers, converted to a system compatible with Edison's. Vitagraph, the other large company, had by ingenious construction of its own camera long been compatible with Edison's equipment, whose projectors their customers used.[25] And the small producers lacked the market strength to be able to hold to their own gauges for long. Far from discouraging Edison from his lawsuits, however, standardisation spurred him to a further costly round of litigation in pursuit of his strategy to exert monopoly control over the industry. We shall see the effects of his action later, but standardisation was made necessary by the demand of movie houses for quantities of films no single producer could supply. With access to the films produced by all the major companies, the exhibitor had a reasonable prospect of securing his needs.

But how was he actually to get his hands on the films? As long as the line of supply led from the producer to every separate exhibitor this was an awkward business. The exhibitor had little idea what the producer had on offer, and might have difficulty contacting smaller production companies in remote states. The producer would have difficulty anticipating demand for each film. Furthermore the outright purchase of a print, at a cost of anything between $50 and $100 was a pointless expense for the exhibitor. As programmes had to be changed with increasing rapidity, exhibitors risked ending up with good prints which were perfectly useless to them.[26] There were ways round these problems – films could be resold, purchased by several exhibitors together, or retained for rescreening at a later date – but the distribution system was inadequate to the demands on it.

It sounds an absurd exaggeration to say that the introduction of the first film exchange began a process that was to bring immense development to the motion picture business, but it is a sensible estimate of what happened. The first exchange specifically established for hiring out films was opened in 1902 in San Francisco by Harry and Herbert Miles. The idea worked so well that by 1907 something between 125 and 150 such exchanges were functioning, serving all parts of the country.[27] Jacobs summarises the attractions of the rental service they offered:

> The exchange man could continue to rent out films long after they had more than paid for themselves: his profits were large. Manufacturers now had one large customer who practically guaranteed to buy most of their output at higher prices; and they enjoyed an increased market for pictures because exhibitors, paying less for pictures, could more frequently change their programmes. To exhibitors the plan meant programmes at much lower cost. A variety of films from several manufacturers could be collected under one roof, and thus the time and trouble involved in the selection of pictures would be reduced.[28]

Though with many imperfections, what emerged in the five years to 1907 was a tripartite industry in which production, distribution and exhibition functioned separately, but with each part dependent on the others. The new arrangement made for greater profits all round, and for their part exhibitors were now changing their programmes daily (some even twice per day), as *Views and Film Index* reported in 1907.[29]

Since the hire of film cost much less than purchase, exhibitors should now have been able to afford to compete with each other, bidding for newer or better films; exchanges too should have been able to compete for product from the suppliers. Market forces were evidently about to make themselves felt, and it can be assumed that in a short time they would have pressurised production companies to adapt their films to meet the anticipated wishes of audiences. Before that could happen, however, those who had been in the film business longest formed a cartel in a final attempt to control it to their benefit through their patents. Their actions temporarily froze the film business into restrictive practices, and locked much of the production sector into its well-established indifference to audience requirements.

3 The Motion Picture Patents Company, 1908–14

Thomas Edison, as we know, had from the earliest days of the cinema aimed for exclusive control of the business. As the years passed and his lawsuits increased in number and expense, expansion of the industry was hindered both by the drain on capital and the want of a stable business environment. Eventually, by 1907, Edison managed to subdue the smaller companies; but litigation against his most powerful rival was proving inconclusive, not least because the American Mutoscope and Biograph Company had designed its own camera in a manner sufficiently different from Edison's that, while it accepted compatible film stock, it escaped his patents.[1] Biograph was making sufficient profit from its film production to be able to afford to contest Edison's lawsuits. As late as 1907 it continued to stand out against him, while most other companies had capitulated and come under his licence. In 1908 Edison changed tactics and proposed to Biograph a truce and the pooling of interests to their mutual profit. Biograph accepted, and in September the Motion Picture Patents Company was formed, embracing not only Biograph and Edison, but all those that had previously come into the Edison orbit.

The Patents Company consisted of ten members. These were firstly the companies that between them held the key patents on equipment – Edison, Biograph, and the Vitagraph Company. With them were conjoined four American film production companies – Essanay, Selig, Lubin, and Kalem – and one distributor, George Kleine. The number was made up to ten with the inclusion of two French companies with a long history of exporting film to the United States – Méliès and Pathé.[2] Paradoxically their inclusion reflected a desire to reduce the share of the American market taken by European films, for one of Edison's motivations in establishing the new cartel was the exclusion of the many small importers. They had found an opening caused by the nickelodeon boom, which stimulated heavy demand for films. Almost all of these companies were refused Patents Company licences, Méliès and Pathé being treated as exceptions because of their relative size. Indeed in 1907–8 Pathé, a well-organised international giant, undercut its rivals and sold more films in the American market than Edison, Biograph or any of the domestic producers.[3]

The Motion Picture Patents Company was set up to act as a cartel and control the industry through an interlocking system of patents and licences. It identified four main parts to the industry, and initially saw control of the first two as most important. Later it was to place a higher priority on the regulation of distribution. The areas in which it meant to intervene were:

1. Manufacture both of motion pictures and of equipment;
2. Access to raw film stock;
3. Film distribution;
4. Regulation and licensing of exhibitors.[4]

The 10 member companies were all licensed to produce films, and thus the cartel, which intended to exclude all other companies, meant to control film production.[5] But although the interests of the new Trust were exclusively the control of the motion picture business (which notionally left its members free to produce films of whatever kind they wished), the financial structure that they had set up exerted formidable pressure on production budgets and distribution schedules so that, albeit inadvertently, the activities of the cartel did constrain the kind of film that was made under its aegis. The Patents Company went further than trying to control the output of film. Royalties were levied on every piece of projection equipment manufactured under the Patents Company licence; exhibitors who bought that equipment had to pay a standing royalty fee of two dollars per week.[6]

The Trust also contracted with the one big American supplier of raw film stock to enter into a monopoly trading agreement. All film stock, whether for production or release prints, was to be supplied by Eastman Kodak; and that firm was to supply no other concerns than members of the Trust. By this agreement the Patents Company intended to exclude any other entrant to the business, and its assumption that it could do so relied upon the technical difficulty of manufacturing raw stock and the fact that Eastman Kodak was already so big and so expert it had all but closed out its competitors from the business. There was, too, money in this agreement for the principal companies in the Trust. Eastman Kodak charged its customers an additional cent per foot as royalty, and passed on to the Patents Company half a cent per foot of film sold.[7] The very considerable royalty revenue received by the Trust from both raw stock and equipment was divided between those four companies that had pooled their patents. As the two most powerful, Edison and Biograph received respectively one-half and one-third in the split.[8]

As far as film distribution was concerned, in the first months of its operations the Trust confined its control to an arrangement whereby it licensed certain exchanges to deal in its films. A total of 116 such exchanges were listed, and the remaining 30 or 40, since in theory they could only deal with imported films and unlicensed movie houses, were supposedly forced out of business. Eighteen months after the inception of these arrangements, however, the Patents Company extended its intervention in the distribution field. It formed the General Film Company in April 1910, funded it to a limit of $1 million, and set about buying up all the 69 licensed exchanges remaining in the business (a considerable number had already had licences revoked for violation of the company's regulations). It completed this programme by the end of 1911, only one licensed exchange in New York remaining outside its embrace.[9]

The General Film Company, owned in equal shares by all 10 members of the Patents Company, regulated film distribution in a way which had particular consequences for film production. It paid production companies a fixed flat rate of 10 cents per foot, no matter what the nature or quality of the films it was buying.[10] This arrangement provided producers with no incentive to improve the quality of their films. On the contrary, the more they spent, the less profit they took, however well a film might do at the box office. Thus the fixed rate of film purchase had the effect of distancing production from market pressures. As longer films tended to require more care in their making, and therefore cost more, the Patents Company system had a built-in bias towards the familiar one-reel film, a bias that was to prove critical in its fortunes. Indeed it tended to encourage mediocrity in production – which is not to say that short films of good quality, or which experimented with new devices, could not be made under its aegis. As we shall see presently, the career of D. W. Griffith at Biograph provides a classic example of extraordinary innovation within a system that was in this respect unhelpful.

How could such an attitude of indifference come to prevail? Jenkins provides an insight which takes account of the Patents Company's financial and structural arrangements in arguing that it depended on the key assumption that the motion picture industry was engaged in selling a standardised, undifferentiated product. Movies were thought of as one reel in length and as saleable by the foot interchangeably. Inherent in this assumption was the notion that the American public would attend movie houses indiscriminately, paying little attention to the personality and talent of the actors, the quality of the screenplay, or the abilities of the director. The problem for the Trust was that these assumptions were to prove false.[11]

However, if the General Film Company did not distinguish between films in what it paid for them, it soon began to distinguish between the theatres to which it rented them. Hitherto theatres had bid against each other to obtain newly released films in a system without much order. Some managers were not above bribing the booking agents to get films first.[12] Deals were struck between other theatre operators whereby they agreed to co-operate so that the theatre with an early booking on a film would let the others use it too so they could screen it earlier than might otherwise have been the case. The General Film Company set about bringing order to this business, and it did so by classifying theatres according to their location and success in drawing audiences. It then fixed release dates according to the class of theatre, and enforced those dates. In doing so it established a system of 'runs'. Furthermore it levied differential rentals for its programmes, ranging from $100 to $125 for the biggest theatres in the best locations (increasingly as the income of the audience improved, the city-centre cinemas), down to $15 for small houses remote from their audiences. And the company also provided theatres in the same neighbourhood with programmes that did not conflict.[13]

The run-zone-clearance system, as it has been called, brought about a significant change in the industry in that it institutionalised a hierarchy among motion picture theatres. This was more than a matter of charging higher rentals to those houses that did better business, since in return for those higher payments chosen cinemas acquired the right to screen films earlier than houses lower down the scale. Thus an order of release, or running, was established, with first-run cinemas, chosen because they did the better business, entitled to screen films before second-run and later-run theatres. Theatres in any given zone were restricted from competing with each other since a period of weeks (the clearance) was enforced before a film could return to a zone for each successive run.

Organisation of the market in this way mattered because it was already apparent that some theatre-goers made a practice of seeking out newly released films. With the new system the public knew where films would be released first, and thus the better cinemas benefited from a mechanism which tended to increase the number of their patrons. Conversely their success tended to reduce the drawing power of fourth-run and fifth-run houses, rendering them less profitable. For the first time, cinema was seen to be a time-based business in which newer product had the greater earning power.

The system as the Trust operated it did not further discriminate between theatres because it did not institutionalise the practice of charging different ticket prices for admission to the different classes of theatre. Although that practice was to become established within about five years, the Patents Company appears not to have further encouraged competition between theatres, even though they had discovered that the commercial value of a film is a function of its age.

In fact the circumstances of exhibitors did change after the formation of the Patents Company. Films produced under licence of the company could only be shown in theatres operated by exhibitors who were themselves licensed. And such licensed exhibitors were prohibited from screening any films other than those produced by licensed manufacturers (that is by the members of the Patents Company). These stipulations theoretically closed the cartel against all competition from without. As compensation for the protection they received, exhibitors had to pay $2 a week for the privilege of the licence, an imposition widely resented.

Just as some exchanges had been refused licences, so not all exhibitors were embraced by the Patents Company. One estimate suggests that about 6000 nickelodeons existed in 1908, and more than 10 000 by 1910.[14] The Trust may have licensed between a half and two-thirds of those in existence a few months after it began operations.[15] It applied a deliberate policy in choosing licensees, and left out two or three thousand storefront nickelodeons, the less salubrious and well-to-do houses, because they did not measure up to the criteria they wanted to nurture in the cartel. Plainly it expected that, like the excluded exchanges, the movie houses it did not license would quickly die, cut off from all film supply other than that of four or five very small American producers outside the Trust,

and some importers.[16] In this assumption too the Trust proved
wrong.

The theatres the Patents Company preferred to license indicate its
bias not only towards nurturing the more profitable venues, but also
towards improving the class of its theatres. It favoured exhibitors
who had moved into 'better' areas or who were based downtown in
the city centres. This was part of a strategy designed to win the
middle-class audience. Trade journals encouraged exhibitors to cater
for the comfort of patrons, and to provide such things as iced water,
comfortable chairs and proper ventilation.[17] The Trust also attempted
to supply better prints of its films; and to advertise screenings and
encourage reviews in the press, which now for the first time was
willing to accept both kinds of placement for movies. And the
strategy had consequences for film production as the Trust recognised
that it stood to win the approval of the middle-class audience by
showing a willingness to co-operate with an imposition that had at
first seemed unwelcome, namely the censorship of movies.[18]

The issue of censorship first came to a head in New York City in
December 1908. The Mayor closed movie houses during Christmas
week, a move symptomatic of anxiety widely felt among the business
and professional classes. This anxiety was of course directed at the
supposed immorality of the movies. And indeed it is clear that
certain movies did attempt to titillate, and were objectionable to a
wider public than the reformers. However, this factor alone does
not explain the intensity of the anxiety. As a young medium, movies
often presented the new mores uncritically, even enthusiastically;
and May suggests that the reformers confused new patterns of
behaviour and styles of dress, particularly among young women on
screen, with what by Victorian standards appeared permissive or
even worse.[19]

The threat of censorship worried the Patents Company just as, at
the end of 1908, it was emerging as a force within the industry. Most
of its members considered themselves to be respectable members of
the very middle-class community that was now challenging the ethics
of their work. But they had business as well as personal reasons for
fearing the attentions of would-be reformers. Above all they wished
to prevent outside interference and to forestall the fearful prospect
of local censorship, which might lead to different cuts being required
in every film in every last local community.

The way the Trust dealt with the threat of censorship indicates very clearly the way it strove to make its products acceptable to the profitable new audience it was trying to tap: it decided to assist the creation of a regulatory body of its own choosing.[20] This was the National Board of Review, whose entire running costs the Trust funded, and with whose work it co-operated.[21] In the event the Board was not overwhelmingly successful as an instrument of censorship, though initially it refused to pass some 20 per cent of the films it saw, usually films concerned with sexuality and crime.[22] However, as an exercise in public relations, co-operation with censorship had advantages which neither the Patents Company nor its rivals could fail to perceive. After 1908 theatres given the Board of Review's seal of approval became acceptable to people who would have shunned them before. Cinemas began to open in the affluent areas of Boston, New York, Chicago and Philadelphia, a move the more pronounced in that few new theatres opened in the poor sections of these cities.[23]

It has often been remarked that the Patents Company perished because it lacked flexibility in its strict methods of business practice. However, within that formula (the one-reel film sold at 10 cents per foot) its members were willing to change their product, as is evident from the speed with which they embraced respectability. But it should not be thought that they acted with uniform virtue. As we have mentioned at least one of the biggest producers, Biograph, continued to make numbers of mildly scandalous films.[24] It is an early example of what was to become a familiar phenomenon, the American film industry seeking to have things both ways and to please more than one audience at a time. Titillation and the exploitation of shocked interest in deviant sexuality remained a continuing theme in films, despite the activities of the National Board of Review. One notorious example, *Traffic in Souls* (1913), was so popular that a number of films followed it on to the market, all exploiting through the same formula public interest in the misfortunes of young women tempted into prostitution. *Traffic in Souls* was advertised as having the censors' approval for its crusade against vice; but in Jacobs's view it emphasised sex heavily, and set itself to interest both the morally concerned and the prurient.[25]

With movies beginning to move upwards in the class ranks, it was necessary, as May says, for producers to do more than act negatively by responding to the pressures of censorship. They had also to create an acceptable product for their new audiences.[26] Jacobs sums up the general moral tenor of the new output succinctly: 'From 1908 to 1914 motion pictures preached.'[27] Of course not all pictures did so, nor was the tendency of those that did exclusively the consequence of the Patents Company's opportunism. Rather, that opportunistic desire to pacify the fears and gratify the sentiments of the new middle-class audience coincided with a period in which optimism, high moral tone and didactic purpose governed both cultural and official life.[28] This was also, it has been argued, a time when a drive began to ensure films had happy endings.[29] Jacobs demonstrates with countless examples of long-forgotten one-reelers that 'strict late nineteenth-century attitudes were the values and homilies preached and defended in films.'[30] Not too surprising then that film ideas often originated from sources that had not previously been tapped. The Bible became a subject for numerous films; the morality of being poor and the dangers of wealth were dwelt on; fortune had a tendency to turn desperate lives to happiness.[31]

Associated with these developments, and no doubt because it both implied high moral tone and provided good plots with narrative structures familiar to middle-class audiences, literature now became a source of ideas for film-makers.[32] Perhaps as a consequence of this, and of improving production values, this era is the one when screenwriters first make their appearance.[33] Still working within the 10–12 minute confines of the single reel, they had to distil an episode from a novel, a short story or play into a scenario which had to be easily enough filmed that the crew could complete two such items each week. Sanctioned by literature or not, film production within the Trust continued to be governed by the flat fee of 10 cents per foot.

An example of the workload of the film-maker is given by the otherwise untypical career of D. W. Griffith, who began to direct as an employee of Biograph in 1908, and made over 400 films in four years. In other words he worked at the pace governed by the requirement that he produce two reels per week, throughout the period when he was making many films remarkable for their stylistic innovation. Of course no director, however energetic, could have made films at this the standard rate of production without the support of a systematic organisation, and Staiger identifies 1909–14 as marking the separation and subdivision of the work of production into compartmentalised specialities with a structural hierarchy. The first elements of a factory system now began to emerge at the large studios.[34] During this time Griffith and his crews made into a routine part of cinematic language many aesthetic devices through which camera and cutting could be integrated into the storytelling process.

Though many, even most of these devices had been introduced singly by others, Griffith's contribution was to systematise them; and Hollywood rapidly took over and naturalised these practices as its own. The narrative style of American cinema swiftly became one of its most marketable qualities.

Griffith's own films celebrated the kind of Victorian morality which the Patents Company, at least with its public relations face in position, wished to be seen to endorse. All his character types would have been familiar to readers of Victorian pulp literature: his young women are innocent and fearfully exposed in a world yet to be cleansed of coarse, bullying males. His youthful heroes are clean and robust, and in sweeping away the villains show up their cowardice; towards their beloveds they behave with ardour qualified by unexceptionable virtue. Thus even before Griffith began to feature starring players, the films had two readily saleable characteristics: first they had their source in popular fiction, and second, their new narrative techniques gave audiences great pleasure, making the camera an instrument which helped move the plot forward and integrate screen action with narrative. However, while Griffith's interests presumably centred on his innovations, Biograph concerned itself merely with the profitability of his output. Its executives appear not to have been persuaded that the quality of his films had anything to do with their success at the box office. It was the issue over which, faced with their obdurate reluctance to have him increase the length of his films and spend more on them, Griffith eventually left the company.

We have remarked already that the distribution arm of the Patents Company, the General Film Company, took over or closed every licensed exchange except one. The exception was the Greater New York Film Rental Company, owned by William Fox and operated to service his chain of more than a dozen theatres. Fox, the only licensee of the Patents Company whose name is still before the movie-going public, had been an exemplary distributor/exhibitor in the Trust's own terms. He had conscientiously moved up-market, having taken over a number of vaudeville theatres that had lost their audiences, and had made them into comfortable movie houses for middle-class audiences. When in December 1908 New York closed the cinemas, it was Fox who led the successful campaign to reopen them.[35] But when General Film insisted on buying up the distribution side of the organisation he had built up, he refused. With his licence cancelled and his film supply threatened, he did two things. He commenced film production as an independent in defiance of the Trust; and he instituted a lawsuit against it, alleging violation of the anti-trust provisions of the Sherman Act. The hearing of this case and the Trust's appeal against the verdict did not come to a conclusion until 1918; but Fox won, and the legal death of the Patents Company ensued.[36]

Although this anti-trust case would have killed it anyway, the Patents Company was dead as an active force in the industry long before that date, in effect by 1914. As early as 1911 it had been obliged to abandon its exclusive arrangements with Eastman Kodak, under threat of anti-trust prosecution.[37] Thus it had long given up the struggle to deny unlicensed production companies raw film stock. But it really expired because its rivals succeeded in changing market demand so that it came to favour kinds of films that the Patents Company refused to produce. However, if in this way the Patents Company proved inadequate to the challenges of the market, in two other ways it had fostered developments upon which the industry was to rely in future years. Firstly the very establishment of the company signifies a recognition that the motion picture industry was potentially a very much larger business than had previously been thought. It sought to stabilise and control it by patents pooling (on the lines of other large American industries) and by centralising a hitherto chaotic industry. Secondly the Trust saw that the industry could be run more efficiently and profitably if it were organised vertically so that either a single company or a closely meshed group controlled more than one of the three main aspects of the business. The Patents Company linked production and distribution, and did so for a while to the mutual advantage of both sides of the operation. Here too it adopted a structure favoured by other large industries, including not only electricity and oil, but also the vaudeville theatre chains.[38] The potential efficacy of such a structure was not missed by those who, at this point the bitter rivals of the Trust, were to succeed it as the new establishment. Though they began as the industry's guerillas, they too were soon to try, though exposing themselves to the risk of anti-trust action, the advantages of vertical organisation and of forming a cartel.

4 Independents, Innovation and the Beginnings of Hollywood, 1908–15

When the Motion Picture Patents Company set up its operation it assumed that a number of factors would protect its business. It expected the exhibitors it did not license would lie down and die; it believed that cornering virtually the entire American market for raw film stock would kill off any attempt to compete in production; and it appears to have thought of film as a commodity to all the qualities of which the public was quite indifferent. In the event it proved to be wrong in all these assumptions.

Undoubtedly some of the poorer nickelodeons must have closed, just as not all the unlicensed exchanges can have survived. But a significant number defended their livelihoods vigorously. What is more, new firms sprang up rapidly. At this time the investment required to start up either in production or distribution was not great enough to discourage new firms, particularly while the market continued to expand. Thus the Patents Company did not enjoy protection such as the studio oligopoly had in the 1920s and 1930s, by which time the movie business had become complex and required heavy investment by any company seeking to break into its ranks on an equal footing.[1]

Within six weeks of the Trust starting in business, a rival, the International Projecting and Producing Company, had begun to supply with imported films the unlicensed sector of the industry. Although its service proved inadequate to supply the market, it did help with the shortage of product during the short year of its existence.[2] One of this company's more influential customers was Carl Laemmle. He had registered with the Patents Company as a licensee, but broke with them in April 1909 because they allowed him no voice in shaping their policies. Sklar describes him as perhaps the only man in a position to break from the Trust at this time – he owned six exchanges in major cities, including Chicago, Minneapolis, Omaha, Salt Lake City, and Portland, Oregon. He also had close contacts with exhibitors in the areas served from those bases: knowledge of their business helped him devise imaginative marketing strategies effective in challenging the Trust's dominance.[3] He deliberately named his new production company the Independent Moving Picture Company, meaning from the outset to make it an IMP to bedevil the Trust.

Not long after he had declared his independence, the French concern Lumière recognised its opportunity and began to export raw stock to the United States. Demand from the self-styled independent companies that sprang up to defy the Trust's monopoly was so great that, even though their stock lacked the quality of Eastman's, Lumière was by 1911 to sell 35 million feet compared with Eastman Kodak's 91 million.[4] Laemmle was among the first to use it; but he did more than merely produce films. Soon his company began a deliberately irritating advertising campaign against the Trust; and sought in particular to arouse support by concentrating on the weekly levy of $2 royalty on exhibitors which was widely hated.

> Good morning! Have you paid two dollars for a license to smoke your own pipe this week? . . . Have you paid your two dollars for a license to breathe this week? . . . I will rot in Hades before I will join the Trust . . . How is *your* backbone?[5]

His tactics were good, for the independent movement commanded considerable support right from the start. A number of other individuals set up production companies almost as quickly as Laemmle; but, added to imports, their combined output would not have sufficed to supply the full needs, often amounting to a daily change of programme, of all the independent exhibitors. In practice some licensees of the Trust helped out, not just through philanthropy, but because they could augment their own income by bootlegging prints of licensed films to independent exchanges or exhibitors.[6] Although the Patents Company ruthlessly expelled licensees when it discovered such infringements of its regulations, in doing so it increased sympathy for the independents, and of course added to their numbers. There is no doubt that an exceedingly bitter patents war developed, which those who lived through it recall with colourful memories.[7] The Trust adopted Edison's familiar tactic by setting in motion lawsuits, while simultaneously attempting to obstruct independent film-making by sending its spies on location. It has often been alleged that these tactics led independent producers to move away from the north-eastern seaboard to escape the Trust's persecution; but as we shall see, there are reasons for regarding such claims with scepticism.

Although there is no evidence that independent productions in their first season (1908–9) were in fact different, the independent exchanges, in their advertisements, puffed the supposed superiority of their releases over the Trust's.[8] Many of them had the wit to undercut the fixed prices charged by the Patents Company members. This lured some theatres into dropping their licences to secure the cheaper independent films.[9] The more farsighted among them realised that they would actually have to produce distinctive entertainment in order to assure themselves of good audiences. It was to help achieve this end that Laemmle arranged in March 1910 the celebrated death of his leading player, Florence Lawrence.

Leading players, at the time he killed her off, rarely received screen credit for their work. Laemmle became aware that the public was giving names of its own to particular favourites among these anonymous actors, which seemed to him a sure sign of their popular appeal. He hired the 'Biograph Girl' to play for IMP, and shortly afterwards covertly planted a newspaper story to the effect that she (now the IMP girl) had been killed in a road accident. This device gave him the chance to claim via one of his advertisements that his enemies (who but the Patents Company?) had fabricated the report. Shortly afterwards Miss Lawrence made a well-publicised appearance in St Louis, and was mobbed by fans.[10]

Together with Miss Lawrence the star system was reborn. For as Laemmle, an experienced showman, plainly knew, stardom was already a familiar phenomenon in the commercial theatre. What his experiment proved to him was that the public responded just as favourably to the presentation of stars in the cinema.[11] Yet Patents Company members, despite the evidence that soon accumulated to show that people went in greater numbers to films featuring players whom they admired, were for the most part reluctant to build the stature of actors even by naming them. They did promote some featured players, but not it seems with the zest or showmanship of the independents. They feared, rightly, that players would demand more money when they saw that their names drew bigger audiences – and of course the flat-rate payment for films made this extra cost difficult to absorb.[12] However, the independents quickly found that much increased takings at the box office made the enlarged costs of actors' wages a very profitable investment. Their system allowed producers to vary the price of films to exchanges so that they too could recoup more from bigger attractions.[13] Encouraged by the prospect of increased rentals from successful films, they were willing to invest more in them. This factor was an essential element in the improvement of their quality. It was too an essential precondition for the development of the feature film which, to keep audience attention throughout its considerable length, had to have better – thus costlier – production values.

Having identified a change in public taste, some of the independents were to set about developing it within a few years. To have done so, however, would not have been possible had they not evolved a more efficient system of distribution than that provided by the scatter of small competing firms that first served the independent network. That network underwent a number of swift transformations under the pressure of need to establish secure business conditions.

Within a few months of the start of independent operations, the small exchanges concerned began to form an alliance. The initially loose organisation of this grouping was tightened, and in spring 1910 the Motion Picture Distributing and Sales Company (usually known as the Sales Company) was established. Within a few months this organisation, set up within a few weeks of the General Film Company, embraced all the major independent interests.[14] Since at first they perceived the market for film in the same way as members of the Patents Company, for a short while the two distribution organisations seem *prima facie* to have run in parallel. The difference between their operations lay in the fact that the Sales Company saw its role merely as supplier to the existing independent exchanges. That is, it distributed films made by production companies to the exchanges but did not, respecting their superior knowledge of the selling territory, attempt to interfere with the supply of films to theatres (which General Film did). However, there was an important similarity in their methods in that they supplied closely comparable packages of films to movie houses.

At this period, exchanges did not so much supply individual films as entire programmes. These as we have seen might consist of a Western, a comedy, possibly a documentary, and a drama – and this pattern of distribution, known as the programme method, was adopted by the independents in imitation of the Patents Company. However, when the independents formed production companies in order to feed their existing exchanges, it seemed logical to arrange for each of them to specialise in at least one type of picture needed to compile a programme, since efficient production should result from familiarity with the genre concerned. The distributor simply collated films from several suppliers to bring together each programme package.[15] Once again we see the industry organising itself on vertical lines. Thus within the independent framework, Laemmle, at the centre of one power block, looked to his own IMP for the provision of dramas, and took the rest of his distribution needs from the Powers, Rex, Champion, Republic and Nestor film companies, as each specialised in dramas, comedies or Westerns.

Laemmle's operations were not, however, the only centre of power within the Sales Company. A second large power block formed around companies set up by John R. Freuler and Harry Aitken, and the rivalry between the two factions destroyed the Sales Company in 1912 when they formed a group called the Mutual Film Corporation, and set about stabilising its operations by buying up additional exchanges.[16] To do this they required financial backing, which they secured from Wall Street bankers Kuhn, Loeb & Co – apparently the first investment by bankers in the industry. It enabled Mutual to supply films from its own cluster of producers to an expanding network of exchanges (and indeed to grow into Canada and Europe too). In return for their investment, Kuhn, Loeb & Co appointed Mutual's company secretary as a means of exercising a measure of financial control.[17] But whatever changes they may have made to the group's business practice, they did not interfere with the programme method of distribution. This was to prove a fatal omission.

Responding to the organisation of Mutual, Laemmle formed his associates into the Universal Film Manufacturing Company (founding a corporate body which, after a multitude of transformations, exists to this day). Thus by late 1912 the industry comprised three large groupings of approximately equal strength, for in four years the independents had taken a great deal from the Patents group. Exhibitors, exchanges, players and production staff had defected and were to continue to do so.[18] Its market share had fallen from almost 100 per cent to about a half.[19]

All three organisations were distributing by the programme method, a fact worth dwelling on because the independents have so often been credited with the innovations that brought the industry forward to its next big change. This general truth should not disguise the fact that in the first years they were quite conservative in their business methods. Indeed the many independents who remained constant to the programme method were to fail – a fact which accounts in part for the near complete transformation of the industry in the years from 1914 to 1918. The weakness of the programme method, as Lyons explains it, was that when a distributor failed, its supplying production companies, lacking any other outlet for their films, went down too.[20] This is precisely what was to happen both to the Patents Company and the groupings of independents that could not adapt to the economic requirements of the feature film. Mutual flourished for a few years, was still expanding in 1916, but foundered utterly in 1918 because by that time the feature film had of commercial necessity called into being new kinds of distribution which by-passed the older exchanges entirely. Inevitably in the wake of Mutual's collapse its contributing production companies toppled.[21] But long before those crashes occurred independent production had entered a second phase.

The rise of Hollywood as a major production centre has tended to become confused with the emergence from 1909 of independent producers. As we have mentioned, they are widely supposed to have chosen Hollywood as a relatively safe refuge from the Trust's raids upon unlicensed production companies during the patents war. This belief was much enhanced by contemporaries' dramatic accounts of events.[22] There must be a measure of truth in these tales of intimidatory tactics practised by gunmen in the pay of both sides in the war; but several factors make it apparent that the foundation of Hollywood had other, more significant causes. Nor was Los Angeles a safe haven: as Sklar remarks, the repeated claim that Hollywood attracted independents because they could bundle their unlicensed equipment into cars and escape the camera-busting raids of the Trust's spies is absurd.[23] In those days the border with Mexico (which they would have had to cross to be in territory where the Trust's patents did not run) was a five-hour drive from Los Angeles. To make the round trip would have cost at least a day's production. And in any case the Trust had a permanent presence in Los Angeles, Selig being the first production company to set up there in 1907. When the first independent company to arrive, the New York Motion Picture Company, set up shop in 1909, it placed itself down the block from them.[24]

From about the time film-makers first appeared in Los Angeles, production companies were also to be found in Maine, Florida, New Mexico, Oregon and Cuba.[25] It is apparent that Southern California had other attractions that these places lacked: Sklar itemises them:

The climate. Southern California enjoyed warm weather and sunshine almost all year round. Although it was not the only part of the United States with a winter climate better suited to film-making than the eastern seaboard, its clear, sharp light was a further attraction.[26]

The terrain. Within easy driving distance of Los Angeles, crews could find many different kinds of landscape suitable for a wide variety of scenes.

Cost of property. Land could be bought inexpensively. When in later years production companies needed to establish studios with vast 'backlots' for outdoor sequences, this factor became especially attractive.

Labour costs. Los Angeles was well known at the time as an open shop, a city without trade unions. It was expanding rapidly with a constant inflow of new residents seeking work, and settling for wages – if they could get them – between a fifth and a third below rates paid in San Francisco (in some cases only half the rate paid in New York). Both the labour surplus and its low cost were to attract the studios as they moved into feature production and required the services of numbers of skilled craftworkers from carpenters to dressmakers and scene painters.[27]

Thus consideration of both the area's topography and plain business advantages made Los Angeles an obvious place to base production companies. Ironically, in recent years the same attraction of low-cost, non-union labour has drawn away a great deal of production from what has long been a unionised city.

In fact by 1913 only four production companies had set up on the west coast.[28] So while the establishment of Hollywood took a somewhat longer time than is sometimes recalled, its symbolic importance for future film production can hardly be overstressed. For in addition to its beautiful climate Los Angeles could present itself as a kind of urban garden.[29] The city had no industry, and with its large residential plots a kind of mediterranean suburban culture developed, more luxurious to look at and much less densely populated than eastern cities. It seems to have resembled a blend of vacation ground and (with its palm trees, orange groves and vineyards) an imaginary Eden. Film-makers were not slow to capitalise on this atmosphere, importing it directly into their films, making its romance a saleable commodity.[30]

This new note, the emphasis on relaxed pleasure and its association with a deliberately glamorous style, would be the key to the way the industry was to present itself in the period from 1915 through to the catastrophe of the Great Depression. Even studio architecture – Laemmle's Universal Studios, built in 1913 in a romantic Spanish style, provide the earliest example – might be married to this ethos.[31] Hollywood in this epoch both propagates and reflects a cultural shift, the desire to enjoy lighthearted pleasures without guilt and to relish the carefree delights with which, from the mid-1910s, glamour began to deck everything the industry touched.

At the end of 1911 the nickelodeon craze had reached its peak. The Patents Company estimated there existed 11 500 motion picture houses across the United States. About 6250 of these were licensees, and the remainder were independent.[32] They required between 100 and 200 reels of film weekly; and each week they drew at the lowest estimate 26 million people through the turnstile.[33] Yet by the end of the First World War the nickelodeon had been extinguished though the film industry continued to thrive. The feature film brought about these immense changes.[34]

Although a few longer films had been screened occasionally, their true advent can be dated from mid-1912 when a conscious attempt was made to distribute them on a regular basis. It is helpful if we recognise (having encountered early instances of vertical organisation) another simple model of economic growth. This model, which makes a tri-partite distinction between invention, innovation, and diffusion or exploitation, was first used in the context of cinema studies by Douglas Gomery.[35] Invention is the first stage in the development of a new product. This is a comparatively small-scale activity, the work either of scientists or specialists, and its key economic characteristic is that it calls for limited financial commitment, requiring the funding of the project itself, but little else. The invention of the feature matters less to us than its 'innovation'. The term refers to the attempt by an entrepreneur to adapt the invention of others to prevailing business conditions, which themselves have to be changed to fit it. Such a process puts the capital of the entrepreneur at risk, but if it succeeds is likely both greatly to enhance the company's profits and to increase its assets. It will also make it possible to raise further venture capital, so that a further product of such risk-taking may be that the successful company moves into a position of market dominance. This enables it to take decisions that affect the behaviour of the market, where formerly the decisions of more powerful companies had delimited its own activities. This was what Adolf Zukor achieved with his business.

Before we look at what he did, we should note that the third stage of the economic model, diffusion or exploitation, describes that phase of business in which most of the rest of the industry follows the example of the market leader, and the new practice becomes the business norm. In the case of the feature film, diffusion followed innovation very quickly. Spectacular economic growth had of course occurred before in the motion picture industry. This, however, is the earliest transformation that it is convenient to explain by Gomery's model because for the first time shifts in capital and power are of a magnitude that cannot be missed.

As Balio notes, the screening of features actually began in 1911 as independents tested the market with European imports. One of them, a nickelodeon owner, Adolf Zukor, had noticed a degree of unrest with current cinema fare among his audiences, and guessed that longer films with more fully expounded plots and star players would be popular. He approached the board of the Patents Company to ask them to consider producing features, but they rebuffed him. So he decided to invest his own money, and bought the rights to distribute a French film in America (not by any means, however, the first imported feature to be released). After some experimentation to find an appropriate method of distribution, it did good business, confirming Zukor's hunch and making it possible for him swiftly to launch his own production company, Famous Players.[36]

The film Zukor imported ran to four reels and starred Sarah Bernhardt in her only screen appearance. It was called *Queen Elizabeth*, and featured a number of elements that were to recur in films of this kind. Firstly both *Queen Elizabeth* and the spate of imports that were released in the wake of its success featured starring players: and Zukor made a point of recruiting stars to his new company. Secondly the imports were plainly theatrical. They used stars of the legitimate stage as players, and they adapted classics either from dramatic or literary sources: *Camille*, *Cleopatra*, and *Quo Vadis* were among the films brought to America in 1912. Typically they were quite crude aesthetically, often relying on long shots and long takes. This failing had at least the compensating advantage that it kept the camera far enough back from the players that the wide gestures their stage training had taught them did not look as absurd as they would have done in close shot. Finally the new films were spectaculars. All these characteristics blended sweetly with the ambitions of the industry to look for the middle-class audience, and to offer it more decorous fare. The classics and middle-class theatre were plainly legitimate, while the sight of expensive sets and costumes provided immediate gratification too.

Zukor and the producers who followed him into feature-film production therefore rushed to sign stage actors, and the drive to imitate the legitimate theatre was so strong, Sklar reckons, that it threatened to turn films into mere records of stage performances.[37] The vogue for theatrical films seems not to have dissipated until 1915, by which time audiences familiar with the vividly cinematic work of such directors as D. W. Griffith, Reginald Barker and Maurice Tourneur found the performance and appearance of stage players inadequate to their new tastes. Harry Aitken, who had set up a production company on the profits from distributing Griffith's *Birth of a Nation* (1915), wrecked it by hiring expensive stage stars just as the vogue for them evaporated.[38] Zukor, only just in time to save his company, directed his famous players to act in accordance with the requirements of the camera rather than of the stage.

As soon as the popularity of the feature (whether theatrical or cinematic) had been demonstrated it exerted irresistible pressure for change upon the structure of the industry; and it did so simply because it ran for a longer time than a programme of shorts. This fact had consequences that shaped the industry for more than three decades, because the length of the feature meant that it could not be shown in nickelodeons. Their 10 cents admission charge was predicated on the speed of audience turnaround in small halls in which programmes lasted about 20 minutes. To hire films running three to four times longer, and costing more to rent, would have forced nickelodeon operators to push their prices way beyond the means of the working class, still by far the largest part of the audience. The advent of the feature was bound to intensify the need to screen in larger motion picture theatres, which were beginning to appear by 1912, particularly in city-centre areas.

The tendency of the feature film to push prices upwards was, however, perfectly acceptable within the industry, provided the audience could afford entry and could be persuaded that they were going to see something pleasing enough to be worth paying for. Inevitably their higher cost tended to select for features a better-off audience; and since such films had to be marketed as something special it was necessary to make them to glossier standards with much improved production values. The demand for higher quality

output in turn called into being a more elaborate production process
in which a number of additional studio crafts became distinct skills.
This division created a newly cxpanded labour elite in which
specialised personnel (handling for example costumes, sets and
make-up) received better pay. In short the studio apparatus began
to develop, as we shall see later.[39]

Initially there were comparatively few movie houses suited to the
screening of features. Sometimes legitimate theatres were booked,
sometimes small-time vaudeville houses. Nor were there enough
features to screen full time. Those cinemas that did take them also
continued to rent from their regular suppliers their normal
programmes of short films, not wanting to disrupt the contracts on
which they had to rely when they could not get features.[40]

Though some of the theatres were able to adapt, none of the old
network of exchanges could, partly because they needed to develop
new financial structures, and partly because each new feature
required individual promotional effort to make the best of its
qualities. Zukor tried two new methods of distribution with *Queen
Elizabeth*. They were to dominate the new market until a more
stable mechanism was established in 1916. The first method was
roadshowing. Still used today to launch specialised films, roadshowing
entails either the producer or, as in Zukor's case, the distributor
taking over the operation of a small number of carefully selected
theatres during the run of the film he is promoting. He would make
himself responsible for publicity, and in these early days might even
run the equipment, paying the theatre owners a rental fee in return.
Though this system did not work for *Queen Elizabeth*, it returned
handsome profits to George Kleine who imported *Quo Vadis* and
played it from spring to autumn 1913 at a Broadway venue. He
charged a dollar, then an enormous sum, for admission to what was
marketed as a prestige event; and his success with this startling
innovation did not pass unnoticed. More than twenty roadshows of
the same feature were soon playing right across North America.[41]
Because roadshowing depended on charging high ticket prices to
amortise the high costs of this method of screening, it worked
profitably only with strong attractions.

Queen Elizabeth eventually made money when Zukor adopted
the suggestion of an enterprising salesman that they sell it by what
became known as the 'states' rights' method. Still used to this day by
small independent producers who cannot interest a major distributor
in their films, this method entails the sale of rental rights to

distributors who cover specifically delimited territories (or states). At this time the initial sale of rights was usually for a fixed fee, which had the disadvantage that the producer did not share in unusually large profits, though he was sheltered from potential loss. The states' rights distributor leased the film to movie houses, either for a flat rental or, ever more commonly as the months passed, for a percentage of box-office takings. This method had the advantage that the distributor could give each film the individual attention it required; he could get to know the houses which in his area screened features, and deal with them. Its disadvantage, however, was to prove such that within four years it became necessary to supersede it with a more efficient system for the supply to cinemas of a regular flow of features. For its inefficiency, arising from the distributor having to deal with every film and every venue separately, meant that the rental price of a film was often not enough to pay for the selling costs involved.[42] A more efficient method was developed in 1916. As we shall see in Chapter 5 it streamlined the movement of features from studio to movie house, centralising control and bringing about changes in the pricing and selling of films which made the industry both more profitable and more powerful.

The advent of the feature film marks a shift between generations in the industry. It killed off the nickelodeon. Very few of the earlier production and distribution companies made the transition to the new era (with only Vitagraph, Universal, and Fox's companies continuing to thrive). And it confirmed the establishment of Hollywood as the single most important site of production.

5 Architecture of the Feature Film, 1915–25

In the period from 1908 to 1914 a number of new motion picture theatres were designed in imitation of fashionable public buildings. Traditionally such designs were based, as May says, on the classical architecture of Greece and Rome.[1] Soon, however, it became possible to find evidence of new motion picture theatres (like Boston's Modern, opened in 1914 to take an audience of 1000 people) in which classicism had become deeply confused with various European styles. The ruling principle of the Modern's architecture was Gothic, but Romanesque and romantic styles were also commonly used.[2] It was not uncommon to find architectural styles thrown together in a mishmash, with the visual excitements of the Gothic or Romanesque oddly framed by 'the Doric, Ionic and Corinthian pillar associated with classicism and reason'.[3]

Here is a further instance of the film industry trying to have things both ways. For it hardly needs stressing that the classic style (which incidentally was also the style of established opera and vaudeville houses) harmonised agreeably with the desire of the industry to appear respectable, and to associate its products with the dignity of literary classics.[4] D. W. Griffith liked the classical setting of such theatres, which seemed to him to provide a proper frame for films advocating a decent morality while remaining true to the democratic spirit of America.[5] But where, as happened increasingly often, a theatre conflated classical with less restrained architecture, the double style held forth through its more exuberant aspects the promise of more immediate (and saleable) gratifications, the arousal of pleasing emotions.

The architectural shift confirms that exhibitors had gradually become aware that most of their clientele sought something more than propriety. Even as late as 1912 while some 5 per cent of New York City audiences comprised the business class, and 25 per cent were clerical workers, about 70 per cent continued to be the oldest audience of the motion picture, the working class. As we have suggested, their interest in propriety had never been as insistent as that of the reformers. Audiences seemed, as the second decade of the century commenced, to have begun looking for not only a

38

release from daily cares, but something of the new glamour of city nightlife.[6] And things were changing rapidly. For instance electricity had enabled the managers of legitimate theatres to transform Broadway from a gloomy gaslit thoroughfare into a brilliant 'Great White Way' which drew excited tributes from many. Movie theatre proprietors followed their example, and decorated their theatre fronts with the sparkling new lights to give the audience an advance taste of the delights that awaited them within. Even the operators of some of the glossier nickelodeons, having dressed their theatre fronts with curious versions of classical (or Moorish, Romanesque or Art Nouveau) architecture, tinselled over their lines with hundreds of electric lights.[7]

Electricity had another use: from about 1912 photoplayers became popular. These automatic instruments played from piano and orchestra rolls, which made it possible for exchanges to supply pre-recorded music with films. In addition operators of the more sophisticated machines could call up a range of 'novelty effects' to embellish the action of the photoplay: bird whistles, horses' hooves, fire alarms, car horns and even the smashing of crockery were within their power. For many movie houses photoplayers had another function at least as important as the accompaniment of films, for instruments were often placed in the lobby (where they might play for twelve hours a day) as a means of attracting patrons to the box office.[8]

Thus even before the construction of the first picture palaces, we find the ambience in which films were screened contributing to the sense of excitement which the movies themselves were to build upon. The place as much as its screenings becomes a part of the package that is sold. It was not unusual for the newer downtown theatres built after 1910 to accommodate 800 customers or more; thus although they had not been designed for that purpose, they were well suited to play feature films. And despite their grandiose associations, these larger theatres for a while kept their prices to a level not much higher – not more than 15 cents – than the nickelodeons, still well within the range of patrons with modest income.

In the early days of feature films the managers of a number of legitimate theatres responded to the fact that the movies were drawing away their audiences. Admissions, which had been estimated at 26 million per week in 1908, had grown according to one (probably generous) estimate to 49 million by 1914.[9] There are plenty of accounts of legitimate theatres converting to the screening of features.[10] Not only were these larger venues suited to the economics of screening the longer picture, through their very size they began to give the film (image, characters and narrative) greater prominence.

Thus several ideas were available for those architects to take up who began, about the time Zukor innovated the feature, to specialise in planning a new generation of extravagant, purpose-built, motion picture theatres that were to contribute substantially to giving the whole industry a new profitability and gloss. The sensational success of Griffith's *Birth of a Nation* much enhanced the enthusiasm of showmen both for converting old theatres and building new cinemas. Against a background of booming income, the exhibition arm of the industry began to reinvest some of its takings in search of yet higher profits. And it did so by increasing the provision of first-run theatres, where audiences already expected to find better and newer releases (including features). They were further prompted to make this end of the market their target because from about 1915–16 the system of price differentials between first-run and later-run theatres became fully institutionalised, with patrons paying more the earlier they saw a film. Already the major profits were to be made from first release, and price differential was becoming one of the means by which the industry was controlled. It follows that owners of cheaper houses that were relegated to lower status and later runs could seldom afford to enter this race to rebuild. Those who could revamped their nickelodeons to make them at least look like first-run houses, but unless they could persuade distributors to give them that status, they could not anticipate making the big profits of the privileged theatres.[11]

During the 1920s the ordering of runs hardened into a complete mechanism for the dominance of exhibition by the big distributors. For not only was each theatre given its designated run, it was held to it by being obliged to observe a clearance – a period of time between successive runs of between seven and thirty days. As we have mentioned, clearances were effective within prescribed zones or territories. Thus the effect of the run-zone-clearance system was to protect first-run cinemas from competition in their own locales. Second-run and later-run theatres could only obtain product at predetermined periods after earlier-run houses had played it – a delaying mechanism that enhanced the profitability of the first-run houses.[12] Thus control of these cinemas meant control of the industry, and they became targets for purchase by the big producer–distributors.

The gap between first-run and late-run theatres now widened to embrace subject matter: by 1914 the National Board of Censorship, now five years old, limited its jurisdiction to the 5 and 10 cents theatres. This created a double standard whereby the costlier theatres were permitted to play films like the white slavery cycle and short films purportedly on sex education that the Board denied the nickelodeons.[13] Evidently the show of respectability on which the newer theatres were founded was sufficient to render wholesome within their walls material that would elsewhere seem salacious.

As May argues, from about 1914 exhibitors began to understand that going to the movies meant much more than simply watching a screen. They also came to understand that the feature film in particular enveloped audiences in an experience that immersed them in the life they saw depicted in light.[14] They realised that they could extend that experience, so that entering a classy movie theatre would be like making an escape from drab reality and becoming part of the fantasy world which both the building and the screen created. Although during the next fifteen years expensive theatres were built in well lit thoroughfares to reassure audiences of their respectability and safety, their architecture and interior design drew moviegoers ever more deeply into dreamland.[15]

This transformation of cinema architecture did not happen all at once. Gradually, however, as Ben Hall shows, a new kind of theatre design established itself, quite different from that of the so-called standard school of classical architecture to whose work we have already referred. The new style became known as 'atmospheric'. Its designers took their ideas from romantic views of nature and ideal landscape gardens. One distinctive feature was that its interior decor relied upon electric lighting to gain its effects. And those effects were startling. As Hall says, the mark of the atmospheric theatre was that one entered and took one's seat apparently in an amphitheatre, Persian court or Spanish patio – this under an open sky that constantly changed, starlight succeeding fluffy clouds or splendid moonlight, all created by intricately programmed effects lights.[16]

The impact of these costly palaces on the luxury end of the market is seen in many factors, not least in the way the standard school itself felt the pressure to change. As the years passed the classical influence waned, and by the end of the 1920s the two styles were indistinguishable, had become altogether more flashy, and exploited Hindu, Chinese, Persian and Spanish as well as Romanesque styles, adapting them to some famous movie theatres.[17] As May remarks, at its most lavish in the city centres the cinema was to be housed among undulating spires and curving pillars, beneath floating ceilings.[18] Alternatively the audience might seem to have stepped back to some perfection of nature, and to have left the city to enter a paradise garden.

By the peak of the silent era, in the mid-1920s, movie palaces stood in all the major cities, either in the urban centres or in outlying business areas which public transport served efficiently. By that time improved transport and, more important, rising levels of private income together with less arduous hours of work meant that costlier downtown entertainment had become accessible to working people. Now the picture palaces emulated the old vaudeville, with programmes running two hours and longer. These programmes even included live acts, though as Gomery points out they seldom accounted for more than a sixth of the performance. No live theatre could imitate a movie palace offering five shows a day, starting at noon and ending near midnight. And because their wages to performers were less, and they could run so many shows, the palaces could charge prices about half the cost of vaudeville theatres.[19] Nonetheless by 1923 the spectator who still wanted to see movies for 10 to 15 cents had to go to a fifth-run house in the side streets. Admission to downtown theatres tended to cost 65 to 75 cents, and to the movie palaces could be as much as a dollar.[20]

Typically their programmes began with a 10 minute overture, sometimes featuring a theme from the main film. Then a newsreel might follow, a live act, and a prologue or song, or there might be a comedy short. The feature would conclude the show; in the afternoons it would be accompanied by an organist, but in the evenings an orchestra of up to 70 players provided the music.[21] Different impresarios offered variant patterns of presentation, but they all featured a full programme. No surprise that, as Gomery records, the picture palace by 1923 was well on the way to swallowing the audience for the vaudeville.[22]

That the marketing strategy for these astonishing movie palaces had been thought through in complete detail is confirmed by the care with which their managers considered the clientele. Their ambitions reached to nothing less than the selling of a total experience. Their staff, neatly dressed and usually young, had to speak to customers in a respectful but friendly way so as to make them feel at ease, and diffuse any nervousness which some might feel in such awesome surroundings.[23] In all the manager had to attend to a multitude of details, the organisation of a large staff, and the co-ordination and promotion of a complex programme: he had become also an impresario. Some, like S. L. Rothapfel, who eventually ran a radio show, became well-known personalities. The slogan he coined characterises the impresario's attitude: 'Don't give the people what they want – give them something better!'[24]

Of course the people were not being given anything. What they got they paid for; and we shall look later at the way the movie palaces boosted the ideology of mass consumption that began to evolve in America after the First World War. For the moment, however, we must consider other connections between these large theatres, the feature film, and business: on these new big screens an image that had altered, the star personality in the extended narrative, was being sold and consumed. Leading players had of course been given star status since Laemmle invented Florence Lawrence; but makers of short films had neither the narrative space, nor with few exceptions the cinematic skills, to endow these stars with screen personality. Two factors changed this. First, the extended narrative, which often concentrated like the nineteenth-century novel on character. And second, the development of a film rhetoric in which the face, clothing and mannerisms of leading players were made fetishes. The star becomes an integral component in the success of the entire business.

Peter Baxter summarises important changes occurring after 1915 in the presentation of stars. He finds this to be a key year because it saw both advances in the electrification of Californian studios and the introduction of new Kleig lights. These were the only lights available that enabled directors and camera operators to work with the kind of precision that became the model for the American industry after the success of several films directed by C. B. De Mille. De Mille's designer Wilfred Buckland had worked with the theatrical impressario David Belasco, and introduced to the screen ideas he had developed for him. This De Mille required because he insisted on creating three-dimensional sets instead of the flat scenery that had previously been acceptable; but illuminating such a space presented problems quite different from those inherent in lighting flats. So his crew began to light in the atmospheric manner of

Belasco, producing lighting patterns which seemed to be natural, and to come from the doors, windows and lamps in shot, but in actuality were highly expressive in augmenting illusions. It was, as Baxter says, this ingenious blend of the seemingly naturalistic with the actually expressive that Hollywood took over as its own.[25] In a sense, too, the light on-screen blends with that off-screen since the wonderful lighting schemes in the atmospheric movie palaces did the same work, creating illusions while seeming merely to illustrate the features of the place.[26]

As lighting became more precise, it became possible not merely to illuminate and mould, but also to leave areas of darkness in the image; but exercising this kind of control required the exclusion of natural light which gave too general an illumination. Thus a change in lighting patterns led to a change in working conditions and encouraged the more prosperous production companies to build studios. It also allowed them to extend the working day on the set well beyond the late afternoon, and made it possible for them to exploit their labour.[27] This was to build up trouble for the future when workers finally unionised themselves in the 1920s.

The new lighting patterns were gradually brought to bear on the human face in a way which transformed the presentation of the star. Hitherto light directed at the faces of actors had of necessity been as flat as that falling on the set. Although the close-up had been a routine expressive device since the early teens, its full impact was at first necessarily muffled by the flatness of both lighting and make-up. The new subtlety in lighting rendered a moulding of brightness and shadow on the face which had not been possible earlier. The face now appears as if in three dimensions. When, after the introduction of panchromatic film stock in the mid-1920s, make-up became less cumbersome, actors could register in close-up fine nuances of facial expression.

Parallel to the working out of techniques which assisted actors in expressing emotions and personalities there developed also, as Baxter argues, an unconscious ideology in which the individuality of the star can come to seem to have a numinosity of its own. The face of the American actor, which usually has more light played on it than the surrounding set, becomes within the image a light source in itself, radiating energy. It is made a fetish, and becomes a shining sign signifying not precisely divinity, but a transcendent power of Great Love. The charisma of the star, Baxter argues, is that of the hero or saint: the aura which surrounds the being believed to be exceptional becomes in cinema an actual aura created by lights, gauzes and processing effects.[28]

This is less remote than it may at first seem from the economics of the film business. First of all, as the objects of desire, stars by definition attracted a wide public. That public could not encounter their heroes and heroines without paying either to get into the cinema or to buy the fan magazines that now became an integral part of the industry. While such magazines had been published since the launching of *Photoplay* in 1911, they first carry evidence from about 1916 that stars had significance in shaping Americans' emotional lives; and from about 1918 stars have clearly become objects of more than intense interest. The ardent devotion that they aroused sharpened the desire of a substantial number of movie-goers to see new releases as soon as possible, and tended to increase further the takings of first-run theatres. Thus stars, too, embodied richly the ethos of consumption in which the industry was now involving itself.[29]

We have seen that the states' rights and roadshowing methods of distribution were too labour-intensive to return profits except in the rental of specially attractive feature films. Inevitably as producers reacted to favourable audience response by increasing their output of features, most of them by definition could not be special. There was a further difficulty in the way of routine feature production, namely the cost of making films of such length, which amounted to between $10 000 and $30 000. The investment they required from producers was so great that they could not afford to turn them out on a regular basis when returns from states' rights distribution were often slow to reach them.

The man who devised a mechanism for dealing with these problems was a discontented exchange operator for the General Film Company in San Francisco, W. W. Hodkinson. He brought about the breakthrough to routine feature-film production and promotion. Unable to convince General Film of the profits to be made from distributing good features, he exploited contacts of his own and in 1914 put together the first national distribution company with the help of a number of businessmen. The new company was called Paramount Pictures Corporation; it was well capitalised, and at once entered into contracts with some of the principal manufacturers of the new feature films. They included Adolf Zukor's Famous Players and others, including the Jesse Lasky/Samuel Goldfish (later

Goldwyn)/C. B. De Mille combination. Having concluded these deals, Hodkinson was able to face the industry with the promise that he could supply year-round a regular flow of two features per week. He achieved this goal not merely by setting up a distribution network, but by arranging to fund producers. Paramount itself invested in advance in the production of contributing companies. In return it took 35 per cent of the gross rental from theatres, passing the balance to the production company. Thus both the distributor and producer would share increased rentals, and both would share the risks. Hodkinson's ideas included one other, upon which the scheme was based – that each film should play for more than one night. When films had run a single night only, those who missed the one day's performances had to wait for the film to show up at a second-run house before they could catch it. The feature film, with the space it offered for narrative development, was likely by its nature to provide more substantial entertainment than short films, and the two films per week pattern of release favoured by Hodkinson allowed word-of-mouth report to build up.[30] Where a star was billed, the new system helped build not only the film's but also the player's reputation. What is more, distributors, who often knew the market well, were now helping fund features and made sure producers knew what kinds of movie they wanted to sell.[31]

Though the Paramount features cost theatres more, they produced greater takings and profits.[32] Audience demand, and the huge success of the new distribution method, attracted wide attention and made the transition from innovation to diffusion swift: other national distributors entered the market. Immense new business was generated, and the feature film took over the market as rapidly as sound was to do a decade later. It soon became apparent that Paramount was in a very powerful position, able not only to take profit but to regulate the industry. Aware of this, Adolf Zukor, whose Famous Players company had by 1916 established itself as the principal contributor to the Paramount programme, proposed to Hodkinson that their production and distribution companies should merge. Hodkinson refused the offer, but Zukor, now a powerful producer thanks to the commercial appeal of new stars he had signed up, succeeded in deposing him from the board of the company he had founded. Thus in 1916 Paramount merged with Famous Players and the Lasky company, with Zukor as president. The first major step towards vertically structuring the feature-film business had been taken.[33]

Zukor had still not completed the cycle of innovation which launch of the feature had commenced. His recent moves had left him in command of a celebrated crew of stars and some of the most exciting directors in the American industry. His stars were a sufficiently novel and irresistible attraction in the late teens that they could be relied on to sell the pictures in which they appeared (a phenomenon which, however, did not hold true indefinitely). Among them were Mary Pickford, Douglas Fairbanks, Gloria Swanson, Norma and Constance Talmadge, William S. Hart and Fatty Arbuckle. Aware of their value to their producers, they were in a position to demand ever higher rewards on the threat of moving to other production companies if their demands were not met. In the period from the start of the World War to 1919 their salaries rose so fast that they became the major factor in the increase of production costs. But if at this period stars sold their pictures and so justified their pay, this still left the industry the problem of doing worthwhile business with films that did not have their presence to make them go. Typically producers who did not own stars tried through fan magazines and publicity to convince the public that their actors were every bit as attractive as the Pickfords and Fairbankses.[34]

To resolve the difficulty of selling films without stars, and to ensure the sale of all Paramount's product, Zukor returned to a method which had been tried in a small way earlier, and imposed it on his clients with a new imperiousness. This method, which exhibitors loathed for the way it curtailed their freedom of choice, is known as block-booking. It became so effective a means of ensuring the continuity or standardisation of business that all the distributors that were to achieve power within the industry were to enforce it upon exhibitors until the practice was outlawed a generation later. Block-booking forced the theatre owner to take an entire package of films if he was to have any one of them: under Zukor such packages were to reach the enormous size of 104 movies, a year's supply for a theatre changing programme twice weekly.

From the distributor's and producers' points of view, the new system was a triumphant success. It was a way of doing business in which the ownership of stars stabilised the entire business so that films without merit would still return profit. It worked so well that by 1918, only the second season after the introduction of block-booking, Paramount distributed no less than 220 features – a huge number. And they managed to sell all the films despite the fact that, as Balio alleges, a major part of their output was second rate.[35]

For the exhibitor the problem was simple. The package would contain star movies that the Pickfords, Swansons and Harts would render very profitable. But such films would be a minority. And while other films in the package would have their merits, yet more would be altogether inferior productions; and films without stars could be uncertain prospects at the box office. Indeed some of the poorer productions might do lamentably. But if he wanted the stars' films, the exhibitor had to take the package. As long as Paramount had the best roster of stars, its attractions, despite the repugnance block-booking aroused, were irresistible. But the fact that the distributor's system trapped them so perfectly added to the rage theatre managers felt.

Two other aspects of the block-booking system enraged exhibitors. As no distributor could afford to stockpile a year's production so that exhibitors could preview it before signing contracts, exhibitors were buying blind. Indeed with much of the package there might be no more than a title and a brief descriptive note. Even features with starring players were largely bought blind. To add to exhibitors' pain, until the 1920s distributors as standard practice required them to pay in advance, on signing contracts, 25 per cent of each film's rental.[36] Thus they were funding product that did not yet exist and which in part they did not want.

Not unnaturally exhibitors always attempted to destroy the blind-bid, block-booking system. In the studio era it dovetailed with the run-zone-clearance system to produce a rigid hierarchy of theatres which the distributors controlled completely, and from which they took the bulk of the profits. These interlocking mechanisms of control assured continuity of business for the big companies. As we shall see, the destruction of this system in the 1940s had serious consequences for the whole industry; and in more recent times distributors have striven with some success to impose blind-bidding once again.

Exhibitors sought a means of resisting Paramount's market dominance, and they found it in the theatre chain. As early as 1912 local chains had become in some areas of the United States an important factor in the film market. By 1916 chains in New Orleans and Philadelphia were strong enough to be able to insist on distributors reducing prices under threat of the chains not booking their product. Plainly horizontal linking of theatres (usually under a holding company since group operation reduced costs) could be a source of strength.[37] Anger aroused by Zukor's imposition of block-booking led a number of exhibitors quickly to react by forming a new kind of chain or circuit on a national basis. With Thomas L. Tally leading the innovation, as he had done with nickelodeons, twenty-six exhibitors joined forces and formed the First National Exhibitors Circuit in 1917. They were not a random gathering of exhibitors, however, but the owners of first-class theatres. Their plan was to buy the rights to films of quality, to screen them in their own theatres, and then to distribute them to theatres in their own areas: clearly they saw what power could be wielded by first-run houses.

Initially the aim of First National was simply to gain access to good films without falling into the restrictive Paramount network. They did not mean to produce their own films – though after a few years they were to do so. However, they intended from the start to finance production, and they succeeded so well that in 1918 they were able to entice Chaplin away from Mutual, and (even more sweetly) won Pickford from Paramount, placing them under contract for $1 million each to make films for First National distribution. Already the First National network encompassed nearly 200 first-run theatres, and had screening agreements with a further 400.[38] It has been estimated that by 1920 they controlled some 3400 theatres.[39]

The way Zukor reacted expressed his own tribute to First National's theft of part of his market. As early as August 1917 he freed Paramount's clients from the requirement to block-book (though the practice was reinstated when he realised he had failed to conciliate his rival).[40] He then in 1919 attempted to do a deal with First National under which their theatre chain would not produce films, and would screen only Famous Players–Lasky productions.[41] Incidentally rumour of this move may have influenced Chaplin, Pickford, Fairbanks and Griffith in forming United Artists in the same year, in that (as the most expensive talents in the industry) they could have been frozen out by such a monopoly.[42] But Zukor's move, which would have merged First National into Paramount, failed, and he turned to open warfare. Taking backing from a stock flotation of $10 million, he commenced an aggressive programme of theatre acquisition which made Paramount by 1926 the owner of a large chain of 1000 theatres.[43]

This new battle for the theatres was again tough. Where Zukor could not persuade owners to sell, he bullied, threatening independents with loss of their livelihoods. And he would carry out those threats if strong-arm persuasion failed, buying up theatres and undercutting his competitors, or building on prime sites and outclassing the other theatres in the vicinity.[44] Thanks to this ruthless policy Paramount became the first vertically integrated company in the feature business, controlling production, distribution and exhibition in a sizeable slice of the industry. Inevitably First National had to respond or succumb, and they added production to their distribution and theatrical interests when in 1922 they built a large studio in Burbank.[45]

Finding the market squeezed by these heavyweight rivals, others joined the rush to merge and expand into vertical organisations; for all the indications were that those who remained independent, in any of the three sectors of the industry, would be shut off from its real profits. This, therefore, is the period when several companies that became major forces in the industry established themselves, often by bringing together fragmentary independent concerns. For example, in 1920 Marcus Loew, who had built up a substantial chain of 100 theatres, bought his corporation, Loew's, into production and distribution by taking over a small company, Metro. In 1924 he purchased two independent companies to strengthen his base in production (Goldwyn Pictures and Louis B. Mayer's company), and from these deals Metro-Goldwyn-Mayer was constructed. In the same period William Fox, who already had strong interests in production and distribution, extended his theatrical holdings by building thirty first-run theatres, each seating from 4 to 5 thousand.[46] Thus in a few years four large companies had been put together, all structured on vertical principles. Paramount, First National and Loew's became the new giants of the industry, with Fox in the next rank of magnitude seeking the means to get on equal terms with the others.

Even though all this activity proceeded on the back of a thriving industry, it required too much investment for profits alone to provide. Some capital was raised by the sale of stock, but large sums were advanced by the banks. Their commitment by the mid-1920s was of two kinds – production financing (that is the funding of single films), and corporate funding. It was one of the advantages of vertical structuring to the emerging movie majors that it allowed bankers to take a greater interest in backing them with general finance of the type needed for capital expansion, because the purchase of theatres furnished them with tangible assets upon which bankers could secure their loans.[47] They further secured their advances by taking seats on the boards of management of the powerful companies they were helping establish in positions of dominance in the industry.[48] The presence for the first time in strength of financial experts in the industry's boardrooms was to have its consequences, not only for production, where as we shall see they reckoned they could devise less extravagant methods of organising film-making, but also in the running of theatre chains. The pressures they exerted moved the industry in the direction of standardisation.

Although the new major companies bought theatres very widely, they tended to concentrate in different parts of the country where each could dominate its local market.[49] Here they needed each other's product to fill their theatres' schedules. They competed in only about thirty metropolitan centres.[50] And although they bought up a range of theatre types, they tended to concentrate on the quality end of the market, and in particular on first-run houses. They did so because the hierarchy of motion picture theatres had long since become a complete system. Gomery shows that by 1926 an average of half the audience each week attended what he calls the key theatres. These were the first-run and second-run houses in the 79 American cities with populations of more than 100 000: in all about 2000 theatres out of a total number that had risen in the same year to about 20 000.[51] When one recalls that audiences would have to pay more to get into such theatres – with movie palaces seating between 1500 and 5000 people taking pride of place – and that those theatres would have returned to distributors a higher percentage of box-office takings than later-run theatres, it becomes apparent that the economic importance of the palaces and early-run metropolitan theatres can hardly be overemphasised.

At this top end of the market the theatre chains had by now (no doubt with the enthusiastic support of the industry's bankers) organised themselves according to principles that derived directly from the most up-to-date retailing organisations of the 1920s, the national chainstores.[52] This, as Gomery shows in his detailed account of the operation of the Balaban and Katz chain, had the double effect of both maximising consumer appeal and reducing costs.[53] When in November 1925 Paramount took over this chain and merged it with their Publix Theatres, Sam Katz extended the same principles to operate throughout the vast organisation, and other companies followed this example.[54] Whereas before 1920 movie exhibition had been primarily a regional business, from the mid-1920s it becomes a national operation. Management functioned centrally, which meant that the Publix business operated from the New York office. Programming, much of the administration, advertising and publicity were run in exact and efficient detail from the centre. By this means fixed overheads were split across the whole organisation; the chain projected a unified image through everything from its advertising campaigns to the billboards and logos of its theatres; and it kept itself informed about local requirements by obliging its theatre managers to return detailed and regular reports.[55] Chain operations of this kind tended to homogenise programmes throughout the country, and thus contributed to the pressure to standardise and routinise the industry.

Before we look at the pressures that this now powerful, well-organised industry exerted on the films themselves, it is worth reminding ourselves that we have been describing the thriving sector of the industry. The small companies left out of the new combinations, the new independents, were altogether more vulnerable to fluctuations in the market. And these did occur. There was a recession in American business in 1921, following the post-war boom; and for a short frightening period over the winter of 1921–2 attendances at theatres began to fall – possibly, as Sklar speculates, exacerbated by other factors including the availability of new kinds of leisure activity. But whether recession, entertainment reaching directly into the home through the radio, or the pleasure of being able to get out and about in the new forms of public and private transport temporarily reduced the movie audience, the effect on small operators was far worse than on the new majors[56] For this recession, which ended abruptly in 1923, coincided with a period of serious overproduction. Over 600 films were being produced each year, more by 150 to 200 than were required to fill the nation's screens. With sales competition fierce, prices charged to theatres dropped, but at a time when production costs had risen sharply. Small producers, some of whom had set up in the post-war boom to take advantage of the growth in the industry, did not have the reserves to enable them to carry losses forward to better times. Small exhibitors, squeezed by theatre chains into late runs, no longer had the profit potential to recover when they lost part of their regular audience. There were a number of bankruptcies.[57]

6 Standardising Production and Consumption, 1915–25

During the decade that followed the introduction of the feature film, the movie business, as we have seen, ceased to comprise firms that were very much the creation of an individual who remained in touch with, and controlled directly, all that he had set up. Instead companies grew so large, employed so many staff, and directed their activities so widely both in territory and in the range of their business, that they became corporate enterprises. In the process they lost a good deal of their freedom to act on the impulse of their owners. Now they began to find themselves obliged to respect various requirements of their new financial partners, the bankers and brokers, including in particular the maintenance of profitability. Since large corporations have commitments to ongoing expenditure which they cannot without difficulty shed (commitments among other things to salaries and wages, rents and rates, power bills, depreciation and maintenance), they have to ensure that they bring in as a matter of routine at least sufficient income to meet these obligations.

For this reason the new major companies took measures to ensure as far as they could that their income was not only as large but also as regular as possible. Block-booking, we have remarked, was a means of spreading risk and organising continuity of film rental; and the studios had other means (stars, genres and marketing) by which they tried to draw custom. Equally they developed methods – the more rigorous the more their bankers involved themselves in studio management – for spreading costs and reducing waste.

The building up and exploitation of stars was an early move to standardise product appeal. In fact the presentation of a star gives a clear indication of what standardisation of the product means in the motion picture industry, for to say that the star remains the same from one movie to another is at one time both accurate and absurd. On the one hand in the marketing of an individual player's work, audiences are encouraged to think of a film as being a Mary Pickford movie, for example. The presence of the actress is understood to be in some way the same as in her last production. That is, certain recognisable character and personality traits associated with her previous roles, publicity, and public appearances will be allowed to show in each new performance. Over the years those characteristics may evolve – and each role will usually call for the representation of an identifiably different character; but audiences may also resist change in certain aspects of the star. Famously, Mary Pickford's audiences would not allow her to get rid of her little-girl image. Thus her case provides a clear instance of the insistent consumption by audiences of a constructed personality. This entailed standardising the star's performances and caused her publicity, in common with that for every star, to dwell both on the sameness of her roles (her recurring presence) and their novelty (she plays a new part in each film).[1] Even when the star was cast against type to vary her roles (as was the case with Bette Davis at Warner Brothers in the 1930s), the counter-character would relate to her dominant character type. In fact the star is defined in part by this extension of a constructed personality beyond the limits of a single film, not only into successive movies, but also into her or his supposedly private life. As Klaprat remarks, this personality was constantly tested against audience response to the star's performances, and was adjusted to maximise market appeal.

Since the protagonist stands at the centre of classical Hollywood narrative and the star's persona moulds the protagonist, the star also shaped the narrative he or she played in. (Thus the Bette Davis vehicle would typically present her as a man-devourer in counterpoint to two men.) Studio screenwriters had to know and be able to develop the star's character. Since to a large extent it preceded the narrative, they had to incorporate its idiosyncrasies into the plot.[2] It follows that stars not only standardised product appeal by making the movies in which they appeared attractive. They also differentiated them. A Bette Davis film is a product quite distinct from that of any other star. Its difference is what makes it desirable, the object of market demand.

The development of a flourishing star system was closely associated, as we have seen, with the innovation of the feature film. But to satisfy market demand more features had to be released than stars could cover, so the industry had to look for additional means to standardise production and maximise income. The block-booking system would not have worked if it had relied for its major attractions only on a relatively small number of star billings scattered thinly across otherwise barren lists: the cinema would have lost its drawing power if audiences had not been able to recognise other attractions in movies lacking stars. The industry (which had always repeated its successes) found in modified repetition another important device for stabilising income. Genres, formula movies, and cycles all became basic elements in studio output from about 1917. Serials, another manifestation of standardised cinema, had been established four years earlier.

The first serial was advanced in its marketing concept, linked as it was to a serialised story in a newspaper. The idea for *The Adventures of Kathlyn* (produced by Selig in 1913) actually came from Walter Howey of the *Chicago Tribune* who reckoned it should be a way of boosting circulation. He was right: the popularity of the screen serialisation helped the *Tribune* greatly, and encouraged the film industry to follow Selig's example. Serials, often with young women as heroines, proliferated.[3]

The enthusiasm of the industry for the serial sprang from the same respect for something which was already pre-sold, as did its liking for genre films. Quite simply if something has sold well already, it seems a lot easier to sell another product whose likeness to its predecessor is greater than its difference. And repetitious work also has the advantage that it speeds production, since crews find they do not have to work out *ab initio* every requirement of the scenario. From at latest 1918, features were classified according to their formula – dramas or melodramas, romances, action pictures, Westerns, comedies or 'shockers' – and every studio planned its output to include a number of films in each category.[4] If a particular cycle suddenly proved immensely popular, as from 1920 in the wake of *The Mark of Zorro* exotic historical romances did, it would be given priority. (Incidentally, these romances, set in imaginary epochs like Hollywood Elizabethan England or Hollywood Renaissance Italy, and starring players with an exotic aura – Ramon Novarro and Rudolf Valentino among them – must have complemented rather well the increasingly hedonistic fantasy of the newer movie palaces.)

From the point of view of the publicity department, stars and genres had much in common. Just as Mary Pickford could only stray a limited distance from the set of meanings her audience had accepted her as signifying, so for example a Western could not be allowed radically to alter the codes of its genre lest it turn into something no longer recognisable as a Western. The likeness increases when we remember that the studios in the 1930s exerted

every control they could enforce upon their stars: they stage-
managed not only their screen but also their social and publicity
appearances, regulating their looks, clothing, and supposed amorous
involvements. Both on and off screen, stars had been turned into
consumable products.

Experts in the marketing of movies have often argued that film
confronts them with a particular problem since each one is unique.
Thus the advertising campaign for a film has to be essentially
different from that which a company like Ford might run for a new
car, because the car, with a finite number of variations, will be
repeated millions of times over. The campaign for Ford, the
argument runs, would seek to sell a massive number of cars, while
that for the film sells just one film, and the next movie will require
an entirely fresh campaign. But the argument relies on inadequate
assumptions, for no fiction is unique – it has to use well-established
coding systems to convey meaning; and to the spectator who did not
have knowledge of such codes as are called into play in, say, the
creation of a plot, the fiction would be incomprehensible. In the
case of a genre movie, the elements that bind it to similar fictions
are stronger than those between films which do not belong to the
genre, for in them a whole range of coded elements have strong
correspondences: narrative, character types, themes, and filmic
control, for instance. For the publicity department this means that
its campaign can concentrate directly on the likenesses between this
film and its predecessors in the kind. In short, the uniqueness of the
product is strikingly de-emphasised.

Broadly speaking this strategy for marketing film has always
worked. A substantial part of the entertainment-seeking public –
usually the major part – tends to look for repeat entertainment,
though the industry is careful not to give the impression it knows
this, preferring to dwell on the novelty of each release. And indeed
Hollywood genre films can permit resolution of the conflict between
the audience's general conservatism and the desire of some film-
makers and part of their audience for innovation. Thus while some
of the more interesting work to come out of the studio system
innovated within the structure of well-defined genres, it remained
possible for publicity departments to market such films as if they
respected the established conventions of the film type.

In recognising that it could sell repeat entertainment, Hollywood
knew of course that it was not limited to working over cycles of
films. By the time the studio system began to take shape, the

industry had also long regarded highly the commercial virtues of well-known novels. These have the marketing advantage of being pre-sold to a substantial audience; and word of their interest often spreads to people who have not got round to reading them and may therefore want to see them as films.

Hollywood also realised early that the same criteria could apply to the legitimate stage production. And the studios kept in close touch with Broadway, just as they had established contracts with literary agencies. Robert McLaughlin discovered that as early as 1915 competition between film production companies for theatrical properties was so intense that screen rights were bought to many plays that had little or no potential film value whatever. This relationship developed to the extent that in some cases Hollywood companies actually financed Broadway productions in order to secure screen rights more cheaply than by bidding for them after the play had become a box-office success. The earliest known venture of this type was undertaken in the 1919–20 season when Famous Players–Lasky provided finance for productions by the Charles Frohman company. Over the next five years an increasing amount of movie money found its way into Broadway productions.[5]

For the purposes of publicity departments, stories could be treated a little like stars: if costly and well known they could be shouted up in the market place; if unknown, the studio would try to pay only a small sum for the rights, and would market other values. Thus the purchase of pre-sold titles, both literary and theatrical, was and continues to be another method by which the film industry attempts to sustain demand for its product. Sometimes the film was used to pre-sell literature. From as early as 1911 the industry had begun to exploit the residual value of plots it had featured, with film scenarios rewritten in the appropriate style for publication in movie magazines that could be sold in theatre foyers. Such tie-ins quickly advanced, and by 1914 book publishers were promoting limited editions of novels illustrated with stills from the film.[6]

By the 1920s the American film industry had adopted methods of cost control that were potentially very sophisticated. Attempts to reduce costs, however, were often resisted by publicity departments which argued that the public usually responded well to the attraction of films marketed as having been made at lavish expense. As Mae Huettig wrote in 1941, 'it is a fixed belief in Hollywood . . . that the quality of film is generally commensurate with its cost.'[7] To draw the

larger audience the extra cost had to show in what the industry
called enhanced 'production value' – either the presence of an
expensive star, or blatant extravagance (lavish sets and costumes,
large crowd scenes or elaborate lighting), or both, would do nicely.
On all these counts the exotic historical romances had high
production values, and were marketed accordingly.

Cost control, as Janet Staiger shows, was merely one aspect of a
system of studio management that had taken its origins from an
industrial method of organising work: the division of labour.[8]
Probably Thomas Ince was first to adopt this system at his Californian
studio, where it was functioning by 1915; but Staiger makes it clear
that other studios were introducing it at much the same time. By the
start of the 1920s it had become an essential element in managing
Hollywood studio production. Division of labour she shows to be
characterised by separation of the work of production into its
constituent elements. Its particular advantages included:

1. The increase in skill of workers who perform repeatedly just
   one aspect of the work;
2. Savings in time – and therefore reduction of costs;
3. The invention of equipment that speeds the labour; and
4. Further savings since only those workers doing difficult parts
   of the work are paid high rates – unskilled workers are paid
   less.[9]

Staiger also shows that division of labour was operated in the film
industry in conjunction with a formal system of planning, originally
dubbed 'scientific management' by Adam Smith. This entails
separation of the creation of ideas from their realisation in
production:

> The concept of control adopted by modern management requires
> that every activity in production have its several parallel activities
> in the management centre . . . The result is that the process of
> production is replicated in paper form before, as, and after it
> takes place in physical form.[10]

Planning in this detail ensures both quality and cost control; it
enables management to preplan the output of a business and to
control its operations so that the required products are made to the
right quality, in proper time, and at acceptable cost.

For the American film industry, paper-planning meant the
continuity script, the detailed shot-by-shot outline of each film

prepared prior to shooting.[11] That script would be accompanied, in increasing detail as the years passed, by a budget which itemised all the costs involved – labour, materials and overheads – and allocated them to the several studio departments involved. Implicit in the budget was a time allotted for each task, whether the shooting of a scene, or the cutting together of the finished film. Ideally each studio production supervisor would ensure that staff in every department were kept fully occupied so as to spread the costs of employment over the maximum number of pictures: in consequence if, for example, a studio had a strong art department, then its management would for cost effectiveness favour film projects which required its use. Thus, as is plainly apparent in the 1930s, each studio began, for economic as well as artistic reasons, to develop its specialisms.

Where, before the division of labour, films had been produced by men and women each working in a variety of roles, from 1915 individuals come to occupy specific posts. As the studio system grew larger and roles were ever more tightly defined, the pay gap between skilled jobs such as the director's and editor's and the relatively unskilled work of carpenters and drivers widened.

As if such pressures were not sufficient to make for standardisation of output, the scriptwriter too was caught up in the division of labour. For however attractive to the industry the purchase of pre-sold stories, they had inherent disadvantages. They cost more – *Variety* reckoned in 1916 that royalties for purchase of screen rights would start with a minimum advance of $1000 and 10 per cent of the producer's gross, whereas a feature film based on a story written by a scenario department would cost no more than $250 to $500.[12] Then, as Staiger shows, the industry could not be sure either of a regular supply of bought-in stories, nor that they would be suitably written for screen adaptation. The work of the scenario department was therefore to deliver at acceptable cost a regular supply of fully detailed continuity scripts prepared according to a uniform pattern which rendered them ready for shooting. This entailed two things: the writing of a story whose plot and character logic it was possible to film; and the provision of a blueprint which told technicians and actors what they had to do.[13]

If these mechanisms for control were relaxed when studios wanted to make films with lavish production values, they tended to be tightened when bankers' funds were involved. Thus, as Jacobs remarks, after the battle of the theatres, when bankers had undertaken extensive corporate funding, their board representatives looked to production supervisors for careful cost control; one effect was a tendency to standardise the output of each studio and to make it more difficult to discern the input of individuals such as directors or writers.[14]

Despite this emphasis on standardisation it should not be thought that the studios had by the mid-1920s returned to the absurd notion of the Patents Company that films were an undifferentiated product. It is not necessary to argue that studio bosses had much respect for their audiences, but they plainly did recognise that the market had certain identifiable requirements. Their every utterance indicated their pride in knowing what could and could not be sold; but more specifically the fact that they marketed both films by genre and actors as stars reveals that they did distinguish film from film. It seems more doubtful, however, that they yet did much to distinguish one audience from another.

The studio's attitude to their overseas markets showed that here too it took time for them to become aware that they were dealing with audiences which would often have specific needs and preferences. At first with very few exceptions they merely replaced title cards with translations, but made no further changes to adapt films to other cultures; and before the First World War even this practice was too demanding for numbers of American producers who sent films with untranslated title cards to Latin American countries. As we know, however, during the war years the American film developed a polished look, with enhanced art direction, camera work and lighting. This combined with narrative action urged on by classic continuity editing in the basic Hollywood formula and proved a sufficient attraction to draw overseas audiences.[15] In fact American films developed a strong enough appeal to overcome what must have been extraordinary incongruities. Sklar has mentioned for instance how odd American melodramas must have looked in countries where the whites were attempting to convince colonial subjects of their innate moral right to rule.[16]

American entry into the overseas market followed swiftly the foundation of the film business. The absence of language difficulties in the silent cinema, and the ease and cheapness of running additional prints for overseas distribution gave the new medium international potential right from the start. Transatlantic business in the early years ran in both directions. We have already mentioned the enthusiasm with which Méliès's films were greeted in America; and there were plenty of other European producers, Lumière and Pathé large among them, eager to export to that substantial market. Although it is generally agreed that European companies supplied the better films until about 1914, American exports were not negligible. As early as 1907 Vitagraph, the biggest American studio after Edison and Biograph, found that its European trade had grown so considerable that in its studio it operated cameras which recorded two negatives, of which one was retained for the domestic market and the other was sent to Paris where the company had built a new laboratory which ran prints for the European market. Within a year the new plant was turning out four times the number of prints supplied by the Flatbush studio to the American market, though print for print they fetched a lower price.[17] This was to be a telling feature of the growing export market for American films, with other companies following Vitagraph's example and printing from second negatives in Europe from 1909.[18] From the earliest days of export, American companies were able to rely upon the vast home market to recoup their costs, and even to put them in profit. As a consequence they were able to rent out films abroad on much cheaper terms than local manufacturers could compete with as they had smaller domestic markets to provide their basic takings.[19] This demographic circumstance was the basis upon which the American industry founded its commercial superiority. It was always able to undercut the overseas opposition on its home ground, which made its product profoundly attractive to exhibitors abroad. In effect even before American films developed particular virtues of their own, like the sophisticated action-narrative of the feature film, the European market was tied firmly to American cinema.

The First World War created the crucial opportunity for the American industry because it so disrupted European production that with few exceptions only simple, inexpensive films were made there.[20] Not only was American feature-film production creating an increasingly sophisticated cinema, its primary markets did not undergo the upheavals of war; and even while the conflict continued American companies benefited as they satisfied demand in other markets that Europe could no longer supply. They also were able to take advantage of a rapid improvement in US shipping facilities, which had hitherto been much inferior to the British commercial fleet. And they learned to handle overseas markets themselves, where previously they had tended to rely on the greater experience of British agents, reaching their overseas markets indirectly through London. From 1916 American firms became altogether more aggressive and effective commercially overseas.[21] They concentrated on expanding non-European markets vigorously, thus cutting the Europeans out of this market for much longer than the duration of the war. For their movement into new markets, for example in Latin America and Asia, coincided with the diffusion of the feature film, a distinctive and expensive product which attracted foreign audiences, and made it worthwhile for US distributors sometimes to send their own representatives abroad to negotiate high prices. This direct sale method worked well with films of the quality of *Birth of a Nation* (1915) and *Civilization* (1916), which did much to confirm foreign demand for American product.[22] Movie exports rose from 36 million feet in 1915 to 159 million feet in 1916.[23] When the war ended American companies moved swiftly to satisfy demand in Europe, while holding on to the new markets they had gained: by 1925 exports had reached 235 million feet.[24]

Activity of this intensity, which the European film industries found themselves helpless to resist, aroused serious concern. As Thomas Guback shows, European fears did not diminish even when their production companies had recovered to the point of making films that could vie with American output. For by that time the American industry had got so far with the process of structuring itself on vertical principles into a cartel that access to the US market was virtually impossible.

By the mid-1920s the big American companies were so powerful in their domestic market that by tacit agreement they supplied their mutual needs all but exclusively. That is, since no single studio could furnish a sufficient supply for its own theatres' requirements, they bought what they lacked from each other. But they did so in a mutually supportive way, and limited outside competition by declining to buy from independents unless the other major companies were unable to fill their needs. This deliberate policy had the effect of weakening independent companies, and of limiting effective competition for the American market to the ten or so big companies that had established themselves by 1925–6. As far as they were concerned, European exporters, who had no contractual arrangements with the big distributors, had no more favourable status than the independents. As Guback says, this is not to argue that American companies had no regard for European cinema – the major studios were quick to hire talented staff and to devour

European innovations in style or narrative. But they had no intention of allowing foreign product equal opportunity for competition. Imports into America actually fell from 16 million feet in 1913 to about 7 million in 1925.[25] Trade had got so one-sided that ultimately several European countries took action to defend their national cinemas. After 1925, Germany, Italy, France and Britain moved to limit film imports, in some instances by outright limits, in others by quotas which sought to restrict imports to a pre-set proportion of local output.[26] In 1926 the US government moved in support of the motion picture industry in its resistance to quota impositions.[27] The reasons for its doing so are not hard to find.

Ironically it had been the overseas market that drew the attention of the industry firmly to its power as an instrument of marketing and propaganda. It was noticed that American films brought in their train American ideas and a desire to imitate their manners and fashions. Exporters became aware about 1912 that demand for American goods followed films into new territories.[28] Thus well before the climax of the silent era the cinema had emerged as an effective means of persuading people to consume. A number of people in the American industry saw the opportunities and exploited them. Advertising through film began as early as 1916, and extended as publicity executives became aware that theatre chains provided them with a means of contacting a national audience.[29] But advertising in the cinema did not become big business until after the introduction of sound, by which time the radio industry had several years start on it (see Chapter 8).

Long before that, however, the cinema had become an agent of domestic consumerism in other, complementary ways. As May argues, Hollywood demonstrated that two major ideals could be attained in real life: one embraced the vision of the modern family breaking free from Victorian constraints; and the other the pleasures of material consumption.[30] Hollywood seemed to prove this to the movie-going public first by its aura and its architecture; second through the lifestyle of its stars and the studio bosses (which was the subject of generous press coverage); and third by, of course, the films themselves.

Most films demonstrated the pleasures of extravagance all too plainly on their surfaces. Since Hampton, commentators have remarked on the wildly spiralling cost of feature-film production – Hampton himself estimating that average costs rose from $10 000–

$30 000 in 1914 to $150 000–$500 000 in 1924, a large increase, even allowing for inflation.[31] We have already mentioned the enthusiasm of publicity departments for extravagance and bigness on the screen, and the manifest display of lavish production values inevitably carried its own ideological charge.

Among the many myths that run through Hollywood films of this epoch, one that winds itself deeply into the luxury of many costlier films is the dream of personal consumption. It was not uncommon for films to become advocates of this pleasure, as could the stars themselves. Sometimes the combination of their on-screen and off-screen roles made a powerful ideological statement. May argues that the lifestyle and work of Douglas Fairbanks and Mary Pickford during the period 1914–18 came to present new role models for young people of each sex, demonstrating on the one hand how post-Victorian values gave individuals more freedom, and on the other how the traditional virtues of marriage could be preserved by a high level of personal income. They seemed to show that, while the newly emancipated individual expected a freer life than that of the previous generation, the pleasures of a rising disposable income made that entirely possible within marriage, in the enjoyment of the many new leisure pursuits that a couple could now share. As stars, the Fairbankses represented both in their on-screen and off-screen lives this model of high-level consumption. Since they could be imitated merely by buying things – which could make one look like them and might endow one with the same aura of freedom – it was an effective model. Advertisers did not fail to see this: Miss Pickford, for instance, was under contract to model clothes, pets, cars and furnishings. Thus in her case advertising converged with the advocacy of conspicuous consumption in her films.[32]

In a cycle of films made between 1918 and 1924, Cecil B. De Mille brought the celebration of unabashed luxury directly to the screen. Whereas the Pickford and Fairbanks image returned their wealth to the service of marital innocence, De Mille gave his representation of contemporary mores deliberately ambiguous meanings. Although as we have seen he could not by any means claim to be the first to treat sexuality with ambivalence, De Mille seems to have been shrewd and unscrupulous enough to realise that films that showed sexual behaviour at variance with accepted mores had a good chance of attracting both those who would approve and others who condemned such conduct. De Mille took pains to shadow out opportunities for spectators to adopt either moral position, thus confirming a formula for ambivalence which worked so well that Hollywood subsequently relied on it countless times. Indeed ambiguity veils Hollywood treatment of many other topics than human sexuality: how many Vietnam movies seem simultaneously to embrace and refute the American consensus on that war?

De Mille's films between 1918 and 1924 included *Old Wives for New* (1918), *Don't Change Your Husband* (1919), *Male and Female* (1919), *Why Change Your Wife?* (1920), *Forbidden Fruit* (1921), and *The Affairs of Anatol* (1921). Typically they deal with crises in marriage which the growing boredom of one partner with the other brings about. As May shows, they often end (after the couple have experienced sexual adventures outside the marriage) with the old relationship rekindled by each partner's discovery of the necessity of pleasing the other. That pleasure is to be given by being more attractive and fun-loving – and for the woman this usually centres on transforming the ambience of the home and becoming more attractive herself, while for the man it entails providing her with the means to do so.[33]

De Mille's films so effectively confronted the anxieties of the many Americans who were abandoning the constraints of the old Victorian morality but feared the unfamiliar behaviour patterns of the jazz age that they were scrutinised by many as arbiters of the right way to act in new social circumstances.[34] In a culture conscious of style, anxiety about the right way to orient one's life extends swiftly to worry about the way one looks. De Mille's films offered the direct resolution to that problem too, for as surely as they indicated new ways in which it would be pleasurable to behave, they showed people how their homes should look. But before all else they showed how women should dress to renew their sexual appeal. Thus much of the activity that movie-goers might undertake in reforming their identities to match the vision De Mille's films projected entailed the purchase of luxury products. Draped and moulded by these goods, they could begin to see themselves in new ways.[35]

It has often been remarked that from the mid-1910s rising standards of living freed increasing numbers of Americans to spend at least a portion of their income, after basic needs had been satisfied, on what they liked. Cinema itself benefited from popular desire to spend such spare money on leisure; and many other industries did so too. Among them were the furnishing, furniture, and auto industries. De Mille's films provided certain of these industries with a massive publicity boost, and none more than the fashion business. His films showcased extravagant apparel, and in doing so did much to motivate the establishment of close links between the two industries, which endured to the benefit of both sides for many years.

In an article on Hollywood's connections with the advertising business in the 1930s, Charles Eckert records that at the turn of the century Hollywood had just one clothing manufacturer, which made shirts. By 1937 the Associated Apparel Manufacturers of Los Angeles listed 130 members (and the city's furniture business had grown rapidly too). As many as 250 of the largest American department stores kept buyers permanently in the city.[36] For Americans and the many throughout Europe who modelled their looks on what they saw in American movies, the centre of the fashion world shifted from Paris to Hollywood – and the films of De Mille started this change. In later years, as the symbiosis between the two industries matured, Los Angeles fashion houses would provide the stars with their costumes for contemporary stories; the films would act as their billboards, and through carefully planned promotions the dressmakers would ensure that women made the connection. It was an obvious extension to move from fashion to other consumables, and in a few years American cinema became a shop window (occasionally as we shall see through cynical deals) for everything from furnishings and furniture, to cars, sports clothes and even domestic architecture.

Even from the earlier years of this liaison, new fashions in a stylish setting comprised one component of the formula that increased the audience for De Mille's films. Inevitably the tie-in with consumer industries had its effect on the films. De Mille recalled later that in his films of the 1918–24 period he dwelt on modern themes as a consequence of pressure from marketing and sales people. They wanted no historical costume drama, but modern photoplays 'with plenty of clothes, rich sets, and action'.[37]

Cinema has been linked with the other mass media of the day – the printed press and commercial radio – as one of the agents that assisted in bringing about certain changes in American culture. It tended to reduce the importance local communities placed on their own interests and entertainments. It sponsored instead an approximately homogenised national culture whose images and sounds took precedence, especially among the young, as sources of influence and models for socialisation over older cultural value systems.[38] The new culture was essentially urban in its tenor. This was apposite to the demographics of the cinema where, despite the fact that in the mid-1920s over half the population of America lived in rural areas, movie-going was an urban phenomenon. In particular the industrial cities were the real centres of movie-going, and here the first-run houses were concentrated. As May shows, in 1928 over half the nation's motion picture theatres were located in the industrial centres of New York State, Pennsylvania, Illinois, Ohio and California. An illustration of seat distribution confirms the point – there being one cinema seat for every 6 residents of New York City, compared with one for every 32 in Birmingham, Alabama. The cinema made its fullest provision for the northern and the west-coast urban markets, precisely the places where people worked the shortest week and took home the higher *per capita* income.[39] Costly and sophisticated features like De Mille's (essentially urban in character) actually had to play to this market to return profit; the film that appealed to the rural audience had either to be made inexpensively or to interest the urban movie-goer.

Cinema probably contributed to another change, for it has been suggested that the relative uniformity of the new culture prepared audiences for their roles as consumers. Mass-production technologies were now turning out products in vast numbers, but in considerable uniformity; and it followed that the desires and habits of consumers needed to be moulded to a comparable degree of sameness. Nationally distributed film, like nationwide advertising, helped expand demand and channel it into national consumption habits.[40]

As has been mentioned, Hollywood came to be seen almost as a mythic place, a garden where the fruits of consumer spending were enjoyed in the highest degree. From about 1917 the personae of many of the stars expressed the happiness of their condition – one in which wealth and luxury combined to make their images the cynosure of American desire.[41] By their nature, however, paradises are out of reach of most of humanity, and perhaps inevitably an emotional backlash occurred. An immediate consequence of this reaction was to be an intensification of demand for censorship of films.

From 1908 to 1915 US film censorship had been carried out with mixed efficacy by the National Board of Review. For two reasons the release of Griffith's *Birth of a Nation* in 1915 all but crippled it. Firstly, it divided its members against themselves over its racism, and some resigned. Secondly, the film was so popular that it made the Board redundant in its primary role, that of legitimising the cinema to the middle classes (see Chapter 3). Griffith's film did this finally, and the middle classes thereafter went to the cinema without the need of the Board's reassurance. For this reason producers no longer found it necessary to obtain its approval.[42]

Not surprisingly some members of the public continued to find objectionable material in some films. Their protests carried sufficient weight that the industry soon saw that it would help to establish its own regulatory body in order to look into complaints. This it achieved in July 1916 in forming the National Association of Motion Picture Industries. It was intended that the new body should not only respond to public complaints, but also work to the benefit of the industry by imposing its own controls on members in order to defuse the threat of federal censorship. Although it managed to furnish the industry with its first set of written standards, it had not been given the powers to enforce them, and for this reason it was, broadly speaking, ineffectual.[43]

Thus in 1921–2 when the industry found itself the object of hostile scrutiny, it was apparent that it lacked effective means of self-regulation. Pressures to censor films were revived not only in response to film content, but partly in reaction to a series of scandals that hit the reputation of a number of stars and their friends. Massive press coverage was given to a number of incidents, most dramatic among them a murder, a suicide, and a supposed rape. In their wake followed a general ground-swell of resentment directed at the extraordinary wealth of the new superstars; and this sullied even the reputation of Pickford and Fairbanks, as people recalled that they had been married to other partners when they began their life together. Formidable pressure built up during 1921 as bills proposing to enforce censorship were introduced to a number of state legislatures.[44] These proposals menaced the industry with the expensive prospect of having to cut films in different ways for the different states; and it realised that it must act effectively if it was not to lose control of its own output. The anxiety of studio executives would have been given a further twist by the fall of attendances at cinemas during the winter of 1921–2. In retrospect that fall can be seen as temporary and as being in part caused by other, economic factors on which we have touched. But at the time the backlash against the movies worried executives so much that it must have seemed to be the only cause of their difficulties.

In 1922 the industry took action. It formed the Motion Picture Producers and Distributors Association (MPPDA) as a new regulatory body. In order to give this organisation the power its predecessors had so patently lacked, the industry's representatives appointed as its president Will Hays, a man with a strong political reputation as a Republican reformer. He took on a number of responsibilities, but the one which was publicised was the organisation of mechanisms by which the industry was to pre-censor its own output to save it from the control of outsiders. His first move was tactically inventive in that he approached the very groups which had been agitating most loudly for control of movies, and enlisted their support. He asked them to help the industry reform itself by monitoring new pictures with its representatives. This system was too cumbersome to prove effective in the longer term, but Hays's approach took the sting out of the attack and gave him time to set up a powerful public relations lobby against state censorship, which proved to be extremely successful.[45]

For the longer term regulation of movies, Hays proposed to both the industry and its critics a process of mutual co-operation – and he signalled to the industry that this would plainly be to its advantage. In 1924 he published a formula whereby production companies agreed to forward to the MPPDA before production a copy of each story property together with the observations of a reader upon any aspects of the treatment which might be considered questionable. Though at this time Hays took no formal powers of control, this step alone at first had an effect, 67 properties being rejected in 1924, 20 in 1925, and 10 in 1926.[46]

Self-regulation amounts of course to a form of censorship. Projects are censored primarily at the pre-production stage, a mechanism which avoids the waste of investment in films that have to be scrapped on a censor's instructions after completion. Major implements of such pre-censorship include the rejection and extensive alteration of projects which seem to offend the standards adopted by the regulatory body. Thus a direct consequence of pre-censorship by the MPPDA was a tendency towards conservatism on the part of executives planning future production. This was to reveal itself very clearly in later years when the industry gave the Hays Office the powers it at first lacked to enforce decisions, and studio production heads showed how strongly they preferred to avoid violating authoritative industry norms. However, in the mid and late 1920s, as the first shock of the public's sudden outrage of 1921–2 dwindled in the industry's memory, commercial pressures and the knowledge that salacious topics sold tickets tempted an increasing number of producers to ignore the Hays Office guidelines.[47] Not that Hays had ever unambiguously expressed a desire to wipe sex from the screen. On the contrary, he said repeatedly and from the moment he took office that films could be made passionate if they were pure, 'giving the public all the sex it wants with compensating values for all those church and women groups'.[48] Of course, as May points out, a formula for forcing this compromise had been worked out, some three or four years before Hays took office, in the films by De Mille to which we have referred.[49] It was easy enough to describe them either as celebrating the old, traditional values that have marriage triumph in the end, or on the contrary as presenting the tempting delights of a new, freer moral code. Self-regulation was indeed consistently through the following three decades to confirm Hollywood's tendency to have moral issues both ways.

Hays firmly believed that the MPPDA should have a wider role than policing cinema's morals. It should also sponsor trade. Shortly after promulgating his formula in 1924, he again approached the reforming groups and suggested to them it would be appropriate that they should show how they could benefit the industry, since the industry was attempting to co-operate with them. He used them as a network for passing the good word about films which seemed to him to be worth attention but which otherwise would have flopped. In this way he mounted an occasional effective rescue operation, as for *Abraham Lincoln* (1924) and a number of other films. Some years later, in the case of Max Reinhardt's *A Midsummer Night's Dream* (1935), his publicity grapevine is thought to have made it possible for an otherwise unlikely box-office prospect to enjoy an American release.[50]

Thus in a number of ways the role of the Hays Office as internal censor had concealed but effective economic functions, protecting and even developing the domestic market. In the late 1920s a Foreign Department of the MPPDA was organised which developed markedly that economic role. It was charged with defending overseas markets against the actions of the several governments which were trying to close their borders against the flood of incoming American films.[51] As we shall see, it had considerable success in supporting Hollywood's exports, working as it did from 1926 with active US government support.

The Hays Office also intervened in industrial relations, though it officially maintained that it did nothing of the sort. However, Will Hays organised the Association of Motion Picture Producers to represent their interests, and it operated out of the same office suite as the MPPDA. Since member companies individually signed agreements with the unions, Hays's role was kept discreet.[52] But through this office he helped extend the cartel among the major producers so that it covered labour relations. For while the studios competed ferociously with their cheque books for the services of stars, and while they paid their senior executives enormous salaries, they did not step out of line with each other in the contracts they offered the overwhelming majority of their staff. Their tacit agreement made it possible for them to keep rates of pay lower than they would otherwise have been. During the period from the late teens to the mid-1920s studio policy of severely over-working employees in return for low pay began to reap its inevitable return. Staff began to unionise, and the industry faced occasional strikes which were less effective than they might have been only because of inter-union strife.[53]

As a shrewd negotiator with the producers' longer term interests at heart, Hays was able to distinguish between fixing rates of pay at a point which was of advantage to the studios, and setting them so low that workers' discontent boiled over into action. Under his leadership the producers came to fresh terms with the unions and in 1926 a Studio Basic Agreement was signed. It reversed the position of people working for the studios in comparison with workers in similar trades in Los Angeles. Now for the first time studio employees enjoyed the better pay and conditions of service. For their part, studio heads had secured not only industrial stability, essential in maintaining continuous production schedules, but also the retention of an open shop, which helped them control the industry for some years.[54]

7 The Coming of Sound, 1926–29

While the structure of the industry that was to endure until the 1950s had largely emerged by 1925, not all the big companies that were to dominate Hollywood from the 1930s had yet established themselves as major powers. Four other companies soon forced themselves into strong positions in a market which Paramount, First National and Loew's (Metro-Goldwyn-Mayer) dominated.

Although it is useful to examine as we have done the economic forces that persuaded the major companies to standardise their production, it has to be remembered that they also took steps to differentiate their films. For in so far as they were in competition with one another that competition centred on production. As new owners of extended theatre chains, they needed as distributors to co-operate to supply each other sufficient films for screening. Partly because each studio developed its specialisms (see Chapter 6), and partly to play to different interests in the audience, each studio put out as a substantial part of its release schedule films that had distinctive differences from the product of all the others. We shall look later at the subtler developments, but one form of product differentiation could not be missed by anybody: one small studio introduced the sound film as a part of its struggle to carve a place among the first rank of companies in the industry.

The invention of the means to record and replay sound was a major technological achievement which, like the development of the photographic moving image, absorbed the labour of many people and the capital outlay of several corporations over at least a twenty-year period. Not unnaturally it has been analysed most frequently in that context, or for the aesthetic changes it brought to the cinema. However, the introduction of sound may also be described as of great moment in the economic development of the industry.

Once again we encounter a process of economic growth in which three distinct phases – invention, innovation and diffusion – are as clearly apparent as in the introduction of the feature film.[1] The clearest evidence of this arises from the fact that an adequate sound system, Lee De Forest's Phonofilm, was available to the industry and operating in a few movie theatres in 1923. But De Forest never

72

managed to secure the massive backing necessary to convert a brilliant invention into a mass-produced, marketable system. Only after Warner Brothers as innovators had demonstrated conclusively the vast profits they could turn with sound, and only at the point when their success began to threaten the audiences of the other studios did the majority of them finally commit themselves to the new systems. That was in 1928.

By the end of 1924 Warner Brothers had established themselves as a modestly successful production studio of the second rank behind the big three. The difficulty which faced them, Gomery establishes, was to find a way to expand – and they could not safely continue at their current size without risking being squeezed out of the market. Lacking guaranteed theatre outlets and a distribution arm of its own, the company could not securely expand into large-scale production without placing its fortunes in the hands of film-buyers for the three big companies.[2] The brothers sought guidance, and impressed the financiers with whom they came into contact by the tight budgetary control they kept over their productions. The investment company whose advice they sought, Goldman, Sachs & Co. of Wall Street, had not previously encountered a studio whose production departments could guarantee they would complete projects within set cash limits.[3] As we shall see later, the rigidity with which Jack Warner insisted on this aspect of control had its influence not only on the production values and appearance of the films, but also on the kinds of theme with which they dealt.

Determined to break into the ranks of the majors, Warner Brothers commenced a diverse programme intended to increase its share of the market. It was a complex strategy all of whose aspects can be seen as complementary. Early in 1925 the company purchased control of Vitagraph, by now an ailing survivor of its great days. This deal secured for Warners not only a studio in New York, another in Hollywood, and a laboratory, but also a sufficient number of exchanges (26 in America, 10 in England and 10 in Europe) to enable the company to begin to distribute its own product.[4] At a cost of $1.8 million, this was the first deal in which Goldman, Sachs & Co. helped raise finance. Rather than stop there, they agreed with the Warners on the raising of more funds to give the company a secure financial base for further expansion, in particular by increasing the number of its exchanges and first-run theatres, improving its production facilities, and enhancing promotion both of its films and its corporate image. During 1925–6 the company made substantial progress on all these fronts so that it began to build a strong, vertically structured organisation on the model of the big three.[5]

However, their new activity did not stop there, and their innovation of sound appears to have come about as an accidental by-product of their publicity programme. By 1925 radio, which had grown with astonishing speed since about 1920, was a rival to Hollywood sufficiently strong that a special programme could keep audiences away from the cinemas for a night.[6] It has been estimated that by the end of 1922 there were 220 stations on the air; by the end of 1923 that number had more than doubled to 556. Manufacturers could scarcely keep up with demand for receivers.[7] The challenge was so strong, it has been suggested, that it roused the film studios to produce their most spectacular and entertaining features, and made the end of the silent era a period of scintillating releases.[8]

Although the new medium was funded by the selling of advertising time, and had an inherently commercial bent, only one or two entrepreneurs had realised that it could be used in the service of the cinema. Foremost among these was 'Roxy' (S. L. Rothapfel, the movie palace impresario) who inaugurated regular radio transmissions from the theatre he ran, New York's Capitol, in November 1922. Initially these shows simply relayed each week the stage show which preceded the film at the Capitol. But by 1923 his shows, featuring Roxy's Gang, were fast becoming a national institution, and were evolving swiftly into an early form of radio variety programme. What the Warner brothers would not have failed to notice was that Roxy made his radio shows a constant platform to remind his listeners to 'get out and go to the movies'; and they boosted the audience at the Capitol very satisfactorily.[9] The Warners decided to follow his example, and to use the station they themselves set up in Los Angeles as a means of publicising their movies.[10] This they did successfully. Their interest in sound films, quite simply, was stimulated by a salesman for the Western Electric equipment that they had installed in their radio station.

Much of the technology needed for sound film was similar to that required for radio – microphones, amplifiers, speakers, and some means of recording. In the larger research establishments the two developments were closely associated. And these were the establishments that had the backing of massive corporations like Western Electric (itself owned by American Telephone and Telegraph) which gave them the muscle to win the battles for control of sound – not only through the quality of their research, but also via the purchase of patents and the financing of mass production. These were the strengths that made Western Electric an attractive partner to Warner Brothers. (Lacking such power the many small inventors like Lee De Forest, no matter how technically accomplished their systems, could not compete.) Warner Brothers were immediately attracted not so much by the aesthetic possibilities of mechanical sound as by the opportunity it gave them to extend their market. They entered complex negotiations with Western Electric, agreeing in June 1925 to a period of experimentation. In April 1926 the production for release of sound films on Western Electric equipment was agreed in return for a guaranteed uptake of the equipment and an 8 per cent royalty fee on the gross revenues of sound films.[11]

Had the Warners' vision of the future held, we should still see nothing but silent films accompanied by synchronised music, for they had no interest in reproducing talk, and meant to use sound only as a means of enabling theatres that could not afford them to do without orchestras. They anticipated that by offering them the chance to save the costs of live musicians, they could place their films where they had not previously been able to get screenings. Such films might be particularly attractive to the struggling independents and small theatre chains that made up a large part of Warner Brothers' clientele.[12]

Their first full programme, a succession of shorts followed by the feature *Don Juan*, had its première in August 1926, using music to the almost total exclusion of speech. Audience response to this film was very encouraging: the programme played for eight months in New York, was seen by over half a million people, and generated almost $800 000 box-office income.[13] Even so the Warners might have postponed entering the talkie era much longer had it not been for the potency of Al Jolson's appeal and the enthusiasm aroused by his ad-libbing a few lines of dialogue in *The Jazz Singer* (premièred in October 1927). For the talkie, on technical and aesthetic grounds, was an entirely different kind of motion picture from the silent film with synchronised music dubbed on. Recording dialogue posed serious technical problems: it is well known that for a while it inhibited movement on screen; conversation became not only possible but virtually mandatory (otherwise what had the talkie to boast of?); and all these factors led directly to the restructuring of narrative.

The stir caused by *The Jazz Singer* even before it came into full-scale release made up the Warners' minds. To them it was clear that sound would attract audiences to every class of theatre, let alone to the small, late-run houses. They announced at the end of November 1927 their intention to shoot twelve talking films in the coming season.[14] Most of the other companies, however, proceeded with much greater caution, a conservatism that is readily explicable. They were making good profits from the silent film, and to enter the sound era would require massive re-equipment at appalling cost. The majors were in a position in which their oligopoly would not be threatened if they allowed a smaller company to take the risk of innovation, meanwhile quietly evaluating both the profit potential and the technical quality of the principal systems on the market. This they did from 1925, postponing their decision until 1928, but ultimately making the transition to sound smoothly and without loss of their market position.[15]

The re-equipment of the studios was one element of the investment required – a considerable undertaking in its own right. But financially the equipping of the theatres for sound playback was an even heavier burden. The cost to the theatre operator of Vitaphone equipment installed by Western Electric was to range between $15 000 and $25 000 according to the acoustics, size, and volume of business of the cinema. Thus for the theatre chains the total investment required was massive. But this was not all. The theatre had to pay to Warner Brothers' Vitaphone Company not only a royalty on every foot of sound film screened, but also a charge of 10 cents per seat each week for the privilege of being allowed to play their films.[16] Exhibitors also worried that there might not be a constant supply of sound films, and Warner Brothers undertook to produce enough films to keep pace with installations in theatres. In their November 1927 announcements, in addition to scheduling twelve talkies they said they would release all twenty-six of what had been planned as silent films with synchronised music tracks.[17]

Warner Brothers began its programme of innovation as one means of attaining economic growth into the first rank of movie majors at a time in the mid-1920s when the market had been static. It succeeded so well in increasing box-office business that its confidence in the market's potential encouraged it to recommence in 1929 the purchase of theatres. It bought the Stanley Company with its chain of 300 theatres on the east coast, and then picked up a substantial part of First National, which had in the meantime been weakened by Paramount's purchase of some of its best theatres. Four years earlier, when in 1925 Warner Brothers had started their programme of expansion, their total assets had amounted to $5 million; in 1930 they totalled $230 million – a huge increase.[18]

Warners Brothers did not, however, enjoy a monopoly on the sound film for long. The Fox Film Corporation, like Warners, was in the mid-1920s one of the companies in the second rank of power behind the big three, and its owner too wanted to break into the first rank. As the owner of no more than the 20 neighbourhood theatres in New York which he had held for some years, William Fox saw the necessity for putting together a theatre chain as one of the methods of gaining this end. As we saw in Chapter 5 he began a programme of theatre purchase and construction at about the time Warner Brothers did, continuing with that expansion through 1926–7. In 1928 he formed an alliance with financiers who enabled him to accelerate this programme.[19]

Fox entered the competition for the sound-film market later than Warner Brothers, but with one advantage. He managed in July 1926 to buy the patents rights to an alternative system of recording sound, which seemed to have greater potential than the sound-on-disc system employed by Vitaphone. The Fox-Case system, soon renamed Movietone, recorded sound on the film itself, which made for simple synchronisation on replay and avoided the problems of setting up and changing discs; but it lacked a good quality amplification system. To gain access to one, Fox signed an agreement with Western Electric in which the parties cross-licensed each other's patents (that is, gave each other rights to the patents they owned). Fox bought Western Electric equipment for his burgeoning chain of cinemas, which he converted as quickly as he could, and guaranteed royalty payments for some eighteen years ahead.[20]

After a period of test production, the company demonstrated its system to the press early in 1927. It observed, however, that Warners had saturated the somewhat limited market for short musical films, and decided to differentiate its own sound output and gain experience in outdoor recording by making newsreels. Having developed both the equipment and practised the new skills needed to do this they launched their first newsreel at the end of April 1927. Movietone's first coup was coverage of Lindbergh's departure on his transatlantic flight three weeks later: Lindbergh took off early in the morning; that evening sound footage of the event played in Fox's Roxy Theatre, New York, to a cheering audience of 6200.[21] The combination of sound with topical actuality proved irresistible. The company took advantage of the good business Movietone News was doing and by the end of 1928 had 50 crews producing two editions weekly; and even that intensity of activity was to increase during the next year. By way of completing the cycle of innovation that supported the recapitalisation of his company and lifted it into a position of authority in the film industry, Fox expanded production in the 1928–9 season into talking features.[22]

The case of one other company is worth highlighting because it was brought into being to secure a part of the market for another massive corporation that had a big commitment to sound recording and broadcasting. That corporation was General Electric, which with its associate Westinghouse had put together the Radio Corporation of America (RCA) as its way of gaining entry into the radio industry. Thus RCA, like Western Electric, had the backing of vast finances. Its research laboratory had developed a complete sound system, Photophone, for recording and reproducing sound on film. From 1926 RCA and Western Electric had cross-licensed each other's patents; and RCA had the technical back-up, the personnel, and the capital to establish manufacturing resources (though it had not yet done so).[23] RCA set about trying to persuade the uncommitted members of the industry to adopt Photophone, and worked at overcoming their conservatism throughout 1927 and on into the following year. Early in 1928, however, it became apparent that the majors were preparing to equip with sound, but that they favoured contracting with Western Electric and its associates on the grounds that they would be charged lower production royalties by them, and Western Electric was already experienced in equipment production. RCA, learning of this development, at once commenced a series of intricate operations which resulted in its putting together its own major film company Radio-Keith-Orpheum (RKO) by October 1928. In effect, though the corporate tactics were covert, to achieve this they took over the Film Booking Office (FBO), a national distributor with its own modest production facility; they added to it two vaudeville circuits, Keith-Albee and Orpheum, with some 200 theatres; and they also got Pathé, which survived as a production company recently bought out by Keith-Albee.[24] Thus a major studio, fully structured on vertical lines, was launched direct into the sound era. It was done to protect and advance the interests of one giant corporate conglomerate backed by Rockefeller money which saw the sound-film market falling under the single influence of another conglomerate which happened to be financed by Morgan money.

This rivalry of two of America's biggest capital groupings ensured that the rights to sound in the movies were not secured by a single monopoly interest. On the other hand the industry required such massive capital assistance in wiring all its theatres, in acquiring yet more of them, in building studios and converting them for sound, that it had to call for massive tranches of capital from Wall Street financiers. Thus the requirements of corporate financing in a period in which many companies massively expanded their operations led to the further penetration into company management of representatives of financial institutions. If for the most part the bankers and financiers did not seek to interfere in creative decisions, they clearly meant, as we have already seen, to secure long-term stability of profits. These pressures led in turn, in the stable market which existed through most of the 1930s, to the firming up of the enlarged cartel or oligopoly which had been forming through the mid and late 1920s.[25]

During the early years of the sound film, the numbers of feature films produced in America showed a distinct decline. Production by the major companies reached 501 films in 1927, and dropped thereafter – to 429 in 1928, 379 in 1929, and 356 in 1930. Output continued to drop until 1933, but the Depression was the significant factor in the continuing decline beyond 1930.[26] More than one commentator has remarked that immediately before the introduction of sound the industry was producing more films than the market could consume; and the arrival of the new technology seems to have provided studios with the occasion to turn to a policy of fewer but better pictures. It may well have seemed a safe policy to produce quality sound pictures since, with the addition of an entire new labour division of skilled sound recordists (largely hired from the telephone, radio and electrical industries), the costs of films inevitably rose, the more so in the early days as for a while the complexities of sound recording slowed production. There was a further reason for producing fewer films, namely, that it provided an opportunity to keep the bigger attractions on screen for longer runs. Until the effects of the Depression made themselves felt, the industry found that good films returned much increased income, a factor which in turn further enhanced the importance of first-run theatres.[27] Not only did the public keep coming to the films it wanted to see, but they came nightly in numbers which filled theatres to a higher capacity than had been the case a couple of years previously.

One other feature of the introduction of sound needs to be remarked on – its speed. The remaining majors having come to their by now inevitable decisions to convert during 1928, by the end of 1930 not one of the Hollywood studios was producing a silent feature film of any kind.[28] The conversion to sound was as rapid as that to feature films had been, and had consequences at least as far-reaching both in the corporate changes we have discussed and for the film-going experience.

The long-established dominance in Hollywood of narrative over other forms of film was massively reinforced by access to dialogue. Now characters could be understood to a depth that had been unattainable even by the finest actors when expression of their meanings was limited to gesture, expression and the title card. Thus the hero of the silent film, the character as type, is soon succeeded by the hero of the sound film, the character as psychologically distinct individual. It is a fundamental change which allows the feature film to follow and in certain ways rival the novel in its familiar concern with the individual as the centre of larger actions. This is more than a matter of theme and aesthetics alone, for it enables the feature-film industry to anchor itself even more deeply in the largest of all genres, that part of the market devoted to story and character. The individual as the centre of action all too often becomes the key to every conflict whether personal or global. Thus Hollywood looks to its heroes and heroines not merely for elaboration of domestic themes, but as the anchors, sufficient reason for, and means of resolving, great problems in the social and historical arenas – war, politics, the professions, crime, medicine, and the conquest of the West. All centre on the response of the hero or heroine to what happens to them. That American films should function in this way was not new. We have already had occasion to remark upon the rise and establishment of the star. Now the introduction of sound reinforces the economic importance of these figures to the industry as it redoubles the authority of their position within narrative cinema. Norman Mailer has expressed the subtle power that invests style, in a society that judges both meaning and moral worth by it. Style in the sense he means is one of the things stars transmit most effectively – as becomes nakedly apparent when players are seen out of their epochs in old movies.

A part of [Mailer] had always tried to believe that the America he saw in family television dramas did not exist, had no power – as of course he knew it did – to direct the styles and the manners and therefore the ideas of America (for in a country where everyone lived so close to their senses, then style, precisely, and manner, precisely, carved ideas into the senses) . . .[29]

Sound not only subtilised narrative, it also let it move faster. The delays for reading title cards vanished; dialogue (for instance in Warner Brothers' films) began to crackle; and the effect of offering a self-containing illusion (towards which Hollywood films had long been tending) was much enhanced. Because movies could now communicate through five 'channels' – the photographic image, graphics, speech, sound effects and music – directors were able to keep spectators fully occupied. It became common practice in the Hollywood studios to do this as a means of sustaining dramatic intensity and keeping audiences entertained. Spectators had little leisure to do more than react emotionally. Contemplation while the film ran became impossible, and cinema moved closer to becoming an engulfing experience. The crime-film cycle that Warner Brothers developed in the early 1930s used all these characteristics, and relied heavily on sound both for explosive dialogue and readily marketable effects (gunfire, the racket of fast cars, and city sounds).[30]

As Harry Warner had intended, the sound film rapidly killed off the live stage show in the cinema: by the end of 1929 only the plushest houses offered live music, and not only was it costly, it began to seem old-fashioned.[31] But ironically, while theatre musicians were being pushed into dole queues just as the Depression struck America, music on screen was thriving. Because initially it had been easier to record music than speech, song and dance routines had from the start been attractive propositions for the production companies (as *The Jazz Singer* itself shows). Producers soon found that such routines performed by attractive girls sold tickets even better; and it was not long before they developed the idea of the chorus-girl show. Warner Brothers pioneered what was to become a very profitable cycle of such movies with *The Desert Song* (1929) and *Gold Diggers of Broadway* (1930). With further development this cycle eventually evolved into the musical. Such films were among the studios' most popular exports during the early years of the talkie, when dubbing was impossible. This factor must have encouraged producers to continue with the genre, for the patience of overseas audiences with untranslated English dialogue declined rapidly as the novelty of the sound film wore off. But the chorus-girl and revue musical continued to prove attractive, either with no translation, or with minimal subtitling; and foreign audiences took pleasure in their music, dance and glamour. Even though satisfactory translation procedures were in operation by 1931, and other genres began to do well abroad, the new genre had become firmly established with audiences in the intervening time.[32]

In addition to its assistance at the launch of a new genre, music had other functions. One was to increase audiences for films which only employed music in the specially composed theme song. While in the first place such songs served to hide gaps in the dialogue of the earliest talkies, the industry quickly noticed that popular pieces were in much demand as sheet music. The thing worked both ways – a well-liked film could render the music popular, or the theme song itself could draw more people to the movie. The connection between the two industries was quickly exploited, and has never been forgotten. Several of the major studios bought into the music business, Warner Brothers, MGM and Paramount all acquiring music publishers so that they could participate in royalties from the sheet-music industry. Because musicals needed songs, the film industry virtually took over Tin Pan Alley. Warner Brothers, for example, soon owned the rights to most of the songs by Jerome Kern, Richard Rodgers, George Gershwin and Cole Porter. During the 1930s the film industry was to make a great deal of money from licensing radio to play music by these composers. This connection, which was to be reinforced in later years when the studios bought into the record business (see Chapter 9), was one of the reasons theme songs and musicals flourished both early and long in the sound era. Westerns, comedies and romances were all so written that principal characters could croon song after song to each other.[33]

In 1928 the American industry experienced a flurry of interest in the colour film when Technicolor released the first feature to be made in their two-colour process. Though this was not by any means the first colour system to reach the market, it had the advantage of being technically reliable and of becoming available at a period when a number of companies were trying to maximise revenue. In its expansionist strategy, Warner Brothers decided that profit might well follow upon innovation in this field too; and they led the big studios in making a commitment to colour as soon as they saw the extra profit returned by *The Desert Song* (1929). Innovating colour had the particular advantage for the studio that it did not require massive capital investment since Technicolor had funded the development of the technology. Even if colour did not draw a larger audience, Warner Brothers would risk no more than the additional cost of making each film in colour. They signed contracts with Technicolor for more than twenty colour features, including *The Gold Diggers of Broadway* (1930) which was to gross $3.5 million. The major studios followed Warners to take advantage of colour's novelty value. However, two-colour films were never entirely satisfactory since they could not reproduce the complete visible spectrum – for all its technical sophistication Technicolor could not render blue. This meant that various tricks, like shooting dawn or dusk scenes, had to be used to escape the problem of registering on film improbable skies. It was one factor which made the garish musical or chorus-girl film, set indoors, an obvious subject for the process. Yet notwithstanding the necessity of using the two-colour system tactfully, it seems that few colour productions of this period showed much evidence of colour artistry.

When Hollywood felt the bite of the Depression in 1931, the majors decided that colour was not the cure-all for their problems. As it entailed extra expense which could readily be cut, they cancelled their contracts with Technicolor. The process was reduced once again to use in a limited number of short subjects.[34]

By the time sound was fully established at the end of 1929, the increased costs it brought were causing smaller companies and theatres either to fall prey to larger corporations and theatre chains, or simply to fade away. The introduction of sound therefore stimulated further consolidation in the industry, a trend which would continue through the Depression years.[35] Warner Brothers, Fox and RKO had joined the older majors, Paramount and MGM–Loew's, in the first rank of power and influence. First National had nearly disappeared, large parts of it having been devoured by Paramount and Warner Brothers. Three companies remained in the second rank of the industry despite possessing relatively few theatres between them. They were Universal, Columbia and United Artists, and the means they discovered to achieve profitability and survival as lesser members of the cartel will draw our attention to the importance in the economic environment of the established studio system of subtle mechanisms for product differentiation.

8 Product Differentiation in the 1930s

We have already referred to the pressures that led the studios to standardise production. If anything, these intensified, for now the industry had more than merely the old profit motive to drive it: it had massive debts to repay, both of capital and interest on the loans it had taken to finance theatre purchases and the installation of sound systems. As we have seen (Chapter 5), the major financiers of the studios made sure that they had representatives on their boards, and these people interested themselves not so much in individual films as in the organisation of production. The studios were expected to use their human and material resources as efficiently as they could.

In the context of production what emerged were studios organised, as Roddick describes it, on the basis of the classic management pyramid.[1] Heading this pyramid would be the studio executive in charge of production, a figure such as Hal B. Wallis at Warners, or Irving Thalberg at MGM. He kept tight control over the broad parameters of the productions under his command – he would supervise the original story material and its refinement through the several stages of scripting, casting and contract negotiations; he would budget and schedule, ensuring that those projections were kept; and would examine each day's rushes, advising editors on how to cut material together. In turn each movie was controlled in detail by a producer responsible to the production executive; and under his authority worked the rest of the crew, including the director who, in standard productions, though he might have a degree of authority over script, sets, and costumes, was usually a studio employee like any other.[2] The control of film production thus shifted after the introduction of sound closer to management; and the pyramid system, centring ultimate responsibility on one executive, of itself tended to impose standardisation. The change is illustrated by Rosten who records that in 1927 Hollywood made 743 pictures with only 34 producers supervising 246 directors. In 1937, 484 movies were made by virtually the same number of directors (234), but their work was now supervised by 220 producers.[3]

It is worth reminding ourselves that at this time studio employees included virtually all the personnel who worked on a film. The studio had under contract its own writers, a constant pool of acting talent and of creative technicians who moved from film to film as required, its own art department, research department, and technicians with particular expertise in costuming, make-up, lighting, camera, and so on. It also had its own publicity organisation which, as Roddick points out, not only functioned to manipulate public taste, but also served to provide the studio with feedback on the success of what it was releasing.[4]

The combination of these factors pulled studios simultaneously in different directions. On the one hand, as we have already seen, they tended to standardise a considerable amount of their production around genres and stars. In this context Roddick argues persuasively that the narrative film itself was a product of the economic system:

> The classic Hollywood style, with its insistence on the unproblematic, seamless narrative whose advancement is controlled by the destiny of one or more individual characters, was determined by the economics of the production system. The need to mass-produce art necessitated a certain approach to storytelling. Studio practice required an economy of production method which in turn created an economy of narrative method. The studio system dictated, by its structure and its gradually established orthodoxies, the making of a particular kind of movie. Formula it may have been, but it is a formula which is now clearly established as the standard approach to movie-making. . . It is, simply, the archetypal form of cinema, the model for most films that have come after it. . .[5]

On the other hand those same economic forces, exerted through the particular stars and production departments of the individual studio, pulled each towards specialising in certain kinds of film. Not only was this a ready way to use human and material resources cost-effectively, but it also gave each studio an identifiable style in relation to substantial parts of its production. The work of the production staff was made easier because they were imitating familiar models; and the publicity department was handling films that were to some degree made recognisable, and thus pre-sold, by the style of their precursors. This style was made easier for the public to recognise in that theatres owned by a studio would show all its output. Thus each studio brand name led the more knowing

members of the audience to expect certain kinds of entertainment
under that flag.

It follows that studio specialism could take a number of forms,
with the repetition of story types just one among them. As we shall
see, some .studios became known for their Westerns, others for
horror films, romantic dramas, and so on. Equally single departments
might achieve a state of unusual competence that invested much of a
studio's output with its distinctive mark. The art department (MGM's
and Paramount's were to do this) might work up a facility for
brilliant, plush interiors. The lighting crew (MGM again) might
develop a style of flooding sets with high-key lighting that enhanced
a look of great opulence. Other specialisms were not necessarily so
visible. Some studios – Warner Brothers, Columbia, and producers
of B movies such as Republic Studios – exercised cost controls so
rigorous that they were able to put their movies into distribution at
much lower rental rates than their rivals, and thus secured a niche
for them in the theatres. For all these specialisms had an economic
as well as an aesthetic function in that they sought to make attractive
the output of each studio in most cases to the first-run and second-
run theatres operated by the other majors. This remained the key to
running a successful production and distribution company in a
vertically organised industry: that one's output included a good
number of films that one's rivals in production would want to rent to
keep their theatres in business. No major could produce sufficient
movies to fill unaided the screening requirements of its own theatres.

Warner Brothers, by innovating sound, had for a while
differentiated their product very successfully. When that success
brought imitation, the studio gradually developed certain kinds of
film that suited their production methods, and which during the
1930s came to characterise a significant part of their release schedule.
Roddick identifies their social dramas, crime movies and newspaper
pictures as distinctive categories.[6] Each of these kinds was given
striking force by the advent of sound, relying as it did upon quick-
fire delivery of terse dialogue and vivid urban sound-effects. And
Warners stamped these movies even more firmly as their own by
creating a dark mood through low-key lighting (which incidentally
made it possible for them to work with cheaply made sets). The
success of such films as *Public Enemy* (1931) and *I am a Fugitive
From a Chain Gang* (1932) established this category of film firmly in
the studio's canon.

Although Warners was one of the studios which most carefully controlled its production costs, it did not limit itself exclusively to turning out low-cost drama. We have already referred to its development of the revue musical (Chapter 7). The brothers knew also that there was an audience for prestige productions, and that such productions could both return profits and the esteem that arose from invading territory which a few years earlier appeared to belong exclusively to the established studios. They made their claim for prestige principally through the colonising of history through biographical pictures and costume dramas, linking the two forms in the 'foreign biopic' which became another identifiable feature of their output.[7] But like all the other majors, however, Warner Brothers not only established its own distinctive lines of production, it also laid claim to common ground. Roddick notes that in common with many other studios it produced a line of action-films, which dealt with action solely for its own sake. And in its production of sentimental movies (like many of the best Bette Davis films), it undertook a type of production associated more readily with MGM or Paramount.[8]

Despite the fact that in its earliest years Paramount's releases had little enough in common to identify them as coming from the same source, this studio had the good fortune during the 1920s, as producer and distributor of Cecil B. De Mille's films, to have a house style established for it. Over the years Paramount, profiting from its success with his movies, came to make a speciality of sophisticated and romantic comedies. It was one of the companies that most extensively recruited talented film-makers from Europe, in particular from Germany and Scandinavia. It did this largely in response to the popularity in America of two German films, *The Last Laugh* (1924) and *Variety* (1925).

Although these two films had been recut to fit with American preferences for swift, flowing narrative, American audiences particularly admired their artwork, photography and acting. The studios for their part seem to have seen an opportunity in this new attraction to help them counter the growing competition they were experiencing from radio in the mid-1920s. Not only does this offer a partial economic explanation for the ubiquity during those years of expressionist devices embedded in Hollywood naturalism, it also helps account for the different working practices at Paramount from those of say Warners and MGM. For having recruited such figures as Ernst Lubitsch, Josef von Sternberg, Erich Pommer and Pola Negri, Paramount had to make use of their talents and allow them to imprint an important part of its product with their distinctive styles. The studio did continue to insist on the modification of European mannerisms to match with American demands for movement and action, but it conceded a measure of artistic independence to some of the key talents. Directors came to expect rather more creative authority at Paramount than elsewhere.[9] Through the 1930s, then, the studio became celebrated for its glittering, sophisticated comedies, whose witty and elegant scripts, embellished with the opulent glow for which its art department was renowned, made for exotic escape from the real problems of the Depression era.[10]

By way of contrast, catering for that section of the audience to whom such material did not appeal, Paramount began in the late 1920s to produce a number of tough movies which by comparison appeared realistic – examples include von Sternberg's *The Dragnet* and *The Docks of New York*, Lewis Milestone's *The Racket*, and William Wellman's *Beggars of Life* (all 1928).[11] In 1930 the studio decided to schedule no more than three-quarters of each year's production in advance so as to leave itself room to react to topical subjects as they developed.[12]

MGM also developed its own specialisms. Like Paramount it went for brilliance and expense in its *mise-en-scène*, and its high-key photographic style, extravagant sets and costumes have long been seen as a trade mark. But the differences between the productions of the two studios were profound. Whereas the keynote of the Paramount movie was sophistication, the creation of an idea of wit, and an aura of worldly knowledge, the glamour of the MGM style served another end. It acted as a façade only, glitter to attract those who desired to know something of the life of the rich. The studio featured 'tastefully mounted high life melodramas and society comedies, alternating between the unrealistically classy and the idealistically folksy.'[13] Its films, it has been said, express typically American impulses in endorsing the virtues of money, position, and honest lust.[14]

To achieve its ends MGM kept a glittering roster of stars, including Jean Harlow, Greta Garbo and Joan Crawford; but by comparison with Paramount, its directors were highly skilled professionals (like Victor Fleming, Clarence Brown, Edmund Goulding, W. S. Dyke) rather than stars. They were expected to concentrate like Warner Brothers' directors on realising the programming ideas of their production executive, Irving Thalberg, rather than expressing their individual preoccupations.[15]

The circumstances of Loew's – the company which owned MGM and the theatre chain to which it was wed – to some extent dictated the studio's production programme. Maltby argues that the corporation derived from film rental a significantly higher share of its total volume of business (about 40 per cent), and of its total profits (about 70 per cent) than the other majors. It did so by charging a higher rental (about 40 per cent of box-office takings for an A feature) than the other companies (which sought about 30 per cent); and it ran the most efficient distribution sales team of any studio. Loew's had to work this way because it had the smallest theatre holdings of the big five – in the late 1930s no more than 139 (half of them first-run houses) compared with Paramount's 1239 and Warner Brothers' 507. Since it had a smaller exhibition base for its product, it had to compensate by securing a greater profit from distribution, and the logical means to enable it to do was to supply a higher quality, more expensive product whose lavishness would draw customers and justify higher rental charges. Hence the MGM style was very much a part of necessary corporate strategy for Loew's.[16] But the studio's output was no less diverse in its full spectrum than Paramount's. Gomery recalls the importance to its box office of the Marie Dressler comedies; the films of the Barrymore family, versions of classic literature, and musicals, all did good business in the 1930s.[17]

Production at RKO did not at any time in its twenty-five-year history get organised into the kind of long-term programme that the other studios arranged. The difference is easily explained. The company, it will be recalled, had been set up in 1928 to exploit RCA's patents on the Photophone system. Within a few months RCA had demonstrated through their new corporation that Photophone could record and replay to audiences good quality sound. By a double strategy involving on the one hand preparing a lawsuit alleging monopolistic practices against Western Electric's owners American Telephone and Telegraph, and on the other offering to lease Photophone to any studio that wanted it, RCA persuaded the majors who had been hesitating before investing in the new technology that it would become a universal phenomenon. Ultimately (though not until 1935) they succeeded in cross-licensing their system with that of Western Electric, and having broken into the market, secured patent revenue from their system.[18] But they do not appear to have had a long-term plan for RKO other than that it should make money. Matters were not helped by the decision in 1931 to buy the former Pathé Studio at Culver City. Although the new facility was impressive (forty acres and eleven sound stages) and freed RKO from working in a very cramped environment, the company was now faced with operating two studios simultaneously. Costs and administrative difficulties increased.[19]

The history of RKO can be read as a demonstration that it is not sufficient to have only the profit motive as goal in the movie business. Commanded by its owners, RKO changed its production heads with such speed that none of them could establish a distinctive pattern to the studio's programming before he was replaced. William LeBaron, David O. Selznick, Merian C. Cooper, and Pandro S. Berman, all better than competent production chiefs, filled the role during the 1930s; none was given sufficient authority, and only Berman held the post for more than eighteen months. Despite this lack of managerial continuity, certain kinds of production were repeated often enough that they plainly come from RKO in the 1930s.

One profitable cycle was built by Berman round its performers Fred Astaire and Ginger Rogers, whose dance routines were featured in a succession of films between 1933 and 1939, from *Flying Down to Rio* to *The Story of Vernon and Irene Castle*. RKO were also particularly strong in women's pictures where, although most of the studios worked in the genre, they were distinctive in producing a number of films on the theme of the fallen woman. In addition the studio was known for the excellence of its artists and technicians. By the end of the 1930s it had built a reputation as a designer's studio, strong in its creation of the fantastic in films as different as *King Kong* (1933), the Rogers and Astaire vehicle *Top Hat* (1935) and *Citizen Kane* (1941).[20]

The three minors, as it now becomes appropriate to call them – United Artists, Universal and Columbia – made their corner in the market precisely by supplying films that were needed to fill cinema screening schedules. For the most part (Universal being the obvious exception), they sought to supply the first-run theatres of the majors, and offered films different enough from their releases to give cinema programmes a variety that would keep the interest of audiences. Since the shared characteristic of the minors was that they owned few theatres, their survival as producer–distributors depended on their identifying unsupplied needs that they could fill.

United Artists (UA) had been set up in 1919 to allow its founder members – Chaplin, Pickford, Fairbanks and Griffith – independently to produce the films they wanted; it continued with this policy through the 1920s and 1930s in association at various times with a succession of producers including Joseph Schenk, Sam Goldwyn, Howard Hughes, Walt Disney, Alexander Korda, David O. Selznick, Walter Wanger and Hal Roach. Thus most of the films the company distributed were made by independent producers, and were sold as films of high quality. Some of the major theatre circuits (Loew's, Publix, Warners, and RKO) formally recognised the calibre of United Artists' releases by contracting around the end of the 1920s to rent agreed numbers of their films over a period of years.[21] Thus the studio had no difficulty differentiating its product. Its principal problems lay in organising the production of a sufficient number of films to keep its distribution arm profitably busy, problems which arose from poor management. As Balio shows, the partners were forever at odds with each other, and agreed only on the exclusion from corporate power of the very newcomers who in the 1930s were generating most of UA's income. This caused deep rancour and wrecked efficient company management.[22]

Universal's features in the mid to late 1920s boasted few stars, apparently because Laemmle imposed a policy of budgeting films too tightly to allow the studio to rival the majors for their services. Unable in most of its films to present players with the charismatic talents of those whom Paramount, Fox or MGM rostered, it chose alternative means to securing a market.[23] Although it released occasional specials which competed for playing time in the majors' first-run houses, Universal decided to make its main income from the rural and small-town market, which it had identified as requiring a less sophisticated product than city audiences. Accordingly in 1925 Laemmle recapitalised the company and commenced buying and building modest theatres in small cities; and elsewhere he cultivated the small exhibitor. Adapting its product to these outlets, Universal made low rental Westerns and comedies – a policy which proved adequate to keep the company trading from what Hampton calls a 'moderately firm' position until the arrival of sound.[24] Thereafter it developed as a specialism the horror movie, and its programme of releases was popular enough to carry it through the Depression. The profitability of this cycle, which ran until the mid-1930s, may have come about because they provided a covert channel for the release through fantasy of fears aroused by the deprivation of the Depression years. The films included *Dracula* and *Frankenstein* (1931), *The Mummy* and *Murders in the Rue Morgue* (1932), featuring actors Bela Lugosi and Boris Karloff, and director James Whale.[25]

Despite the success of the horror film, Universal's overall strategy did not survive the short term, and the Depression put paid to it. By 1933 the company had sold its 300 American theatres.[26] Quite simply the first-run market it had ignored was essential to give routine films the audience penetration needed to make profit. Not only did first-run houses return a higher rental, but their screenings obtained an intensity of publicity that small houses could not provide. Films whose screen life began on the small circuits automatically seemed to the majors to lack prestige; therefore they did not take them up for later big-city exploitation.[27] The loss of revenue caused by this misjudgement combined with the effects of inefficient management and the decline in box-office revenue during the Depression to bring Universal into receivership after several years of losses.

Laemmle was bought out in 1936, and Universal passed into the control of a syndicate financially backed by some big interests in the film world – Western Electric's film-sound equipment subsidiary, Eastman Kodak, and J. Arthur Rank. The first two companies were not only extending their investments, but also protecting their royalties and sales; the British distributor intended to secure an invaluable entry into the American market.[28] After a couple of years of continuing difficulties, the new management in 1938 tried what has sometimes been described as a novel approach: they put in charge of production two executives whose experience lay in exhibition. Thus although they did not know about film-making (other executives in the meantime took a firm grip of production schedules and costs), they could discern what stars and stories the public wanted to see in various territories, and so could advise the company how to match its product to various markets. Actually this idea was no more than an extension of the kind of experience Laemmle and his fellow independents had originally brought to production in challenging the monopoly of the Patents Company. Where the new management did innovate was in devising means of contracting with stars whose services they could not afford. Instead of offering long-term contracts, they squeezed their shooting, in imitation of Columbia's practice, into very tight schedules; but then they went further and made the proposition attractive by not only paying stars for their time, but giving them also a percentage of profits. By deferring a part of their cost they secured for various films stars as popular as Bing Crosby and W. C. Fields, and did so at very little risk and every advantage to the company. They brought Universal back into profit by keeping costs ruthlessly low and expanding from horror into the market for cheap musicals, farce, and subjects like comic-strip serials which had the benefit of a tie-up with radio productions.[29]

The third of the minors, Columbia, is another studio that secured its place in the market through careful cost control of high quality product. Formed in 1924, by 1935 its turnover amounted to $16 million, no more than 4 per cent of the total volume of business done by the industry.[30] The screwball comedies of Frank Capra are its best-remembered product of the Depression years, although they actually formed only a small part of the studio's diverse output. There is a double irony latent in Capra's delightful films about idealistic bucolics triumphing over corrupt urban businessmen and politicians. Not only were the films' escapist values naive in Depression America, but they came out of the studio run by Harry Cohn, notoriously the most ruthless of all the movie bosses. However, what kept the studio in routine income, year after year through the 1930s were its Westerns, shorts and serials, the Westerns with stars Buck Jones, Tim McCoy, Ken Maynard, Bob Allen and Charles Starrett.[31]

In terms of the studio's output, that ruthlessness showed itself in rigorous application of pre-production techniques. It was one of the first companies to shoot in complete detail on paper, preparing in advance not only scripts, but artwork and storyboard, shooting schedules and budget; and it insisted on keeping films within tight budgetary limits. It has been said that Cohn valued writers more than stars on the grounds that the best stars cannot make a good movie if it has a weak plot. And more than a decade before Universal, Columbia was hiring big-name artists by the day instead of the week. Sometimes the studio would borrow players from other Hollywood companies. If it had to sign talent, it kept to short-term contracts for one or two films.[32] It also learnt to catch actors either as they were on the way up to stardom or as they declined from former fame. Either way the studio got them relatively cheaply.[33]

Although methods of preplanning and cost control were by the end of the 1920s universally applied, they were not by any means practised with constant rigour. As we shall see (Chapter 9) bankers found when the Depression hit the industry that that they needed to renew their vigilance because some studios had become luxuriously extravagant (indeed some of them boasted of it) in their production regimes. In the conflict between the impulse towards cost effectiveness and the contrary belief that extravagant production values sold movies, economic practice was often undercut. Nonetheless the factory system ruled the preparation of story material; as Roddick says it processed reality:

> To make the material process of film production as economical as possible, a standard code of practice was adopted in terms of decision-taking, planning, scripting, shooting, editing, publicity and release. This necessarily involved fitting the variable story material into as regular a narrative pattern and cinematic style as possible, with the crux of the plot – whether it was a social problem, a scientist's life or the career of a medieval outlaw – illuminated through a central character whose response to physical obstacles was action and whose experience of emotional life was romantic.[34]

Since films were targeted at a mass audience their scenes and characters were usually so written that the broadest possible group of people could identify with them. Characters with broad appeal could not be, as O'Connor has written, too radical or intellectual; their personalities should be simple, their loyalties unconfused. There should be no subtleties to trouble the audience, which was generally assumed to be comfortable with stereotypes. Action was arranged to heighten excitement and sharpen climaxes: history and biography had to bend to meet these requirements.[35] Thus the economic system, which incidentally continued to require the selection and shaping of many stories in such a way as to showcase each studio's stars, impinged on narrative.[36] The broad flow of product from the studio system is described within these paradigms.

9 Depression and the Mature Oligopoly, the 1930s

Thus far our account of the way the studios angled their product at the market has ignored the impact of significant social pressures. The Depression and Roosevelt's New Deal both had direct economic consequences for the fortunes of the motion picture industry. As the case history of the Fox Film Corporation shows, the disarray of the majors was not brought about merely by trading losses in the film business.

Fox, it will be recalled, was before 1925 a relatively small company centred on a production facility, and owning few theatres. Around 1926 the company began to put out quality pictures, and in the following year its subsidiary Fox Theater Corporation commenced investing massively in independent theatre chains, soon bringing more than 550 cinemas under its wing, and adding to this a one-third interest in First National Pictures.[1] The studio's innovation of sound via the newsreel, a project which immediately won audience approval, confirmed the company's rise in stature to the ranks of the majors. In 1929 Fox raised a further $36.5 million to finance the construction of more studio space and theatres.

All these activities depended on the availability of finance, much of which was raised in the form of bonds and debentures by the banking firm Halsey, Stuart & Co.[2] Had the Fox companies ceased expansion at this point it is possible they could have survived, though even this is doubtful. However, Fox's ambitions ran even higher, and in 1929 he bought for $50 million (again with funds raised by long-term and short-term loans) a controlling interest in Loew's, and with further advances a controlling interest in the British Gaumont theatre chain.

The problem which most of the majors faced when panic set in with the Wall Street crash of October 1929 (Fox was simply an extreme case) derived from the fact that, in order to keep corporate control in the hands of the original stockholders, they financed their expansion programmes not by issuing new shares to increase their companies' paid-up capital, but by raising various forms of loan. On average in 1931 debts amounted to some 47 per cent of the majors' sources of capital, while stock supplied no more than 52 per cent.[3] The massive interest repayment on those debts could just be sustained when business was flourishing, but not when it diminished.[4]

The excitement caused by the novelty of the sound film had kept people coming through the box office in numbers which at first suggested the industry might escape the heavy fall in turnover experienced by the American economy at large. In the event, trouble was merely postponed until 1931, when Fox made a loss of $3 million, RKO of $5.6 million, and Warner Brothers of $7.9 million.[5] In short order, staff were laid off, ticket prices were cut by up to 25 cents to bolster patronage, and innovations introduced with sound (colour and the Magnascope widescreen system) were relinquished if they cost more but did not bring dramatic increase in profits.[6] But the damage ran much further and the industry was to suffer badly till 1933 when box-office receipts fell to their lowest – one estimate puts them at only 40 per cent of what they had been two years earlier.[7] Theatres were at the centre of the trouble, with takings inadequate to cover loans raised to purchase them; in general the more cinemas a major owned, the deeper its difficulties. *Film Daily* estimated 5000 out of 16 000 theatres had closed by mid-1933, with even some chains collapsing.[8] Warners made a succession of heavy losses and saved itself from reorganisation only by reducing the numbers of its theatres from 700 to 400 and selling off assets to pay its debts.[9] RKO went into receivership; Paramount lost $21 million in 1932, went into receivership, then bankruptcy; and Fox was in equally desperate trouble.[10] Yet the studios survived, apparently undamaged. How did it happen?

With the market collapse Fox found it impossible to cover all its financial debts – William Fox entered a long and bitter period of complex and reportedly doubtful dealing. In the end, however, control of the Fox companies and of the shares in Loew's that William Fox had tried to buy passed into the hands of the Chase National Bank, where it remained for a number of years. As with the other majors in trouble, control passed from the original shareholders to those who bought up their debts and refinanced the companies by the issue of new stock or debentures. The Chase National Bank, for example, held in 1933 almost $90 million worth of investments in Fox companies, which it retained until it had the group firmly back into profit.[11]

We have mentioned that the banks' new commitment to the

majors led them to tighten up their operations, maximise profits and reduce costs: as major stockholders they now stood to participate in profits. As Wasko records, production units were merged, distribution operations were trimmed, and some theatres were sold. The Chase National changed accounting procedures in the several companies in which it now had interests, putting them on a more realistic basis. And they enforced studio budgeting systems, often demanding reduction in personnel, other cuts in overheads, and smaller picture budgets.[12] Fairly quickly however, the banks discovered that running a film studio required more than skill in business management alone.[13] The Chase National for instance soon replaced its own man at Fox with Sidney Kent, who had an impressive record at Paramount. Under his guidance (and more particularly that of Darryl Zanuck who joined as head of production when in 1935 Fox merged with his production company Twentieth Century), the studio began once again to produce films with a distinct style. Having been for some while much sustained by Shirley Temple fripperies, it began to put out serious dramas, big city movies, musicals and costume dramas. Zanuck set about finding stars, and soon signed up Alice Faye, Sonja Henie and Tyrone Power. In the meantime he further differentiated the studio's product by making more extensive use of Technicolor than its rivals.[14]

Two factors had saved the majors. Firstly, the vast commitments by banks and other financiers in loans and debentures raised for theatre purchase and conversion to sound forced them to secure their capital by refinancing and reorganising those movie majors that got into trouble – Fox, RKO, and Paramount. Secondly, the industry was by this date extremely strong. This is to say more than that not all the studios went through reorganisation (Warners, Columbia, United Artists and Loew's emerged with no significant change of management or control, Loew's apparently unaffected by Fox's dealings in its shares).[15] Additional strength lay in the collective grouping which it now becomes appropriate to refer to as a mature oligopoly, the structure towards which the studios had been tending since the early 1920s and which survived until 1948.

The term 'oligopoly' refers as Strick says, to an industry in which there are only a few large producers, who make similar products and collude, either openly or simply by observing each other's behaviour, to their mutual advantage. Firms comprising the industry recognise their interdependence and that the policies of one will affect the others.[16] Crucially they come to realise, in Litman's words, that

every price cut, every new advertising campaign, and every new
product innovation results in reaction in kind from one's
competitors. While the firm initiating the action may achieve a
gain in sales, that gain will be short-lived . . . When all the dust
has settled, relative market shares may be just about the same,
but costs have risen, prices have fallen, and profits have
significantly decreased.[17]

Thus in an oligopoly companies collude to maintain high price levels
and profitability. Collectively they have the power to deny other
firms entry to their sector of the market by controlling prices and
access. When they grow big (as the movie majors now had done),
even their size obstructs the entry of others. We have seen (Chapter
6) how the movie majors kept foreign producers out of the American
market. They were equally effective in excluding small domestic
competitors. In recent years the only new entrants to the magic
circle either had massive capitalisation (RKO) or were absorbed by
merger (Twentieth Century–Fox).

There were two forms of collusion open to the studios. Firstly,
they needed to do no more than observe each other's product,
practices and prices, and judge their own accordingly without open
consultation. This they have always done.[18] More formally, as
Staiger says, with the growth of external financing and joint-stock
corporations, collusion could be direct. 'Financiers could place
representatives on boards of directors and control the industry . . .
through interlocking directorships.'[19]

Depression brought alterations to film exhibition. We have mentioned
in passing some of the changes in audience taste that occurred; and
exhibitors worked hard to boost audience numbers. Having reduced
ticket prices, some operators reverted to changing programmes
twice a week. In 1931 an ingenious exhibitor in New England
experimented with a new pattern of screening by showing double
features; and this format was so widely imitated that it became the
norm for the industry until the end of the 1940s. The three-hour
programme gave the movie-goer the sense, important in a time of
financial stringency, of getting good value for the ticket price, which
stayed at the same level as for a single feature.[20]

This development at once affected the economic infrastructure of
the industry and led to the production of a new kind of film – the B
movie. It did so because, with the theatre operator charging an

unchanged admission price, his rental payments now had to be divided between two films; and those rentals were increased relatively little through the drawing power of the double bill as more and more theatres adopted the same screening pattern. Few exhibitors could afford two top quality movies, and distributors saw no advantage in screening two good movies together for one admission fee when by separating them they could get the customer to pay twice.[21] It was quickly realised, however, that the quality film guaranteed the distribution of the inferior movie coupled to it. The practice arose of charging a flat, fixed rental for the B feature, while the A feature continued to attract the percentage of box-office takings set by its distributor to reflect the level of business it was thought likely to generate.[22]

Much B-movie production was undertaken by small companies that did nothing else, and had to survive on the low but comparatively stable returns provided by these films in this era. Many small companies entered this field, but few survived for long. Principal among those that did were Republic and Monogram. Several of the big studios (Fox, Warner Brothers, RKO, Columbia and Universal) ran their own B units during the 1930s and in some cases on into the next decade. They did so to provide a complete service (most of the studios also had units regularly releasing either serials, short subjects, or cartoons). Providing a complete programme was a further means of maintaining control in the market, and distributors forced exhibitors to screen their shorts as a precondition to obtaining features. Although the direct profits returned by most B pictures and shorts were not to be compared with those of the A picture, the studios gained an incidental advantage from running these units in using them for the training of new talent and experimentation with ideas. Both people and ideas could then be tested cheaply on audiences with a view to future feature programming.[23]

The mark of the B movie was its cheapness. Specialist B production units perfected cost-saving techniques for every aspect of production. They were shot to absolutely rigid budgets and schedules, with minimal sets, and often at night to use facilities and staff to the maximum. Night-shooting was impossibly expensive for most units because they had to pay overtime. Not so for the B-picture units which paid flat rates for all hours worked. Hence the *film-noir* milieu that B-picture makers developed as part of their expressive vocabulary was as much an economy as an aesthetic mode. It required few lights, and often merely impressionistic sets.[24] Every means of avoiding retakes was exploited: stage business (entrances, exits, unnecessary transactions) was severely restricted to cut down the risk of fumbling.[25] Crowded scenes were avoided to keep the wages bill low; extras if used were cheaper silent than speaking; actors were asked to wear their own clothes wherever possible (most B movies had present-day plots to reduce costs); sets were borrowed from other productions; and stock footage of places and events was cut in (often with massive errors of continuity) to save the expense of shooting them.[26]

As a natural corollary to these practices, scripts also became formulaic. Republic, for instance, specialised in serials, mysteries, and before all else, action films and Westerns. It had the doubtful distinction of innovating and popularising the singing Western.[27] Not for B movies the adaptation from best-selling novel or Broadway play: the entire production would cost less than one of these properties. Their sources might be something by a freelance writer, a magazine short story, a pulp novel, or a radio playlet. It would be given to a studio writer who would have no more than six weeks to complete the script. He would probably, like the writers of the Roy Rogers Westerns at Republic, regard the characters of the hero and his friends, and the basic plot, as fixed formulas. Therefore the villains' characters and actions were used to introduce variety into these films. Thus cost-saving formulas reached into the heart of the B movie, and the same was true of the series and serials.[28] Action was kept punchy. The good guy came out on top (appropriately in the New Deal era in which Republic was founded). Characters were simply good or bad, without psychological complexity. Above all, films were generic: in its twenty-year history this one small studio made 386 Westerns, 56 with Gene Autry and 81 with Roy Rogers. They were immensely popular, especially in neighbourhood theatres, small towns and rural locations – and in Saturday matinées everywhere.[29]

In the effort to sustain trade, exhibitors did more than introduce the B movie, though that was their most effective ploy. They realised that movie-going was no longer an automatic habit, and introduced gimmicks to bring people in. Ticket-holders with lucky numbers won cash prizes on Bank Nights. Other enticements included Screeno, Bingo and the giving away of crockery. As Bergman says, in a period when people were glad of the smallest windfall, these draws were a great success.[30] In the early 1930s most cinemas built refreshment stands. Previously patrons of almost all movie houses had purchased confections outside the cinema and brought them in. Now exhibitors could use the interval between the two parts of the double bill to encourage people to spend money on leisure foods. Suddenly even in the classiest cinemas, which in better times would have thought such things cheapening to their image, sweets, popcorn and soft drinks were sold. The high returns earned by sales of these 'concessions' (over 100 per cent net on popcorn) meant for many theatres the difference between making profit or closing.[31] Last but not least, the theatres cut costs. Celebrated in the 1920s for their service to customers, in the 1930s even the movie palaces fired their ushers, turned up the lights, and let patrons find their own seats.[32]

During the Depression years stars were not the object of envy. Rather they inspired admiration because their wealth gave them a status almost godlike. Fan magazines augmented their epic stature and confirmed them as creatures of fantasy. As employees, however, their power declined with the drop in ticket sales and the concentration of control in a few studios. Their salaries were (like other studio costs) cut back, and most were offered seven-year contracts, renewable annually by the studios. If they were successful they were bound, if they failed, they were released. During the studio era stars became commodities, in Kindem's words, to be shaped, manipulated, exhausted and discarded. The highest salaries were limited to $10 000 per week (actually less than the principal stars of the 'teens), and most of those who earned this well did not hold on to their positions for long. The huge earners were the chief executives – the presidents and production chiefs – of the studios. These men were rewarded far more generously than the norm in much larger corporations; some of them served for long periods.[33]

At about this time advertising, which had been tried during the silent era, began to be a significant source of funds. By 1930 it was of course a commonplace that trade followed American pictures because they raised in the minds of their audiences the desire to possess the goods (and live in the manner) they depicted.[34] The studios now integrated themselves further with the consumer-oriented economy by arranging tie-ins with manufacturers. At their crudest, as Eckert shows, these amounted to nothing more than turning short fictions into giant billboards in which naked ads were strung together round a feeble plot. Such shorts were prominent in Paramount and Warner release schedules for 1931; but they aroused a furious campaign by independent exhibitors (who thought they would annoy audiences) and newspapers (fearful of losing advertising revenue to the cinema), and they were stopped.[35] Tie-ins became more sophisticated.

The showcasing of goods, particularly of fashions, cosmetics and furnishings, became very subtle in the 1930s. As we have noted (Chapter 6) the manufacture and wholesale of fashion-wear expanded explosively in Los Angeles in the late 1920s. Two brands were set up to market styles modelled by individual stars, and clothing manufacturers began to promote such style lines nationally. From 1930 the Modern Merchandising Bureau acted as fashion middle-man for most of the major studios, receiving sketches from them of costumes to be worn in future films, and contracting with manufacturers to have them ready for sale in time for each film's release date. It prepared a promotional campaign linking pictures of the clothes with the stars who would be wearing them, with the film, the studio, and the local theatre where it would play. In the early 1930s the Bureau marketed these fashions to wealthy women through an exclusive nationwide chain of 'Cinema Fashion' shops. Later it added a second chain which sold informal styles at popular prices. The studios were not paid cash for the huge publicity they gave these products (cosmetics were marketed in a comparable way). Instead they got massive, well-timed publicity for their films.[36]

All manner of manufacturing companies approached the studios offering their products as furnishings, props, vehicles, or whatever. The deal was much the same – these items appeared on screen without overt hyping (though the observant spectator would have noticed for example a proliferation of General Electric fridges and Buick cars in Warner Brothers' films between 1933 and 1935). The manufacturing partner then undertook, without charge, an intense programme of publicity linking his product to the movie.

An alternative pattern of tie-in is instanced in the agreement between Coca-Cola and MGM in 1933 whereby the soft-drinks company funded the studio with $0.5 million in return for the endorsement of its product by MGM stars. That year Coca-Cola was deeply involved, right down to local level, in the promotion of *Dinner at Eight* – through national magazine ads, and placards carried by delivery trucks and local dealers, all tying together Jean Harlow, the drink, and the film. The film itself, quite typically, was tied to a number of other products. And it became practice for studio heads of exploitation to co-ordinate scriptwriting with a breakdown of products and services for which sponsorship might be sought.[37]

About this time a small specialist studio, Walt Disney, commenced systematic marketing of the rights to use its cartoon characters. By 1934 about 80 American companies including General Foods, RCA Victor, and Ingersoll Watches (this last corporation owing its rescue from deep trouble to Mickey Mouse's boost to its sales) were paying royalties of between $2\frac{1}{2}$ to 5 per cent on products sold with the aid of Disney designs. Merchandising, as it became known, raised income for the company of some $300 000 (in that year one-third of its net profit) and brought security to an independent whose profits from animated film production were not yet regular. It was to continue to have this significance in the Disney accounts for years.[38]

The symbiosis of the motion picture industry and consumerism was further enhanced in the 1930s by Hollywood's vigorous exploitation of radio. At the start of the decade the studios still regarded it as a rival which could best be used (as by Warners through its local radio station, or Paramount taking advantage of the half interest it owned at the time in CBS) to advertise their movies. RKO, however, was early in recognising a new possibility when it drew on its affiliate NBC (another subsidiary of RCA) for a new breed of film star, the radio personality – Amos and Andy were examples.[39] In 1932 NBC opened a studio in Hollywood with one staff member. By 1937 it had constructed a major sound studio employing 100 staff. The same five-year period saw a massive growth to some 700 hours of radio programming originated from Hollywood. Film stars gave interviews, regularly appeared both hosting shows for sponsors and endorsing their products, and played in radio dramas sponsored by commercial giants. To Hollywood the direct benefits included income from the contracts which the movie studios signed with radio for the services of their stars; free publicity, often tied to specific films; and recruitment of radio stars, like Bing Crosby and Bob Hope to Paramount, one of the studios that most actively exploited links with the other medium. On the one hand more and more films imitated the radio variety-show format (such as Hope's début at Paramount, *The Big Broadcast of 1938*). On the other, radio drama was deeply influenced by the formulaic creation and resolution of simple problems. Sometimes it even inherited generic formulas, as in the case of the CBS series *The Lone Ranger*.[40]

During the 1930s Hollywood controlled Tin Pan Alley (see

Chapter 7). Thus it took substantial income from music royalties paid by the radio companies, an arrangement which satisfied all parties to it as long as they all made money. And during the epoch when film stars (Eddie Cantor, Deanna Durbin, Rudy Vallee, Fred Astaire, Bing Crosby and many others) were also highly popular recording artists, radio, cinema and the music industry all supported each other. Towards the end of the decade, however, big band swing began to pull dancers and listeners alike; but the film studios found they could not feature these bands other than in short films. For band leaders could not be groomed for film stardom, though they could be broadcast cheaply by live relay from dance halls.

The Hollywood studios agreed among themselves to compensate for the loss of film revenue by doubling royalty charges on ASCAP (American Society of Composers, Authors and Performers) music. They calculated that through ASCAP (which they controlled via Tin Pan Alley) they commanded virtually all the popular music played by radio. This may have been the case, but the radio companies got wind of the ASCAP proposals and bought music rights from other sources. They were able to react to the imposition of doubled royalties in January 1941 by banning all ASCAP music from the air. Shepherd argues that three things happened: country and western, and rhythm and blues music, which for the first time got extensive airtime, quickly rose in popularity; and the film companies backed down after a few months; but Tin Pan Alley's music did not recover its old popularity, and Hollywood's grip on the radio industry slackened to some degree.[41]

As in the 1920s, Hollywood's links with the advertising and broadcasting industries continued in the 1930s to encourage a preference in the movie studios for contemporary subjects. More significantly, it furthered the process whereby the skills of many talented movie artists and craftsmen had been lent to what Eckert calls a massive sales effort using covert techniques to associate products with the gratifying and pleasurable experience films provided. What followed was '. . . the establishment of powerful bonds between the emotional, fantasy-generating substance of films, and the material objects those films contained.' It was, he concludes, a spectacularly successful exercise in consumer manipulation, not to be surpassed until the advent of television.[42] For much of mainline Hollywood cinema it meant that the fetishism of the actor developed into the fetishism of man-made objects which themselves now became invested with the projected desires of the aroused libido.

The audience is now drawn to react emotionally to objects on screen as well as to characters.

As the Depression hit the industry some producers reverted to old exploitation tactics, reintroduced sex appeal, and 'discovered' violence. The musical with its chorus line-ups made a ready vehicle for sexual display; and the cinema could do what the stage could not, combining skimpy costumes with revealing close-ups of the female body. In turn these elements could be co-ordinated into erotic routines like those choreographed by Busby Berkeley.[43] In 1932 Mae West made her first film and became for about five years Paramount's most popular star. Her films expressed female desire with a shocking frankness previously open only to male characters.

The gangster film also shocked some people, sometimes for its acknowledgement of sexual desire, but usually because such films as *Little Caesar*, *Public Enemy* and *Scarface* were built around bad men whose lives had vivid glamour: Edward G. Robinson's Rico, and James Cagney's Tommy became instant archetypes. Those who believed that these films set out to entice an entire generation to licentious and criminal conduct were appalled. The studios faced once again an urgent clamour for the censorship of these dangerous products.

At first it seemed to the industry on the basis of its previous experience that the pressure for censorship would be no more than a temporary inconvenience. Even after the establishment of the Hays Office, the most insistent pressure for reform had obliged the studios to do little more than clean up their product for a few months, after which 'forbidden' matter quietly edged back on to the screen. The theoretical guidelines were clear enough – the Hays Office had issued in 1927 a list of 'Don'ts and Be Carefuls', comprising eleven things the members of the MPPDA agreed with the coming of sound not to do. But not only did half the member companies not co-operate, the Hays Office simply did not have the machinery to enable it to supervise all the films that were made.[44] In 1930 the Office acted, but it did not take to itself greater powers. Instead it issued a new and longer Production Code which combined general prohibitions against movie immorality with twelve specific clauses. Among the latter it included an attack on screen lawlessness, and sought to regulate films so that crime should not be shown in such a way as to elicit sympathy or imitation.[45] On sexual matters, the Code recognised the financial pressures on studios and attempted to reconcile religious morality (it was written by a Catholic layman and a Jesuit) with box-office necessity. Although Hays sponsored the code, recognising the political necessity for doing so, the studios, faced with falling admissions, had no qualms about ignoring it.[46]

On this occasion, however, they misjudged the opposition. For during the next five years public opinion shifted significantly. Two factors contributed to that change. Firstly, among the long-established protest groups, the Catholics now organised themselves into an effective pressure group, the Legion of Decency.[47] In April 1934 bishops distributed, to the faithful, forms pledging support for a boycott organised by the Church, and within ten weeks 11 million people had signed. They then informed the Hays Office that henceforth the Catholic Church would review all films and classify them according to its own standards. Those of which it disapproved would be boycotted by the Legion of Decency. Given that the industry was at its lowest economic ebb, and that it was, as we shall see, dealing with new macro-economic circumstances, this threat from a highly organised campaign proved decisive. In July 1934 Hays and the MPPDA board amended the Production Code to endow it with powers.[48]

From that date no film could be distributed or screened by a member of the MPPDA (no matter who produced it) unless it carried the Production Code Administration (PCA) seal. That seal was given only to those films that fell within the terms of the Code, and now for the first time a penalty of $25 000 could be levied by the PCA on members who transgressed. As all the majors (and thus their theatres) belonged to the MPPDA, PCA approval became all but universal.[49] That approval was much more than a matter of review. Censorship of completed films, even industry self-censorship, can be a catastrophically expensive intervention because it may lead to re-shooting large sections of a movie, or even the scrapping of a finished film. The PCA therefore practised pre-censorship. From 1935 every producer kept in touch with the PCA from the moment he took up a film project. Every stage of production – outline, script development, plans for costumes and sets, rough-cut sequences and the final cut – was supervised in minute detail. Every stage had to receive written approval before production could continue and the PCA seal be granted.[50] Inevitably this degree of control had a considerable impact on the kinds of film that were produced, as we are to see.

The second new factor influencing the industry in the years

1933–5 arose through the election of Franklin D. Roosevelt as US President. For the implementation of the Production Code was assisted by what is generally recognised as a change of perceived needs on the part of an altogether wider audience than that represented by the Legion of Decency. As Sklar observes, movie-makers suddenly found it better (i.e. safer and more profitable) to support middle-class values than to defy them, and to boost social morale by fostering a spirit of patriotism.[51] From about 1935 a number of well-documented changes in genre production took place in response to the way audiences showed their new enthusiasms at the box office. To take just one example of many detailed by Bergman, the gangster movie shifted ground significantly so that from 1936 Cagney and Robinson played not the the gang bosses, but FBI men. They were actually seen to change sides on screen, Cagney in *G Men* and Robinson in *Bullets or Ballots* (both Warner Brothers).[52] Where formerly the corruption of the society in which the gangsters move seemed greater than their own evil, now these one-time heroes seem less attractive than the agents of federal law.[53] Bergman shows parallel shifts in a number of other genres.[54]

These changes, which arose from the impact of cultural rather than directly economic forces, tended to make for a new moralism and dignity in American cinemas. Its obverse face was a certain blandness which the application of the Production Code brought about. Mae West, for example, was prevented by the PCA from expressing the raucous independent sexuality that had made her famous. As Sklar says, she had to become instead merely a self-deprecating comic, a bad girl on her way to redemption, and her movie career was over by 1938.[55] When one sees what the PCA could require of a relatively innocent musical, this is hardly surprising. For example, having examined the shooting script and songs for *On the Town*, it insisted that the phrase 'New York, New York, it's a helluva town!' was unacceptable. It also made a point of directing the attention of the producers:

> to the need for the greatest possible care in the selection and photographing of the dresses and costumes of your women. The Production Code makes it mandatory that the intimate parts of the body – specifically, the breasts of women – be fully covered at all times. Any compromise with this regulation will compel us to withhold approval of your picture . . .

The kissing . . . throughout this production should not be unduly passionate, prolonged or open-mouth.[56]

As Balio writes, the Code severely restricted the subject-matter that American films could deal with. Well into the 1950s the industry was to rely on the supposedly undifferentiated mass audience for its main box-office income. The 'family' film might boast expensive production values and high technical gloss; but it would certainly not deal with topics that concerned people in their daily lives.[57] For more than two decades sexuality was replaced by coyness, and controversy by blandness.

These several pressures no doubt help explain the renewed popularity with the studios of costume drama, which was once again popular with audiences. There was also an additional business factor in their favour. Production chiefs noticed during the Depression era that only the costly or the very cheap film was likely to make profit. Given that to draw audiences willing to pay first-run prices movies had to build a reputation, most medium-price pictures simply were not good enough to pay back their costs. (Cheap movies had a better chance of doing so in neighbourhood and small-town theatres.) Costume dramas, however, cost a lot, and the studios did all they could to make them attractive so that even the mediocre ones returned their costs, while good films could make a fortune. As Sklar adds in making this point, famous novels and historical themes once again lent themselves to big budget treatment because they showed off their enhanced production values with their costumes, exotic sets and large casts. And as before they had by virtue of their literary status the requisite dignity and seriousness. In particular Thalberg and Selznick at MGM, and Zanuck at Twentieth Century–Fox made distinguished films from such sources, among them *The Barretts of Wimpole Street* (1934), *David Copperfield*, *Anna Karenina* (1935), *Mutiny on the Bounty* and *A Tale of Two Cities* (1936).[58]

The policies of the New Deal did have a direct impact on the economy of the industry. The new administration sought to shift the film business, in common with the rest of American industry, into a different economic environment where notionally it would eschew cut-throat rivalry in favour of fair competition. The new administration failed in this aim for at least two reasons. Firstly, the measures it introduced in the National Industrial Recovery Act (NIRA) of June 1933, were repealed by the Supreme Court in May

1935. It did so on the grounds that they violated the anti-trust provisions of the constitution by allowing businessmen to collude in regulating their own industries. And secondly of course, most of the business done by the American film industry was not subject to cut-throat competition. Indeed the NIRA actually reinforced the oligopoly, not least because the MPPDA, which in effect represented the five majors and three minors, drafted the *Code of Fair Practice for the Motion Picture Industry*. Despite the protests of the independent sectors in exhibition, which saw their existence marginalised by it, the new Code was brought into law. Its fairness was reserved for the eight studios whose status as a collusive cartel it enhanced.[59] *Inter alia* the NIRA code:

1. Accepted the vertical integration of the majors;
2. Legitimised block-booking and blind-bidding (which in practice were only operated in respect of bookings by the weaker independent theatres and chains since the majors had the pick of each other's schedules, and strong independent chains had sufficient purchasing clout usually to get what they wanted);[60] and
3. Confirmed as instruments of these policies the classification of theatres by run (giving cinemas a pre-ordained place in the order of release); the enforcement of clearance (the period of time, between 7 and 30 days, that must elapse before a lower-run house could advertise or screen a film its immediate precursor had finished with); and enforcement of zones, the geographical limits within which clearance applied to each theatre.

The terms of the NIRA Code continued in all essentials to govern the industry even after the Act had been invalidated. They enabled the oligopoly to control the industry, despite challenges from the law, for a further fifteen years.[61]

In one respect only did the Roosevelt administration weaken the control of the studios – on the labour front. Soon after his election the President declared a bank moratorium, and the studios devised a plan to cope in part with the interruption of cash flow by cutting the pay of staff. This proposal angered Hollywood's workforce the more in that it was made by the trade union set up by the studios, the Academy of Motion Picture Arts and Sciences. The highest-paid employees of the studios successfully lobbied Roosevelt in defence of their own interests. Rank and file staff learnt sharply the value of effective representation, and the episode was the stimulus to a prolonged period of activity which, after much struggle, brought full and strong unionisation to Hollywood.[62]

10 War, Prosperity, Divorce and Loss, 1939–48

No doubt studio production schedules would have altered in the 1940s, whatever had occurred in that decade; but the war brought specific pressures to bear. Of these some were explicitly political: for instance when America joined the war, the government outlined six basic themes on which it suggested Hollywood producers should concentrate as part of their contribution to the war effort. However, economic pressures exerted at least equal influence at a time when the industry was facing the loss of much of its overseas market, together with striking changes in the composition and needs of audiences at home.

The industry seems to have been slow to respond to direct political pressure, possibly in part because the war seemed remote to Americans before 1943. Until that year producers did little to illuminate the government's themes:

1. The reasons for America joining the struggle;
2. The nature of the enemy – his ideology, objectives and methods;
3. America's allies in arms;
4. The work of those producing materials required for the war effort;
5. The Home Front – the duties of civilians; and
6. The allied fighting forces.

Although about one-quarter of Hollywood's output as late as the 1941–2 season related in some way to the war, Jacobs describes the bulk of it as puerile. Stock characters and formulaic action were merely translated into a military context: the sheriff and the private eye, equally with the blonde in the silk négligée, now appeared in uniform.[1] Only after the army decided to give the studios the indoctrination new military recruits received did feature films begin to treat the war with the kind of responsibility the government required. But by this time Hollywood had been exposed to the criticism of men and women who had experienced combat and were offended by the falsity of what they saw in films.[2]

Though they were politically gauche, the studios remained alert to economic changes. Well before the formal declaration of hostilities, the studios were aware of the erosion of their overseas audience. Foreign markets had for years supplied the American film industry with about a third of its revenue, despite the sporadic imposition of import restraints by nations attempting to protect their own film industries.[3] Now as the Axis powers invaded country after country, they shut out Hollywood's product. By the end of 1940 the whole of continental Europe (apart from Sweden, Switzerland and Portugal) was closed to American film.[4] To make matters worse, late in 1939 the British government imposed restrictions on the export of currency, and the American industry found itself deprived of about half its earnings in this important market, until 1943 when Will Hays persuaded the British to revoke the controls.[5] With the Commonwealth and Far Eastern markets also badly hit, Hollywood found it would have to rely on Latin-American audiences for most of its overseas income.

The government assisted the industry to export its newsreels to South America because they were seen as a means of countering Axis propaganda. But in order to sell features, it had to change its offensive, cardboard stereotype of the Latin-American as a bloodthirsty villain and produce films better adapted to this audience.[6] Twentieth Century-Fox realised this and recruited Carmen Miranda to instant stardom in a number of films such as *Down Argentine Way* (1940) and *That Night in Rio* (1941) which used Latin-American locales and themes.[7] Business in the sub-continent did improve steadily throughout the war, but did not compensate for all that Hollywood had lost abroad, firstly because local production also expanded, and secondly American distributors had trouble getting their product through reliably.[8]

In these circumstances the domestic North American market, always the base upon which the industry had founded its profitability, became so important (despite a resurgence of business in Britain) that producers were able to think almost exclusively in terms of American demands. This made it possible for instance, for the studios, with little regard for tact or truth, repeatedly to show US forces winning the war single-handed.[9] And it has been argued that Greta Garbo's career came to an end because, with the loss of her European audience, MGM decided to change her haunting presence into the persona of the all-American comedienne in *Two-Faced Woman* (1941) – a mask that did not suit her.[10] But as we shall see, the alteration in Hollywood's audience also encouraged more attractive developments.

Happily for the industry, domestic box-office receipts improved substantially from 1940 as America stepped up its war effort. Unemployment fell, and many workers received increased wages. As men enlisted, women took their places on production lines. People went to the movies more than ever before, an interest sponsored by the fact that alternative activities became hard to find. Nightclubs and restaurants closed, goods and petrol were in short supply: the new affluence of wage earners had fewer outlets, yet after the long hours of overtime which the wartime economy required, the need for recreation was all the more strongly felt. The movies benefited.[11] Takings began to soar until, boosted by the return of servicemen, they reached a peak at $1692 million in 1946, and attracted customers (about 85 or 90 million per week) in numbers that cinemas have not seen since.

Improvement at the box office had immediate consequences. Theatre operators abandoned all the old gimmicks designed to draw audiences – Screeno, Bingo and free crockery. Only the double bill survived. In towns where war industries created booming economies, movie theatres stayed open round the clock to accommodate changing workshifts. And the cinema became more than ever a place where people could give vent to their emotions, sharing sadness and pleasure, often responding rowdily to the screen.[12]

The industry itself, however, remained cautious, and its approach to films about the war illustrates its continuing concern with box-office takings rather than social realities. Shindler says that the studios began the summer of 1939 by being uncertain whether war would break out. Then when it did they feared it might end or change drastically so as to wreck any movies in the pipeline. Eventually they released a spate of films about the conflict; but in the first months these, as we have mentioned, were mostly melodramas – plots about spies, saboteurs and refugees – and satires on military training.[13] The industry remembered the huge profits it had made from films about the First World War, and did not want to miss the chance to repeat such business. But it experienced countervailing fears: that it might be accused of encouraging war, that actual news from the front might discourage audiences from watching fictions, and worst of all that the public might simply prefer the old kinds of escapist entertainment. And indeed the bestsellers of 1940 were films like *Strike Up The Band*, *Boom Town*, and *Rebecca*, though to the studio's relief people did not stay away from such anti-Nazi films (including Chaplin's *The Great Dictator*) as were released.[14] In general the majors once again sought safety at the box office by following rather than leading public opinion. Hence the obvious disparity between what Hollywood showed and the actualities of news reports dealing with life in Europe.[15]

Thus only after America had entered the war did the industry in 1943 find the courage to reflect the contemporary events more accurately and seriously, often in terms which the Office of War Information had recommended. Even then its courage did not last long as, with memories of the way the industry had been left at the end of the First World War with numbers of unsaleable films, the studios stopped making war films as soon as they could foresee an Allied victory, which they did some time before the conflict ended.[16] Then they sought out stories that dealt with the problems facing returning servicemen, latching onto a dimension of post-war society that could clearly be seen in advance.[17]

The studios should have been well informed about the ways their domestic audience had changed, for from just before the war they began to make increasing use of audience research techniques. The business had at last grown so massive that some studio bosses seem to have had to concede the need of more than just their famous intuition to guide programming policy.[18] But the two surveys conducted in 1941 and 1943 appear merely to have renewed their complacency – for there is little evidence of their having reacted to the more detailed findings of these and other surveys over the next few years. Indeed this early research was deeply comforting in that it showed that, as opposed to the way movie-goers behaved in the Depression, fewer than a quarter now took note of what was on at their cinema before buying tickets. The majority went to the movies no matter what was showing. But members of higher income groups were more selective than the less well paid.[19] Presumably their need for recreation was less insistent.

With or without surveys, the studios knew that wartime enlistment meant that perhaps as many as 600 000 Americans a night saw movies on 16mm prints as part of the armed forces entertainment programme.[20] They also knew that women comprised an ever more important part of the audience. In fact the studios had believed for some years that in the better class of cinema it was often women who 'set the type of picture that will go'. Through the 1930s they had marketed films to married middle-class women in the expectation that they would act as opinion-formers for a wider audience. In that decade women's films had usually stimulated reverie, offering an escape from a dull life into an imaginary luxury greater than anything spectators might know at home. Such fantasies were often rounded out with fictional husbands infinitely more solicitous of their wives' desires than the average male.[21] But during the war women's pictures changed to reflect the altered circumstances of the audience and showed women coping with a new independence in both their private and working lives. A few films, like *Tender Comrade* (RKO, 1944) with Ginger Rogers, actually paid tribute to the new working role of American womanhood. And for the first time exhibitors were faced with the problem of finding marketing devices to attract the single woman – distributors encouraged them to display glamour pictures of male stars outside theatres.[22]

The independent role of women during the Second World War has sometimes been emphasised to the point where it is forgotten that, as we have already remarked, the cinema also provided people with a haven in which they could enjoy a sense of community. Loneliness was not the only theme of wartime cinema. Many films ritualised the sharing of hardship in a common cause. So many families were broken (whether for the duration or permanently) that it is tempting to speculate that the cinema may have been for many a family substitute. The *film noir*, with its emphasis on the threatening sexuality of woman and the treachery even to himself of the hero, has often been read as a covert rebuttal of women's new independence. It can equally well be glossed as indicating the deep desire for the restoration of the family based on traditional values: woman's domesticity, man's honourable authority.[23] Much of the power of the genre springs from the denial of mores which the dominant part of American society continued to find natural and right at least until the end of the 1950s.

These values were to reassert themselves immediately the war ended, and were among the factors that contributed to a decline in the cinema audience from the peak attendance of 1946. Great numbers of young people whose lives had been disrupted soon set up home and started families. For many, home became the centre of their lives, and over the following decade young families moved into the suburbs there to seek a life as neat and ordered as their tidy gardens and carefully planned streets. The baby boom, the cost of new mortgages and of transport into the city centre for work left many with less to spend on entertainment than during the war years. And new leisure activities and sports were being developed that competed with cinema for people's spending money. The most effective new counter-attraction to the cinema was increasingly, of course, television – cheap visual entertainment in the home.[24]

For the movie industry the immediate effect was that as attendance declined, the audience once again became selective. Outstanding films continued to draw custom, but suddenly the average film could not be relied on to return its costs. The studios did not apply the lessons of audience research and appeared not to have any grasp of the great social changes that were under way. Towards the end of the 1940s, research indicated that the demography of the audience was undergoing another sea change. Now the better educated and the more well-to-do individuals were, the *more* they went to the movies. And young people were going to the cinema more than older folk.[25] But during this era the studios made no attempt to win the better educated audience, persisting Sklar says in thinking of intellectuals as antagonists.[26] And they left it to a small poverty-row studio, Allied Artists, to demonstrate as late as 1954 that there was a market for films that exploited young people's tastes.[27]

Instead the studios responded to the tastes of certain large minority audiences at the expense of others. They continued to favour the small town and rural audience, which though substantial by definition did not patronise the first-run houses where big money was made. As we have seen, this audience was well known to the studios for its dislike of the subtle, the exotic or the unexpected, and its preference for what was already familiar, easy and glamorous. These values seemed to the studios both profitable and comfortable. They could accommodate them within a scarcely changing pattern of generic production, concentrating in particular on Westerns and horror movies.[28]

The accommodation of this market contrasts vividly with the studios' behaviour towards black American audiences. In effect they ignored this large community, producing no films for it (Zanuck's social consciousness movies at Warners and Fox were built on liberal ethics for the white audience), and casting very few black actors in any other than demeaning 'coon' and 'Uncle Tom' roles. In the South some exhibitors did take note of the black audience, but only to the extent of excluding them from cinemas, or putting them in segregated seats.[29] As Cripps remarks, studio executives were as blind to the true conditions in their regional markets as they were to the true feelings of blacks. They had no accurate data for the South, misread what they had, and failed to realise that they could have helped rather than hindered the post-war shift in American racial attitudes. It was enough for them that the trade press held the Southern market in contempt for its low volume of business.[30] Hollywood only developed black movies decades later when it finally saw the possibility of taking profit from black audiences.

Faced with unmistakable evidence of audience decline from 1947, the industry concentrated on combating factors which its executives could readily understand as causing its problems. The number and severity of these difficulties was great enough to explain why company chiefs did not look further for hidden causes. They had to deal with circumstances which would affect both the way films were released, and ultimately the kinds of film that reached the screen. These factors included firstly new problems in their European markets; secondly the succession of anti-trust cases brought against them by the Justice Department; and thirdly the growing competition from television. They reacted to these 'visible' troubles with all the more urgency in that their bankers were themselves concerned by what was in 1947–9 an unexpected phenomenon, the failure of a number of films produced with bank loans to return funds sufficient to repay those debts.[31]

First, then, film exports. At the end of the war the American film industry had moved to recover its overseas markets and exploit them once again as a source of all but 'free' profits on films which had already earned income in the United States. The European industries had been devastated by war – suffering damage to plant, loss of personnel, and scarcity of capital to invest in production. These and a number of other factors made the American industry almost unstoppable. For it was encouraged to do abroad what the US government expressly sought to stop it doing at home – to act as a cartel. In 1945 the old MPPDA was reorganised, and it emerged as the Motion Picture Association of America. One wing of this association was established to handle exports – the Motion Picture Export Association (MPEA). This department worked closely with the US government in its dealings overseas, and the liaison gave it great power since in some territories film deals could be coupled with the promise of aid under the Marshall Plan. The film industry got improved access, particularly to Western Europe, and won a powerful ally in resisting post-war import quotas which a number of countries soon sought to impose. For its part the US government secured an equally powerful ally in its tacit propaganda programme in Western Europe, in which it used every communications channel it could to persuade European voters newly freed from Nazi tyranny not to vote left-wing parties into power in reaction to Fascism. Not that Hollywood films (with relatively few exceptions) intentionally incorporated propaganda. Rather, as Guback says, the basic assumption of all parties was that American feature films already adequately represented Americanism and no additional steps needed to be taken to enhance their content. This suited the studios, who did not wish to put at risk their films' profitability by subordinating entertainment to political messages.[32]

During the war Hollywood had built up a huge backlog of films that had not been shown in countries controlled by the Axis powers. The MPEA sought to get unlimited access to these markets, and where it succeeded a flood of pictures followed. Italy received an average of 570 American films in each of the four years following the war. Having earned their profits at home these films were dumped on the French, Italian and German markets.[33] Local distributors had no hope of competing with their rental prices. And exhibitors had more than cost alone to discourage them from hiring local product. Typically American movies were the more popular. They had driving narratives, plenty of action, and vivid character development of strongly marked and melodramatic personalities. To popular audiences local films seemed at best a pale copy of the real American thing.

Nowhere was this attitude more fixed than in Britain; and in 1947 the British government was the first to take action against American hegemony, even though it was not the victim of wholesale dumping. It was followed in 1948 by France and Italy. All three nations hoped to save their domestic film industries from probable extinction; to prevent the drain to the United States of currency no European nation could afford to spend on entertainment after a devastating war; and incidentally to inhibit American cultural imperialism. They placed limits on the amount of the studios' earnings that could be exported (the British, for instance, eventually settling for an arrangement that prevented the American industry from repatriating more than $17 million each year).[34] This was not of course the first time European film industries had resisted Hollywood, but it was the first occasion in peacetime this particular device had been used. In the long term it led to a change in the studios' operations as they used the money they could not bring home to fund production abroad. Runaway production, as it became known, took advantage of cheaper overseas labour rates, and eventually helped organise the American industry into a consolidated international operation. But this was to happen in the 1950s and 1960s: in 1949 runaway production accounted only for 19 Hollywood productions; by 1969 there were 183.[35] In the meantime the movie business had to face more immediate worries.

Those worries arose at the end of a period in which, despite the disruption of war, the industry had run on stable and profitable lines. The improvement of business from the start of the war had a further consequence in that pictures ran for longer seasons to capacity houses, and the demand for films dropped. The eight studios released 388 films in 1939, but only 252 in 1946. Thus, until the decline set in, each movie tended during the 1940s to take larger rentals. At a time when Hollywood lost about a quarter of its personnel to the armed forces, it was convenient to be able to reduce the volume of output. Moreover from the start of 1943 the government imposed a 25 per cent cut in the industry's allocation of raw stock. Because they had anticipated this the studios did not face great difficulty – they refined their shooting techniques to use less stock, reduced their output, and made up their release schedules to the required numbers by drawing on a hoard of more than 100 films they had stored against such a need. Even at a time when inflation hit the US economy sharply and production costs rose, these several factors led to the eight studios making much enhanced profits.[36]

On the production side most of the studios seem to have tried to continue their former programming policies with as little change as possible other than to take account of shifts in audience tastes. For example, after the appointment in 1939 of Arthur Freed as producer, MGM continued to make musicals, but their tenor changed. After the fluffy Nelson Eddy/Jeanette MacDonald films of the 1930s, the musicals of the 1940s were altogether more vigorous and energetic, but no less sophisticated. At Paramount the elegant satire of Preston Sturges and the cynicism of Wilder followed Lubitsch's wit. And the anarchy of the Marx Brothers gave way to the series of highly profitable *Road* movies with Bing Crosby, Bob Hope and Dorothy Lamour – but comedy remained a major theme in the studio's programme.

There were no dramatic changes of policy at Warners or Fox. Columbia lost Capra in 1939, but continued with its policy of making tightly costed, slick B pictures; and it found in Rita Hayworth an actress who could be exploited both as a wartime pin-up and star of a series of musicals.[37] United Artists continued to be the most erratic studio. Ever declining in prestige and profitability through the extraordinary wrangling of its owners, it actually managed to make a small loss in 1944 when every other company was booming. During the 1940s it parted company with, among others, Samuel Goldwyn, Alexander Korda, Walter Wanger, Arthur Rank, and David O. Selznick. As before, these ruptures left the company for prolonged periods with too few films to distribute, and relying increasingly on B-picture material for survival.[38]

At two studios policies did change. In 1946 Universal merged with an independent production company, International Pictures. Its former owners William Goetz and Leo Spitz were placed in charge of production for the new combine, and they developed a strategy intended to force for Universal-International Pictures a place alongside the five majors. These tactics (which failed commercially, Universal having to close temporarily in 1949) caused the studio to discard its earlier successes – Abbott and Costello, Deanna Durbin, B films, Westerns and serials – and to substitute a big-budget production schedule just at the time the industry ran into difficulties.[39]

Production policy also changed at RKO, when in 1942 Floyd Odlum's Atlas Group gained control of the company. The new management team set about making quickie features instead of the quality films that RCA had preferred.[40] And, with the company plunging $2 million into debt, they took one stage further a policy which had been evolving for some time and committed the studio heavily to B feature production with the appointment of Val Lewton and a support unit.[41]

In 1938 the US Justice Department initiated a long process of anti-trust litigation which culminated in the decisions of 1948 and 1949 in the *Paramount* case. It intended nothing less than the break up of the studio oligopoly. This became one of the major challenges faced by the studios post war. As early as 1940 the Department won the agreement of the five majors to a number of changes in business practice; and had the three minors accepted them, it might have ceased its suits against the industry. In the event the minors refused to sign the required Consent Decree, and from June 1942 business slowly returned to its former patterns – except that the B feature was affected lastingly.

Under the Decree, distributors could no longer force exhibitors to screen their shorts as a condition of obtaining features. Furthermore blind-bidding was banned, and they could no longer force bookings in blocks larger than five films.[42] Since these conditions applied to B as well as A features, it made their quality important as they too had to be sold individually. Relatively rapidly B pictures were encouraged to become increasingly distinctive and competitive.[43] The A/B distinction became more flexible, and the B category enlarged.

One consequence of the Justice Department's first victory was the evolution of what Kerr calls the 'ambitious B', the best known of which today are the B *films noirs* of the 1940s. An interesting shift in the conditions of the market was taking place. Although audiences still preferred a double bill to a single feature accompanied by a short, the basic economics of the industry had not changed, so the B film was still paid for by a flat rate rental. Thus its potential revenue remained limited, and it had still to be made cheaply. But, freed from the constraints of block-booking and blind-bidding, theatre operators who wanted to screen improved programmes to their audiences (no doubt principally in first-run cinemas) now created a significant demand for better quality films to supply the bottom half of the bill. The ambitious B film, Kerr argues, was one that bid for critical and commercial prestige, and this altered the sub-genre.[44]

When double features first became popular, B movies had been made as cheap copies of the A genres. From the end of the 1930s, however, the better ones in particular began to distinguish themselves from A movies by playing with the genres. Paradoxically, given that they continued to work under rigid budgetary restraints, B units were sometimes left to get on with their work in relative freedom. Not only did they continue as the industry's unofficial training schools, but they were able to experiment, sometimes with a degree of autonomy that would not have been granted to more expensive productions. Val Lewton's experiments at RKO with horror films laden with menace and tension are a case in point.[45]

Except for its impact on the B movie, the 1940 Consent Decree implicated the studios in an episode of only short-lived consequences. It never had teeth, being drafted complete with escape clauses to relieve the companies of difficulties if any of its provisions should actually bite. Specifically if the ban on block-booking and blind-bidding should succeed in nurturing competition, the majors were to be permitted to resume those practices in order to stifle it![46] One remembers that the government wanted the co-operation of the motion picture industry in the war effort.

As the war drew to a close and the government no longer had this need, the Justice Department resumed its suits in earnest. The practice of block-booking had by then been re-established, and the Federal District Court in a judgment of 1946 outlawed it once again. Although this ruling restored to independent theatres the right to rent the best films on the market (a factor which substantially encouraged post-war independent film production), it did not satisfy the Justice Department because it failed to attack at root the vertical structure that underpinned the oligopoly. It set in motion an appeal to the Supreme Court.

The Supreme Court reached its decision in the *Paramount* case in May 1948; and its verdict was confirmed by the District Court in July 1949, some eleven years after litigation began. (Compliance took some of the majors almost as long again.) In their judgment the Courts prohibited:

(1) block booking;
(2) the fixing of admission prices by anyone other than exhibitors;
(3) unfair runs and clearances between theatres in the same towns; and
(4) discriminatory pricing arrangements that favoured affiliated theatres at the expense of independent exhibitors.

Thus the Courts meant to end unfair distribution practices and to ensure each picture would be rented separately, theatre by theatre, without regard for other films or the ownership of cinemas.[47] However, the decisions which made the impact of these rulings so much heavier than those of earlier judgments concerned the vertical and horizontal relations of the eight companies with the theatres. They sought to sever production–distribution from exhibition by ordering:

(5) each of the eight companies to bring about *divorcement* by splitting itself into separate production–distribution and theatre companies. Here the courts attempted to break the industry's vertical structure.

They also sought to weaken the stranglehold both of the theatre chains formerly affiliated to the majors and the big independent circuits. For although in 1945 the majors owned or leased only 3137 out of 18 076 theatres, they thereby controlled at least 70 per cent of first-run houses in cities of more than 100 000 people, and almost 60 per cent of those in towns of 25–100 000. The courts required:

(6) that they (and some big independent chains) *divest* themselves of all cinemas operated in pools with other companies; and of one or more cinemas in towns which they had closed against outside competition by owning or controlling all the outlets. In this the Courts attempted to break some of the industry's horizontal links.

Finally, as a means of keeping the newly severed units apart, the Courts required:

(7) that they should remain isolated from each other by special trust requirements so that common control could not be exercised by common shareholders; and they were not to share interlocking directors or officers.[48]

The position of the three minors was anomalous in so far as they had no theatre chains from which they could divorce themselves. But as suppliers of product essential to the maintenance of the oligopoly they were held to be implicated in it, and were subjected to the same restrictions in trade practice.[49]

Divorcement and divestiture were painful and slow, taking the companies some ten years to complete. Some, like MGM-Loew's dragged their feet. Two, RKO and Paramount, quickly began negotiations for Consent Decrees. Borneman says that these two were in due course rewarded with a concession that the three recalcitrant majors did not receive – tacit permission for the new production–distribution outfits to buy a number of theatres, and for the new theatre companies to become involved again in production. That is, they were in time permitted once again to violate the spirit of anti-trust legislation.[50]

Divorcement was difficult because the two parts of the split majors had unequal earning power. As ever theatres contributed more dramatically to the profit and loss sheet than production and distribution. For example, in recent years RKO had been kept alive only by the profits of its theatres; its production and distribution operations made substantial losses. On divorcement the latter division found itself faced with demands from anxious creditors for the repayment of $8.5 million in loans. Under Howard Hughes' ownership it never again proved viable; by 1957 he had dismantled it. Even in more profitable concerns like Warner Brothers the fact that the company's cinemas earned 62 per cent of corporate profits created problems for the severed production–distribution arm.[51]

The Courts' decisions had direct consequences not only for the corporate structure of the eight companies, but for the main activities of the industry – distribution, production and exhibition. For the eight as distributors a direct consequence was that, deprived of profits from their theatres, they had to charge more in rentals for their movies. Whereas before divorcement they had (with the exception of the higher-priced Loew's) charged about 30 per cent of admission grosses, by the mid-1950s that figure had risen to 36 per cent, with popular films asking anything from 50 per cent to 70 per cent.[52] In order to be able to charge such rentals distributors had to pack their release schedules with films of supposedly sure box-office appeal. For as theatres could no longer be compelled to take product, distributors had to tempt them with the prospect of profits. Therefore they put pressure on production units to turn out 'sure things' rather than 'prestige items'. Experimentation was taboo.[53]

Because the majors could not be sure of guaranteed sales for the movies they released, they reduced production, cut out pot-boilers, and lost interest in the B picture. The double bill died because the studios no longer had a vested interest in theatres of their own; while, facing higher rentals for features, the theatres could no longer afford the second film. After releasing 243 films in 1940, the five majors reduced their production and in 1956 put out only 116.[54] However, with the decline in attendance most films were not able to sustain the kind of extended runs customary during the war. Thus falling numbers of spectators actually produced an increased demand for product just as the big five cut output. To some extent the shortfall was made up by the minors, who now had unimpeded access to the theatres. Columbia's domestic rentals increased 39 per cent from 1946 to 1954, and Universal's performance was comparable. Although they continued to release low-cost productions and ambitious B films, these two companies greatly expanded their output of first-class features, Columbia with such movies as *Born Yesterday*, *All About Eve*, *Sunset Boulevard* (1950) and *Death of a Salesman* (1951). And United Artists, working from a weak base, improved its rentals 80 per cent between 1945 and 1957.[55] Of no less significance was the development for the first time since the establishment of the studio system of independent film production on a substantial scale.

For these reasons the five majors *as producers* suffered serious setbacks from divorcement – which were exacerbated by the effects of the shrinking audience (403 million fewer seats were sold in 1947 than the previous year), and the strengthening rivalry of television.[56] As they cut back production, their fixed costs (wages of staff, rates, power, maintenance of studios, etc.,) had to be allocated between fewer films so that each movie tended to cost more. By about 1950 most of them had taken radical steps to reduce overheads. They fired staff: much of their labour was employed casually, and was first to suffer. Employment in the craft unions fell from 22 100 in 1946 to 13 500 in 1949.[57] Contracts with players – whether stars or rank-and-file actors – were not renewed. And some studios did the almost unthinkable and reduced the salaries of executives. They trimmed budgets, and required detailed planning for efficiency to resolve all difficulties before productions came to the studio floor. For a while certain kinds of film were eschewed – such as epics requiring large crowds, massive and costly sets, and intricate costumes. Films which emphasised contemporary realism were favoured, and many of them were shot on location.[58] The success of these measures through the late 1940s and early 1950s shows up in reducing average negative costs. Then from 1954 average costs began to rise again after the introduction of widescreen, and with more films being shot in colour.[59] And the epic made a spectacular return; but by then the majors were negotiating a further change in the market.

Despite every difficulty, and the fact that these developments represented no more than the beginning of a process of rapid change that was to alter radically some of the functions of the studios, the eight companies (the new majors of the 1950s) actually adapted well to their new conditions. The former minors enjoyed sharply rising earnings; and the profits of the old majors (expressed as the ratio of net income to shareholders' investment) compare closely in the years following divorcement with those of the years 1937–41.[60] *As distributors* the eight emerged from divorcement relatively strong, and took steps to retain their control of the entire industry despite the change in its structures and practices. In this the evolution of independent film production assisted them greatly.

The term 'independent production' describes the work of companies that neither own nor are owned by a distribution company.[61] Although we have encountered it in an earlier epoch, independence had almost to be re-invented in the 1940s, so successful had the studios been in buying up and controlling talent. By the end of the silent era they had virtually eradicated independent producers other than those who struggled to release through the uncertain mechanisms of United Artists, the one company set up purposely to distribute such films. The other majors dealt only occasionally with independents. These circumstances were altered by the coincidence of a number of factors. Firstly, as we have seen, the Consent Decree of 1940 temporarily ended block-booking and opened the way for exhibitors to select films on the basis of their excellence. The demand for quality put a premium on talent so that stars, directors, producers and even some principal technicians could bargain for greater recognition – either in cash or in artistic independence.[62] Secondly, the effect of the majors reducing output during the war years while exhibition was booming was to create a market vacuum which the independents filled. The third factor was the desire of some talented people to find a degree of creative freedom in their work – although in time this prospect proved for many to be a mirage. Fourthly, independence had big potential tax advantages. At a time when individuals were liable to pay 90 per cent rates if they fell within the top income bracket, the operator of a production company could reduce his or her tax to 60 per cent. Moreover, by forgoing a salary, listing profits as capital gains, and selling one's interest in a film as a capital asset, the individual was liable only for capital gains at 25 per cent.[63]

By 1945 there were about 40 independent producers, 70 the following year, 90 in 1947, and about 165 a decade later.[64] Many well-known people had opted for independence by the end of the war – including Constance Bennett, Frank Capra, Gary Cooper, Bing Crosby, Joan Fontaine, Bob Hope, Hedy Lamarr, Fred MacMurray, Ginger Rogers, George Stevens, Hunt Stromberg and John Wayne. Recognising the trend, most studios granted semi-independence to some of their most talented people. It was a way of keeping them within a studio's orbit, and conferred on the individual profit-participation and greater responsibility for artistic decisions. Cecil B. De Mille and Hal Wallis at Paramount; Bette Davis and Errol Flynn at Warners; Dudley Nichols and Leo McCarey at RKO; and Mervyn LeRoy and Mark Hellinger at Universal had this status.[65]

In practice after 1947 independent producers seldom strayed far from the studios' orbit because they needed to use them as distributors. During the boom years this had not been a problem as every film could make its money back; but as soon as business began to contract independents felt the consequences. Whereas previously the banks had been eager to lend production funds to every kind of operation, when films began to lose money, independents were worse hit than studios. The bigger organisations simply offset losses on one production against profits on others, and the banks' advances were safe. But many independents were set up to produce a handful of films, or even one. Losses from them could be terminal, and some producers defaulted on loans, particularly during the three or four years when the speed of audience shrinkage took the industry by surprise. Films made in 1947 with that year's audience in mind were being released a year later (a typical lead time) to much smaller houses. In three or four years around 230 films gave the banks enough cause for anxiety to get them involved in actively trying to recoup losses, even to the extent of ordering distributors to adopt specific marketing strategies for particular movies. Among those made by independents that run into trouble were some of the most progressive of the period, like two films from Enterprise Pictures, Robert Rossen's *Body and Soul* (1947) and Abraham Polonsky's *Force of Evil* (1949).[66]

Banks quickly became reluctant to advance funds for the production of single pictures. Where they did so they lent less and charged more, taking a direct interest in every aspect of production, including the script. It was not so much that they told producers what to do as that they made them avoid anything financially the least risky. And to seem safe independent productions had to be as conservative as mainline studio output.

In practice the trend in funding independents now moved away from sole funding by banks towards substantial investment by the studios. This did not make, however, for a break with conservatism – for the funding studio would contract to distribute the picture. Therefore it would exert control over every aspect of the production, and would decline to support projects that did not seem likely to do good business.

For the studios this new pattern of business had many advantages. Typically they would furnish a large part of what is known as 'second money' (that is the money that is repaid second, and stands at greater risk than 'first money'). This the banks might still furnish to a limit of perhaps 60 per cent of budgeted production costs. In effect the guarantee of second money would finance a film because, once it was found, first money could easily be raised. When the studios were involved not all the second money need be advanced as cash, since part might be contributed by the producer, director or stars agreeing to defer payment of part of their salaries in return for a profit-sharing contract.[67] As we shall see (in Chapter 12), the advantages of independent production to the studios did not end with these beneficial funding arrangements.

Although divorcement did not of itself restore to the industry's creative talents the artistic freedom they had hoped for, independent production became from the 1950s one of the two standard ways of making films. And it did so for economic reasons. The independents could make films less expensively than the studios – and that advantage increased as the volume of studio production fell. They could do so because they had no fixed overheads, and no massive administrative offices. They hired labour, technicians, actors and directors on a freelance basis only when they needed them. They paid for studio space only when they meant to shoot film – and indeed lacking studio space of their own, they were part of the late 1940s movement to shoot on location and save expense. When they came to post-production they rented editing and dubbing suites by the day from the studios, who could also, if required, supply the staff to man them. Conant reports that in 1950 the average negative cost (that is complete production costs) of films by independent producers turned out at $800 000. By comparison Paramount's costs averaged £1 144 000 for their 25 productions; while for the other majors whose output was smaller, average negative costs were estimated to be as much as $1 800 000.[68]

The relative cheapness of independent production must be seen as a direct corollary of the under-employment and unemployment of workers at every level of the industry. It was made possible only because the studios had sacked their employees and created a large pool of freelance workers. For although freelancers charged more when they were in work, their increased day rates did not by any means make up for the fact that most of them spent half the year out of work waiting for a call. Ultimately both they and their old employers would benefit from a continuing expansion of television production, which brought with it the need both for full-time staff and for the constant availability of sound stages.

There were exceptions to the general shift towards a pattern of production in which two-thirds of feature films came from independent and often increasingly well-established producers. Right through the 1950s MGM held on to its contract players and directors – but its pictures often seemed old fashioned in the post-war world. Universal, having once again discovered an unexploited corner of the market, also continued for the decade following divorcement to function as an unreconstructed studio. But for the others the change was so profound that, although they continued to produce some films on their own behalf, the major aesthetic consequence of divorcement can be identified as nothing less than the erasure of virtually all the marks of difference by which each studio had distinguished its product from the others'. Having broken up the creative departments and teams that made their films look and sound the way they did, they could neither recreate those effects in their own films, nor expect independents to do so working with pick-up freelance crews. It is this visible factor that made clear to every film-goer the end of the studio era.

Divorcement and divestiture had some unforseen effects on the theatres. The five former chains of the majors (United Paramount Theatres, National Theatres (formerly Twentieth Century-Fox), Loew's, RKO Theatres, and the Stanley Warner Corporation) faced increasing problems as they prepared for divestiture because their market value plummeted as box-office takings went into relentless decline. Thus after their divorcement all five chains were granted extensions so that they might have time to negotiate the sale of cinemas at a fair price. However, these extensions gave the five an additional decade to dominate American exhibition. And when they did sell, they had had plenty of time to decide which cinemas would be most profitable in the light of the demographic changes which were sweeping through urban America, and to which we have referred.[69] They were then in a good position to perpetuate their dominance by retaining first-run and second-run houses, and selling the rest. In the event declining revenues persuaded the chains to dispose of more cinemas than were specified in the Decrees. From the 3137 theatres they had owned before the *Paramount* case, they had been required to reduce their holdings to 1541. In fact by 1957 they retained only 1334.[70]

Divorcement and divestiture do seem to have brought about certain changes in exhibition patterns, though these were not as dramatic as those caused by the shrinkage of the audience. Now that exhibitors found themselves for the first time in decades in competition with one another, many operators of later-run houses wanted to upgrade their status to that of second-run cinemas. And a considerable number did so, even though the major distributors were not willing to supply all theatres on a first-run or second-run basis. In some areas multiple first and second runs were innovated, with several theatres in the zone playing the same film simultaneously. The effect was market saturation after first and second runs. Ever fewer patrons wanted to see films in the small theatres, and with the closure of more than 4000 in the years to 1956, the B movie, by now of diminishing importance to big producers, lost much of its staple theatrical audience. In many cases the knock-on impact on small producers of B movies was fatal.[71]

In some ways things did not change for exhibitors. Although price-fixing by distributors had been prohibited, it continued in all but name because they refused to license films to theatres whose prices they thought too low. The public, far from enjoying cheaper admission, tended to have to pay more as the small, late-run cinemas closed and distributors increased their rental charges.[72] Meanwhile the large theatre chains had been left sufficiently strong to be able to force distributors to give them preferential treatment. While they could continue as before to negotiate advantageous rental and clearance terms, the independent exhibitor had no equivalent means of persuasion until some years later the practice became common of reviewing contracts with distributors in the light of each film's actual box-office performance. Many independent operators complained vociferously that the market was anything but free. And when after 1956 some of the divorced chains were allowed to buy both conventional four-wall and drive-in theatres (which reversed the process of divestiture), many observers reckoned this further limited competition.[73]

One further consequence of the *Paramount* case needs to be remarked on because of its influence on the future economy of the industry. Severance of production and distribution from exhibition destroyed the logic of self-regulation (or pre-censorship) which the Hays Office had set up under the Production Code Administration. Since cinemas were no longer obliged to rent from the big eight distributors (and began both to use small independent distributors and to import from Britain and Europe), the eight and the PCA could not impose standards on them. Moreover the Supreme Court had in the *Paramount* verdict granted the industry one small victory: it indicated that it should have the same protection as the First Amendment extended to freedom of speech.[74] Although this ruling was not tested until 1952 in a case concerning Vittorio de Sica's *Miracle in Milan*, it led directly to the freeing of the subject-matter of films from the cloying restrictions of the PCA. Shortly after this decision, films made by Hollywood began to appear without the sanction of the PCA. First of these was Otto Preminger's *The Moon Is Blue* (United Artists, 1953), notorious for its use of two dirty words – 'virgin' and 'mistress'. But from this uncertain start, American cinema discovered new material, themes and styles – and a new audience which in the 1950s and 1960s television could not steal. Preminger himself violated the Code altogether more adventurously in bringing the topic of drug abuse to the screen in *The Man with the Golden Arm* (United Artists, 1955).

11 Hollywood in Transition, 1949–55

While television had the most obvious impact on the kinds of film that were made in the 1950s, its rise coincided with the Cold War era during which Hollywood came under politically motivated investigation. Although the political doings of the Senate's House Committee on Un-American Activities (HUAC) have no direct place in this study, its massively publicised investigations of alleged left-wing activity in Hollywood had an economic impact in that, once again, the spectre of a boycott of movies raised itself in the minds of industry executives. It did so because HUAC's interrogations of Hollywood personnel came at a time when the idea that Communist powers had a demonic capability to infiltrate the minds of a freedom-loving American people had itself deeply infiltrated those minds. It was a time of engulfing social paranoia, and HUAC showed itself willing (if not always skilfully) to heighten popular fears. The argument ran that Hollywood personnel had all the techniques required to make them dangerous propagandists – their *pro*-government activities in the war just ended proved this. Since there were Communists in Hollywood (this had been true between the 1930s and the start of the Cold War), it followed that the studios were a likely site for fifth-column infiltration to start.

However absurd this fear seems now, given the nature of the films the studios were producing, it carried conviction then. Charles Chaplin's *Monsieur Verdoux* (United Artists, 1947) was the target of a successful boycott campaign. Partly it was started to vilify Chaplin's alleged sexual immorality (he had recently been defendant in a sensational paternity case). Partly it was orchestrated by members of HUAC, with chairman J. Parnell Thomas announcing his intention of calling Chaplin before the committee. A vicious hate campaign developed with the right-wing Catholic War Veterans and the American Legion in the lead. In two years *Monsieur Verdoux* played only 2075 dates and grossed only $325 000 in US domestic rentals. Abroad, however, it grossed $1.5 million.[1]

The spectre of picketed theatres and intemperate petitions frightened producers and their bankers inordinately. It became yet another factor making it all but impossible for the independent producer to raise funds for a single film, boycott of which would leave bankers with an unrecoverable debt. As Wasko speculates, the anxieties of bankers may have pushed the studios into a fearful change of policy. Initially the companies had voiced their support for those who in October 1947 were called before HUAC, assuring them their jobs were safe. In November they changed their minds and sacked the ten people who had refused to answer the questions of HUAC. Though their employees had not yet been tried, studio bosses proclaimed loudly that they would not knowingly employ Communists. And they incited the industry's trade unions (some of which like IATSE [the International Alliance of Theatrical Stage Employees] had taken an aggressively anti-Communist stand) to help them eliminate the subversives in their ranks. Wasko thinks that this reversal of policy (which prepared the ground for the witch hunts of 1951–4) is likely to have been a capitulation either to what bankers demanded, or more likely to what the studio bosses anticipated they would want as a means of securing their investment and limiting the risk of boycott.[2] But this pusillanimous action was positively courageous compared with their behaviour during the 1951–4 investigations. Then they dismissed all 212 of their employees named by witnesses to HUAC. As before nothing concerning either the conduct or affiliations of these people was proved – it was enough for them to be named to earn dismissal.

A rumpus this big – social paranoia on this scale – the fearful obsequiousness of studio bosses was bound to have its effect on at least some aspects of film production. Immediate attempts were made to placate anti-Communist activists. Eric Johnston, successor to Will Hays as President of the Motion Picture Association of America (MPAA), helped orchestrate this move by, for instance, advising scenarists to write films that showed Communism not merely to be subversive but also ridiculous.[3] The studios dutifully put into production a number of such films, which started to appear in 1949. Typically they relied on established genres which they simply switched to serve a new purpose – often with extraordinary results. *The Iron Curtain* (Twentieth Century-Fox) drew its espionage motif from *Confessions of a Nazi Spy* (1939), both films being scripted by the same writer. *The Red Menace* (Republic) revived the Mata Hari stereotype, this time making the seductress a Communist agent. Some of the films were badly enough written to be absurd; most advanced fiercely melodramatic notions of what Communism did to its victims.[4]

This cycle of anti-Communist films ran on till 1954, sanctioned from mid-1950 by the Korean War.[5] It ended when the Senate rebuked McCarthy late in 1954.[6] Despite the clamour of a substantial section of the American public for anti-Communist films, the studios noticed that people did not actually attend them in large numbers. Although the films demonstrated the studios' *bona fide* support for the American way of life (at a time when, from 1951, activists had returned to picket films to which 'named' Communists had contributed), they did not make profit.

Probably the effect of the HUAC investigations which lasted longest and ultimately did the most damage to the majors was the caution it inflicted upon them. In general, though there were honourable exceptions, safety became the watchword, and the middle-of-the-road family audience the mark to aim at. Hindsight reveals the weakness of this policy, for the 1950s was the decade when the family audience was withdrawing from the cinema and could more often be reached by television in the living-room. As we shall see, the majors still had much to learn about the changing audience of this decade.

The other overriding concern of studio executives was of course the erosion of its audiences by television. In fact a simple tabulation of the decline in box-office takings against the sales of television sets reveals two important facts about the relationship between the film and television industries. Firstly, the decline in cinema audiences had begun well before sufficient receivers had been sold to make television a serious rival. Secondly, that decline continued long after television sets had been bought by most households, which implies that the new medium grew increasingly effective in holding on to its audiences, and that those audiences found new ways of spending their spare cash in the affluent 1950s and 1960s. In 1946 Americans had spent at the cinema nearly 20 per cent of their outgoings on recreation, and just under 15 per cent on radios, television and records. By 1957 the equivalent figure for the cinema had dropped to 7 per cent, while expenditure on radio and allied industries rose to almost 23 per cent.[7]

Having said this, it is clear that the advent of television did contribute largely to the decline in the film industry's fortunes, particularly of its exhibition wing. But the inroads it made into the cinema audience were uneven. Where television penetration exceeded 60 per cent, cinema takings shrank – for example, by 1954 it had markedly hit audiences in the New England states, in most of which takings per head of population had fallen by more than 20 per cent. On the other hand, given that all exhibitors had raised their admission prices to protect their operations in difficult times, takings in some states, notably in the south and west, had actually risen, with those who went to the cinema spending more on it, contrary to the national trend.[8]

How did the eight majors react? Not, as is often said, first by resisting television and then from about 1955 learning to live with it. This is altogether too simplistic. Each company devised its own strategy: some arms of the film industry fought the new medium while others wooed it. From a very early date some of the majors tried to buy their way in. Paramount had invested in it since 1938, and in 1940 established the first TV station in Chicago. But the *Paramount* case of 1948 could hardly have come at a worse time in this respect, for the film studios remained the subject of anti-trust surveillance, and the Federal Communications Commission (which governs American broadcasting) exercised its power to prevent companies convicted of monopolistic practices from large-scale entry into television.[9] The radio industry (no doubt remembering earlier conflict with Hollywood) lobbied hard, and was encouraged by the government to take secure hold of the television industry. The most the movie companies could do at first was to buy stock in some local TV stations, taking extreme care to have no part in their management.[10] Only years later, when the *Paramount* case had virtually been forgotten, did they manage to link forces with television in a number of ingenious ways.

Having failed to buy into television, the eight majors tried to better it. They attempted to innovate theatre television, that is to sell television programmes as a distinctive cinema product. Paramount led the field in June 1949 with screenings originated from its Chicago TV station. In due course other companies followed. Programmes almost always consisted of sports events, and picture quality was said to rival newsreel images (but not those of features) for tone, depth and brilliance. At one point before 1952 when the project was abandoned, as many as 75 theatres had been wired into a network. Gomery argues that as a challenge to domestic television the innovation failed simply because screenings always lost money. Programmes were limited in range and number and they were expensive, not least because trade unions claimed pay increases for operating the new system.[11]

Broadcast television soon developed an insatiable appetite for programming material; and its purchasing power grew significantly in 1951 with the completion of the microwave network system across America.[12] The film companies took differing decisions in the early years about providing product. Most of them found unattractive the opportunity to supply local television with what it needed – short films made rapidly and on low budgets. Unexpectedly, in view of its general commercial amateurishness, United Artists did get involved early, and in 1948 set up a television department not to produce but to distribute such telefilms to local studios. For a number of years it made losses, but it did get the company into television.[13] The only other of the eight companies to act this early was Columbia Pictures, which in 1949 formed a subsidiary, Screen Gems Inc., to produce telefilms and TV commercials. In June 1952 it announced a $1 million deal with the Ford Motor Company to produce 39 half-hour films for 'The Ford Theatre'. Thereafter it moved into production in a big way, producing a number of popular TV series – *Rin Tin Tin*, *Captain Midnight* and *Father Knows Best*.[14]

The indifference of most of the film companies to producing for television was equalled by their reluctance to release their old films to it. Only Monogram and Republic (both seriously undercapitalised Poverty Row studios that needed the extra income) sold their old films almost at once. In doing so they omitted to see that the demand from television would be incessant and that in the long run they would have made more by renting rather than selling their product. The majors held back until 1955, when significant sales of older films were agreed.

The eight majors resisted television in one other way in its early years – they prohibited their stars from appearing on it. As a consequence TV became for a few years the employer of one-time movies stars like Gloria Swanson, Wendie Barrie and Faye Emerson who had nothing to lose from defying the ban – and who knew how to work with the camera. But the film studios' ban was soon undercut by their own need to free players of their contracts as a way of reducing costs.[15]

The studios worked hard at providing for cinema patrons pleasures domestic television could not rival, in the hope that this would keep them coming through the turnstiles. They tried both technological and thematic means of drawing attention to their films. Colour was one of these means, since it was available only to a small minority of viewers. Although three-colour Technicolor had been innovated by

Walt Disney in 1932, and released to the market in 1935, a variety of economic factors had discouraged the studios from making heavy use of it until they felt the force of TV's challenge for their audiences. But by 1955 just over 50 per cent of features were being produced in colour.[16]

Unlike two-colour Technicolor which the industry had exploited in the late 1920s (see Chapter 7), three-colour Technicolor produced tones across the full range of the visible spectrum. Disney, whose eagerness to exploit new technology was untypical of his peers, signed a three-year contract for exclusive rights for his cartoons, and grossed a quarter of a million dollars with *Three Little Pigs* which cost only $22 000 to make. The interest of the industry was not aroused, however, until David O. Selznick released three successive Technicolor features that did strikingly good business: *A Star is Born* (1937, *The Adventures of Tom Sawyer* (1938) and *Gone With The Wind* (MGM, 1939).[17] Nevertheless colour production continued at less than 10 per cent of feature-film output until after the war. There were a variety of inhibitions about its use. Not only did it cost more, but there was no certainty in a period when black and white productions were doing very well at the box office that those extra costs would be recovered. In its early years it was technically difficult to manage and surrounded with secrecy. Production companies did not in fact have control over their own colour requirements because Technicolor insisted on supplying an entire package – not only the patented three-strip camera that had to be used with this system, but also its operators *and* a colour consultant. Colour films tended until after the war to have much the same look, no matter who produced them, because Technicolor's consultants adopted unvarying criteria for the acceptable image (high-key lighting and fully saturated colour); they actively discouraged experimentation.

This centralised control had another consequence. It meant, since it was equally available to all the studios, that none of them could expect to gain at the expense of the others by launching a massive programme of colour production – for the others would simply have followed suit and pulled back the advantage. Costs would have risen with no sure corresponding increase in profits. Thus until the audience began to shrink there was no strong incentive to invest in colour production. And there was a disincentive in that Technicolor was a small company lacking the capital to exploit its invention fully: in the late 1930s it could not keep up with the demand for stock, and during the war shortage of materials and the requisition of their plant by the military held up developments.

A further breakthrough in colour production occurred in 1949 when Eastman-Kodak brought out a cheaper and readily available photochemical film which could be run through a conventional movie camera. Eastman-Kodak had a major advantage over Technicolor: the massive resources required to back further research into photochemical colour and to capitalise mass production and distribution.[18] In 1939 no more than 18 colour features had been made, and that figure had risen no higher than 29 in 1945. In 1952 some 100 films were made in Technicolor alone – and as we have said the following year about 50 per cent of features were in colour.[19]

Because before 1948 the studios were inhibited from using colour as the basis for full-blooded competition, they developed from an early date a tendency to deploy colour as a means of differentiating certain genres to increase their market. First of these was the musical which as we have seen (Chapter 7) had been made in two-colour Technicolor as much for technical as aesthetic reasons. The associations this connection generated between colour and fantasy endured.[20] Technicolor's high-key lighting practice displayed the human form to unnatural advantage. As colour processes became more reliable, formerly gaudy images became glamorous. Productions were lavish, often set in exotic locations and elaborately costumed: by definition spectacular, they enticed the eye with action as vivid as their imagery. Progressively into the later 1940s these values became attached to the Western, the epic, and the historical drama.[21]

When patrons became more selective in their movie-going after the war, the studios found that the lavish movie that displayed its costly production values tended to produce longer runs and higher grosses. (This held true even while studios were trying to reduce budgets.) Thus even before it felt the challenge of television, the industry discovered an urgent need for colour – a need which intensified in the early 1950s. In retrospect it can also be seen to have begun once again to harbour the need to do things big – that is, big in cost, spectacle and gesture. The belief in bigness was to harden into something like a habit in the new Hollywood.

There is an unexpected twist in the exploitation of colour which follows from the fact that the majors began in a big way from 1956 to sell rights to their pre-1948 features to television. One of the effects of doing so appears to have been that still more people stayed home to watch reruns of old movies. With cinema audiences continuing to decline, the majors sought ways of cutting costs without putting at risk their new television market. They appear to have identified colour as an area of cost-saving, and for a few years colour production declined markedly.[22] Finally when all the American television networks switched to colour in 1965–70, the impact on Hollywood film production was unmistakable. Colour production had dropped to about 25 per cent of features in 1958, but rose sharply to 75 per cent by 1967 and 94 per cent by 1970.[23]

The film industry also sought to protect itself by innovating widescreen systems, since television could not imitate this format. By a narrow margin the first system to be launched was Cinerama, premièred in September 1952 in New York. It relied on an invention developed for military use in aerial gunnery simulators.[24] Films were thrown by three interlocked projectors on to a huge curved screen accompanied by hi-fi stereo sound, to give audiences a sense of depth not previously experienced. Audiences loved the effect. Nonetheless the system was adopted only by about 200 theatres, and rarely more than one in each city. For conversion was always costly, even when in later years no more than a single projector capable of taking 70mm film was required. The system only suited the biggest theatres, which had not only to buy the vast Cinerama screen and rewire for multi-directional sound, but often to undergo structural alteration. Because the new screen was so tall, balconies and proscenium arches all got in the way. Ideally Cinerama required building anew, but after divorcement exhibitors were their own, unaided masters, and needed to be sure that investment on this scale would pay them. As companies releasing in Cinerama soon began to duplicate their films in other formats for the rest of the market, the incentive to make the conversion was weakened. Although Cinerama continued for a number of years, it did not get beyond the innovatory phase of economic development. Most exhibitors looked round for a cheaper alternative.

One such was 3-D, first screened to the public in late 1952. Its innovation seems to have taken the industry by surprise, urged on as it was not by a giant corporation but by a tiny concern owned by two brothers. In fact the Gunzbergs did not invent 3-D, but revitalised a system first demonstrated by Polaroid in 1939 which had attracted little attention. The Gunzbergs' venture, however, was spotted by an independent director who saw the possibility of drawing an audience by the aggressive use of the illusion of three dimensions. Arch Oboler made *Bwana Devil* on a minute budget, and launched it in two Los Angeles theatres where it took $150 000 in two weeks despite the universal hostility of critics. United Artists bought the rights to the film, and most of the other majors rushed to follow this lead – which in retrospect explains why, a year later, they were cautious about following Twentieth Century-Fox with CinemaScope. For the 3-D craze lasted no more than some six months. The studios were so keen to exploit the system that arguably they killed it by sacrificing plot, character and quality to cheap screenplays that arbitrarily contrived a succession of excuses for hurling objects at the audience. Add to that the discomfort some people suffered from the spectacles, and the doubling of the image where projection was imprecise, and you have the probable causes of the short life of this phenomenon. The one consolation for exhibitors was that its launch had not taken massive investment: only a special projector and the sale to patrons of polaroid spectacles.[25]

A third new format was commercially more successful. It relied on the principle of anamorphosis, which obtains a wide aspect ratio by means of a distorting lens. This principle was patented in 1862, and was demonstrated to the film industry in 1898 and again in 1930. Although a year later Paramount took out an option on a rival system developed by Henri Chrétien, it did not develop it. It lay dormant for a further twenty years until in 1952 Spyros Skouras bought, innovated and exploited it for Twentieth Century-Fox under the new name CinemaScope. In yet another instance the industry had ignored an invention until pressing need urged innovation upon it.[26]

CinemaScope inherited the goodwill earned by Cinerama, but though costlier than 3-D, it was relatively cheap at $10–25 000 to install. While conversion meant buying a screen, the new one was no taller than the old, and no alteration to auditoria was required. Existing projectors could be used, with the addition of a new lens. Initially CinemaScope features were released with sound recorded on stereo magnetic tracks, and the established mono-optical system was not used. However, when exhibitors objected to having to meet the cost of buying stereo equipment, Fox relented. From 1954 it distributed Scope prints with both kinds of soundtrack. Furthermore theatres could rely on a regular supply of good quality features, so they were less likely to risk investing in a passing fad.

The introduction of CinemaScope was a well-planned operation, quite different from the scramble for quick money that surrounded

3-D. Superficially it was riskier: Skouras is often alleged to have staked the company's entire future on it because in spring 1953 he announced that all future productions of Twentieth Century-Fox would be in this format. However, in this 'gamble' (as it had done twenty-five years earlier in innovating sound) the company enjoyed substantial support from its bankers. These included the Bank of America and the Chase Manhattan, both experienced in funding the motion picture industry. All these parties knew that one of the virtues of the new system was that, whatever its commercial success, films could be re-released in standard format to cinemas that had not made the conversion.

Twentieth Century-Fox took two further steps to foster CinemaScope. It used the lead time before the release of its first widescreen films to ensure that it was launched with screenplays of strong market potential, having plots, characters and action suited to the new screen. In this it succeeded. Secondly, far from trying to shut out the other studios by waging the kind of patents war that had accompanied earlier technical developments, Fox actually encouraged widespread adoption of the system by leasing CinemaScope cameras and lenses to its rivals.[27] This too tended to reassure exhibitors. For its part Fox stood to enhance its profits through its lead in the market, through equipment sales and lease contracts, through the quality of its films, and not least through the readiness of Skouras's brother Charles to have the divorced Fox theatres, now the National chain, rent CinemaScope films. The first film in the new aspect ratio was *The Robe* (1953), an epic set in the years immediately following Christ's Crucifixion. Made at a cost of $4 million, it did extremely good business, netting $16 million by the end of the year from runs in 400 theatres. A year later more than 10 000 theatres had been converted, and all the majors except RKO and Paramount (which developed VistaVision, its own variant that gave a cleaner image) were making films with the new system.[28]

Although the early response to widescreen was dramatic, it did not halt the reduction in admissions. However, it allowed cinemas to increase ticket prices, and this for a couple of years (1952–3) held box-office grosses level.[29] Thereafter the decline continued, but for a complex of reasons the widescreen phenomenon encouraged a trend to big productions. The markedly good takings of early widescreen pictures (including *How to Marry a Millionaire* (Twentieth Century-Fox, 1953), and *White Christmas* (Paramount, 1954)) reinforced a growing belief that big movies did the best business. Before 1953 only about 100 films had ever grossed more than $5 million. In the first year and a half of CinemaScope more than 30 films did so, most of them widescreen productions. One effect was to link Hollywood's old obsessions with spectacle to increasingly opulent and expensive pictures.[30]

This passion for costly production values was to grow, and the reasoning behind the trend was simple. The industry had figures demonstrating that the big film tended to be more profitable than the little one because many of the costs associated with its distribution remained constant or grew at a much slower rate than the increase in its takings. Paramount furnished one writer with figures for profit and loss on typical pictures in the mid-1950s as shown in Table 11.1.[31]

Table 11.1   Profit and loss on films in the mid-1950s (in US dollars)

	Little picture	Big picture
Negative cost	700 000	3 000 000
Distribution charges	480 000	1 800 000
Prints	250 000	300 000
Advertising and publicity	260 000	400 000
Total costs	1 690 000	5 500 000
Gross rentals	1 600 000	6 000 000
(Loss)/Profit	(90 000)	500 000

The problem with belief in the inherent efficiency of large-scale productions is that it becomes hard to decide what should be the limit of size. Every time a new blockbuster turned massive profits, the limits were revised upwards as rival studios sought comparable profits. This was a mechanism by which Hollywood productions grew ever costlier and often, since money was being spent freely, more wasteful. However, there were other economic forces governing distribution and we shall see that the majors still needed small films.

The very dimensions of the CinemaScope screen made the treatment of intimate or small subjects absurd, and *The Robe* was merely the first of a succession of epics, often set in Biblical or Roman times, which peaked with *Ben Hur* (MGM, 1959). This cycle was killed by the catastrophic failure of *Cleopatra* (Twentieth Century-Fox, 1963). But there were others and for some years the widescreen was the site of costly spectaculars: epic Westerns (*Bad*

Day at Black Rock, (MGM, 1954), *The Searchers* (Warner, 1956), *The Alamo* (UA, 1960)); war films (*Bridge on the River Kwai* (Columbia, 1957)); exotic adventure (*Beneath the Twelve Mile Reef* (Twentieth Century-Fox, 1953), *The Roots of Heaven* (Twentieth Century-Fox, 1958)); and sex comedies (Monroe, Grable and Bacall in *How to Marry a Millionaire*, and Mansfield in *The Girl Can't Help It* (Twentieth Century-Fox, 1956)). Celebration of the large scale led the industry.

We have mentioned that the industry had not yet proved itself adept at registering changes in the desires of its patrons. If the full-colour, widescreen epic did good business, there were other tastes among would-be movie-goers that the majors were slow to recognise. But there were one or two hints that observant producers picked up. Prominent among those hints was the fact that the exhibition business was altering, the clearest symptom of which was the closure of certain kinds of theatre. Between 1948 and 1954, 3095 four-wall cinemas shut, a decline that was to continue through the 1950s.[32]

In 1953 of all cinemas only 32.4 per cent were making profit from the sale of tickets; a further 38.4 per cent were losing money at the box office, but returned profits overall through refreshment sales; the remaining 29.2 per cent made a loss. Most of the loss-makers were small neighbourhood theatres which had made a living screening third-run and B movies. The newly extended first and second runs (see Chapter 10) effectively killed their old business. Lacking product attractive enough to draw audiences away from the small screen, these were the theatres that tended to close (closures which by 1955 ended the cinema life of the B movie).[33]

Had the studios examined the underlying social changes behind the folding of the small theatres they might have found information valuable to their programme planning. Flynn and McCarthy speculate that these closures and the death of the theatrical B movie may have been linked to upward social mobility as the lower middle class was absorbed into the new broad middle class, which began to seek more sophisticated entertainments.[34]

Another change in the audience was reflected in the increase in drive-in theatres. Despite the considerable number of four-wall cinemas closing between 1948 and 1954, the total number of US theatres fell by only 140 to almost 18 500. This is explained by the opening of some 3000 drive-ins, which brought the total number of such cinemas operating in 1954 to nearly 3800. As Stuart observes, the fact that the total numbers of older venues closing coincides with the numbers of drive-in cinemas opening should not be taken to mean that one replaced the other. Drive-ins were seldom in the same location as neighbourhood theatres; their sites were chosen with climate and population concentrations in mind. They proved most popular in warmer parts of the States, and in areas with large rural populations. And they played to distinct audiences.[35]

The drive-in idea had been innovated in 1933 but by the end of the war only about 100 had been built, largely because of wartime restrictions on the use of private transport. The great increase in their number coincides with an increase in private ownership of cars and with the changes in patterns of family life to which reference has been made. Drive-in theatres attracted particular audiences. Among them were families, often with children too young for conventional cinemas. The drive-in saved them the cost of a baby-sitter; and since they could bring their own food, made for a cheap and pleasant night out. Since drive-in cinemas were ideal sites for huge screens, the big widescreen production found a natural home there. Musicals, epics, Westerns, all played to this audience so successfully that in the 1950s drive-ins started to compete with four-wall cinemas for the first run of movies. By 1958 some 20 per cent of all US film revenues came from drive-ins, a level which they held or exceeded for the next twenty years. Only the reluctance of older theatres to accept for second runs films that had first been released this way limited the number of new films seen in these vast arenas.[36]

During the 1960s and 1970s drive-ins became popular venues for working-class patrons. Movies made with their preferences in mind sometimes did good business there which eluded them elsewhere. But one other significant audience emerged in these auditoria during the 1950s – the teenage audience. The drive-in made an even more attractive escape from home than the four-wall theatre: courting couples could be fairly private, other youngsters could make all the noise they wanted without bothering their neighbours. In film as in the clothing and popular music industries this audience was, with the new affluence of young people, becoming an attractive, indentifiable market. But it was left to a few small production companies specifically to tailor films to meet their supposed desires.

One of those companies, American International Pictures (AIP), released its first movie in 1954. It was a minuscule operation, having been set up only two years earlier by two producers with $3000 and four employees. Like Allied Artists (formerly Monogram), this company specialised in low budget films (horror, science fiction and teenpix) which made a fetish of passing fashions in the teenage world. Films were marketed so as to promise sensational experiences, but their publicity often aroused expectations the movies did not fulfil. Producers courted topicality, making a film of a new dance craze or fashion, then ruthlessly moving on to something else when that fashion ended. In this respect production for teenagers differed not only from that of the majors (which in general adapted slowly), but also from that of the old B-movie makers. The successor in cinemas to the old B movie, these films were known as exploitation movies partly because they attempted to profit from the passing fads of a mass audience, partly because they were made very cheaply at great speed (often with the thinnest of plots), and were expected to turn profit. AIP did not between 1954 and 1960 make a film that lost money. By contrast Republic, the second oldest B-movie studio after Monogram, did not adapt its product. Despite the interest of television in its old films, it rapidly lost its cinema audiences, and in 1959 it ceased production.

The production methods of AIP and their star producer Roger Corman reveal a good deal about their approach to the market. For cheapness they worked in black and white. When planning pictures they first selected titles (*I Was a Teenage Werewolf*, *Night of the Blood Beast*, *Hot Rod Girl*). Next outline themes were developed, and only then were writer, director and players engaged. Production was mercilessly swift, and the Corman unit became in effect a new training unit for the industry because it required novices to perfect skills under pressure. Its films differed in other ways from the 'classic' B picture in that from their inception they were designed to support each other as a double bill. Furthermore they were rented for a percentage of house takings, not for a flat fee. AIP's films tended to run in series – *Teenage Werewolf* being followed by *Teenage Monster* and *Teenage Frankenstein* (1957), *Teenage Caveman* (1958) and *Teenage Zombies* (1959). When one 'instalment' had run its term at the top of a bill, it would return after a discreet interval as support for a newer one. Weak in plot, the films made a vivid impact on the eye with strong, often violent or horrific images. This visual impact became a saleable part of their stock-in-trade and enabled them to compete with the other attractions of the drive-in: food, drink, friends and lovers.

As the cycle continued so its constituent formulas shifted, and fashions arose and faded for rock music, wild youth, juvenile delinquency, beach parties and the personality film, often built round a rock star. Many films exploited a contrast between 'wild youth' (designed for sensational appeal) and 'mild youth' (intended to appeal to the family audience). The former are sexy, have menacing clothes and hairstyles, and speak hip dialogue. The latter look like younger versions of their parents, and speak much as they do.[37]

Although these films identified the drive-in audience as their target, and developed that market with great success, they were also rented by small cinemas desperate for product. And when the majors noticed this activity they too started to make teenage films, like *The Blackboard Jungle* (MGM, 1955) and *Rebel Without a Cause* (Warner, 1955): costlier and of higher quality, their films were aimed at the top end of the market. And their decision to enter this market was the more confident in that it was one for which in the 1950s television not could conceivably cater.

The success of the teen picture in every reach of the market meant that a deluge of films followed. As Dowdy remarks, by the end of the decade every studio was producing films which implied that in a world of drunk, dense or vicious adults only young people preserved style and wit.[38] Inevitably older audiences protested both at the sensationalism and at the loss of their generation's dignity. But though the MPAA made rumbling threats about tightening censorship, not surprisingly nothing was done. Not only had the MPAA little power, but the industry had at last become wide awake to at least one finding of research – that by far the greatest part of the movie-going audience comprised people under 30 years. In 1957 an Opinion Research Corporation survey showed where the money lay: 52 per cent of the audience was under 20, and 72 per cent was under 29.[39] Nevertheless AIP, against whose teenpix much of the criticism had been directed, instituted a series of films which neatly defused that anger, to the benefit of their turnover. Under Roger Corman they released a number of fantastic, sometimes mysterious films based on stories by Edgar Allan Poe. By tempting adolescents to sit down and read the books, they suddenly made AIP seem respectable. In effect, as Pye and Myles remark, the company had involved in its sales effort schools and libraries (where lurid posters for the films could be seen alongside the books).[40]

It has been argued that the studios' commitment to making films for a young audience that they did not fully understand affected the scripting of films in subtle ways. Writers were obliged to transform their stories into myths and to alter the traits of characters, draining them of the peculiarities of actual human behaviour and rendering them as ideal types, whether heroic or villainous. Writing in 1950, Seldes argued that in order to make as broad an appeal to young audiences as possible, American movies tended not to reflect the changes that come about as people mature and grow older. Instead the hero myth (James Dean's roles were to be examples) underlay a great deal of movie fiction.[41]

However, Hollywood was gradually finding out how diverse its audiences were becoming, for as it discovered teenagers so too it began to identify a demand from adults for distinctive films. The discovery of this new audience can be attributed to some of the small neighbourhood cinemas that desperately needed product and patrons. A few of them (typically located in university towns and large cities) found that by the early 1950s a sufficient interest had developed in British-made and foreign-language films to draw a constant audience. Further they could charge them more than for the old double bills because these were new releases. This, says Sklar, was the beginning of the 'art house' movement, with initially perhaps no more than fifty or sixty such theatres across the States – just enough to make it worthwhile for small independent distributors to bring in foreign films. But this innovation also demonstrated to the majors the possibility of screening to distinct adult audiences, and gave them ideas as to how to keep their distribution arms busy and fill screens when they lacked American product – so that in time they too found it profitable to help popularise European film as domestic production declined with the shrinking audience.[42] The very fact that foreign producers were thus able to gain access to the American audience was yet another consequence of the *Paramount* case, for before divorcement the majors had closed out their pictures. In 1963 about eighty small distributors released a total of some 800 foreign films, and the art-house circuit had grown to over 500 cinemas, and was still growing.[43]

At these early art-house screenings an educated audience was seeing some of the best European product. Since it liked what it saw, it endowed European cinema with a cachet (not realising that it was not seeing run-of-the-mill films) that kept enthusiasm for imported movies alive. However, a number of these films were sexually explicit in ways American movies, regulated by the Production Code, were not. Realising that their audiences enjoyed their comparative frankness, some importers brought in films with scenes played (at this time) naked to the waist. As independent distributors they were free to take the risk of releasing without the Production Code seal of approval. That risk was well rewarded since the notoriety of the films made them highly profitable.[44]

From these small beginnings this market grew, and a division opened between sophisticated foreign-language features requiring an educated attention (the 'art' film), and the sexploitation piece (the so-called 'adult' movie). As we have seen (Chapter 10), the Production Code began to come under attack in the early 1950s. And in 1956 under a new head, Geoffrey Shurlock, the Production Code Administration began to reassess its role. Before the year was out it once again came into conflict with the Catholic Legion of Decency over its decision to approve Elia Kazan's *Baby Doll* (Warner), a representation of sexual malaise and decay. This time, however, the Church did not win another victory over the film industry; and it failed because the Church itself decided that it should not interfere in the business of an independent private enterprise. This extraordinary transformation in Catholic thinking appears to have been motivated by the clergy's recognition that the time had passed when they could successfully get their congregations involved in the boycott of films without increasing both the notoriety of the movies and the desire of many people to see them.[45]

In December 1956 the Production Code was revised. Changes in specific clauses (which for instance permitted representation of drug-trafficking, prostitution and kidnapping) were less important in themselves than for the broad freedom of expression they implied was open to cinema.[46] The following year, in a judgment concerning the publication of magazines and books, the Supreme Court ruled that although obscenity was outside the law, obscenity and the representation of sexuality were not the same thing.[47] The revision of the Code and this judgment signalled to Hollywood opportunities for new kinds of exploitation which were to make the licence of the 1950s seem pallid. But as so often before, the majors allowed a small concern to try out the ground first. The Hollywood majors tried until the 1960s to avoid court battles over censorship because of the size of their investment in their movies. Ayer *et al.* argue that since films could not be shown while the subject of litigation, and interest on production loans still had to be paid, court cases could cost them dearly. Smaller companies on the other hand could find that a legal case might bring their film a notoriety that would boost its box-office takings as effectively as an advertising campaign more costly than they could afford.[48]

Russ Meyer, a freelance photographer, took the opportunity, always expecting the majors to buy him out if he succeeded. In 1959 he produced for a mere $24 000 *The Immoral Mr Teas*, and managed to find outlets for it in San Francisco and Seattle. The film met great demand, playing first run for weeks, and ultimately running for years. It grossed more than $2 million in rentals.[49] In the 1960s the market for pornography was to build upon these beginnings.

With both the European and the 'adult' movie the industry had not only identified a change in audience demand, but had found yet another way of differentiating its product from anything television could mimic. Precisely as a consequence of its continuing success in stealing the family audience, television was precluded from showing foreign-language material, anything that could remotely be described as difficult viewing, and above all else, anything admitting active human sexuality.

When these developments are compared with the findings of audience research, they reveal, as has been hinted (Chapter 10) the absurdity of trying to run an industry of this scale by trial and error. The majors appear to have ignored the early post-war findings (confirmed by further research in 1957) of such organisations as Opinion Research.[50] But in the end what they discovered the hard way coincided closely with the reports of researchers – namely that male and female patronage was about equal, but younger, single people made up a very large part of the audience; and the better educated and paid went to the movies more often than others, paying more for their tickets. Such findings embrace the teen picture and the art-house movie very neatly.[51]

It was also found that movie-goers were likely to be frequent users of radio and newspapers, a factor observed by Handel; and he deduced that the media stimulated interest in each other, partly through reviews, advertisements and interviews, partly through their shared concentration on narrative and drama.[52] As we shall see, the studios were slowly learning that even television could be exploited to their advantage. And from the late 1940s they had begun to take note of at least one kind of research – the canvassing of preview audiences to discover whether the film had satisfied the emotional needs it aroused in them. Not a new technique, it was increasingly employed by senior executives as a test by which they licensed themselves radically to change a film should it fail to please. Thus by degrees the studios came to take note of more scientific methods of aligning their product with potential audience needs. In the 1960s and 1970s they integrated these techniques into their scheduling and marketing routines.

All these changes, however, did not proceed at an even pace. Two studios held on to the old contract system longer than the others. Universal reverted to its practice of providing films for neighbourhood theatres because many of them were in rural areas which did not get television till 1955–6. It produced many films whose values held loyal to the family and ignored the sophistication of the city in favour of the less cultivated pleasures of the small town. In the early years of the decade it survived on the *Ma and Pa Kettle* series, *Francis the Talking Mule* (until he transferred to TV), and a whole series of cheap and cheerful Westerns. While other studios were releasing their players, Universal actually took on and developed new talent – Jeff Chandler, Tony Curtis and Rock Hudson.[53]

The other studio to try to keep to the old ways was MGM, which continued to act as if nothing had changed until their Head of Production, Dore Schary, left them in 1956. But while MGM still sustained an expensive list of contract players and stars, most studios had radically reduced theirs: in 1947 a total of 742 players were under contract, a number which had shrunk to 229 by 1956.[54] For MGM, failure to abandon the contract system meant that at a time of reducing output they had high fixed overheads which made profit almost impossible. Making a limited number of films, the company was paying dearly for underused people and equipment. It kept afloat only through the runaway success of a few films (including *Cat on a Hot Tin Roof* (1958) and *Ben Hur* (1959)), and through the decisions taken after Schary's departure to sign independent film-makers and rent its facilities to television producers.[55] However, in the latter half of the 1950s MGM finally began to release players as their contracts expired. With these changes the factory system was at last brought to an end and, as we have mentioned, with it went the homogenous coding of studio output which (with for example forty or so departments at MGM providing films with standardised inputs) had often made the studio itself seem as much the author of its films as any of the individuals that worked on them.[56]

12 The New Order, 1955–68

We have already seen (Chapter 10) that after the war and divorcement, independent production became an increasingly common way of making feature films. By the late 1950s, with admissions falling, well over half of American releases were being produced in this way and the proportion was rising.[1] Thus in some ways the industry at large was adopting a business model long since established at United Artists, which for decades had been distributing the work of such producers. But in the 1950s the business practice of even that company was altering.

United Artists was returned to fiscal health rapidly following the belated agreement in 1950 of the original owners Chaplin and Pickford to admit new management. The two lawyers, Arthur B. Krim and Robert Benjamin, who were to run the corporation for the next generation, instituted a vigorous programme of production and distribution which brought the accounts back into profit by 1951. They bought themselves a majority interest, refinanced the company, and introduced new patterns of business. By 1953 they were setting up a broad production financing programme, bringing together producer, director, stars and banking institutions, with the object of agreeing on story, cast and budget, and arranging to underwrite funds. In this they acted very much like the rest of the industry, except that they initiated projects whereas elsewhere outside agents brought projects to the studios.

United Artists also differed from other studios by seeking to give the producer as great a degree of autonomy as possible in bringing in the picture; the company tried, by encouraging its producers to take a share in the risks and profits, to give them a financial incentive. And it was distinctive too in allowing many of its independents to appoint their own sales representatives to collaborate in the distribution process.[2] Other studios kept control of distribution themselves and charged their independent clients for handling their films. Or to be more accurate, they levied distribution and a variety of other charges.

MGM for example, when after 1956 it began contracting with independents, would firstly add, depending upon how much its own facilities had been used, about 25 per cent to production costs by way of rental. Such a figure would comprise not only a charge for every camera, light and nail used on the production, but over and above that a general and large overhead fee. (Since many producers think of this charge as 'legalised larceny' as it has no basis in actual use of facilities, it seemed to many a positive advantage that United Artists did not own a studio.)[3]

The typical studio, such as MGM, then took as distributor 30–35 per cent of net box-office takings after the theatre had taken its share. Furthermore if it had invested in production it made sure debts owing it were settled before passing any surplus to the independent's production office. And finally if the film should move into profit and MGM had a financial interest, it might take 50 per cent of those profits.[4] Figures like these help explain how the majors did better than merely survive the problems of the 1950s, continuing to control the motion picture industry. From the 1960s they were to demand even higher returns, to the outrage of both independent producers and the exhibition sector of the industry. We shall see (in Chapter 13) the justifications they advanced for doing so, and how these demands affected the kinds of film made and the manner of their screening.

As we have said, United Artists differed from most of the other studios in that it appears at this time to have initiated a high proportion of its projects itself. Although the other majors did continue at a much reduced rate to produce a limited number of films, in general they gradually moved over to a more passive role in which rather than generating film projects internally in a scriptwriters' department, they responded to ideas – packages, as they became known – brought to them by outsiders. But from the 1950s these outsiders were seldom writers. Rather they were people who had found a new influence within the industry – agents.

By no means newcomers to the business (stars, for instance, having since the peak of the silent era used their services to negotiate good terms of contract with studios), agents moved into greater prominence when the majors stopped issuing long-term contracts. With more freelance talent looking for work than there were jobs, the agent with good connections (who would be looking for new work while his or her clients fulfilled current obligations), became an essential component of their careers. Since producers, directors, writers, and principal technicians such as lighting cameramen were now hired under the same contractual conditions as actors (freelancing without long-term contracts), they too sought the help of agencies. Rank-and-file technicians on the other hand, lacking individually identifiable talents, simply had to wait until producers called them.

A good agent could now prove invaluable in launching a movie project, offering not merely players to cast it, but much of the crucial talent required to bring it into being. The studios gradually began to rely on this and, realising it, the more powerful agencies developed new services that made them indispensable to the industry. They began to offer an entire package which studios could buy either whole or in part. Such a package might offer a studio an entire deal, including not only the lead players, director and producer, but also the writer and the rights to his or her script. Sometimes the package would be even more complete, including also part of the financial backing for the film. Often, however, agents relied on studios to advance second money and to arrange bank funding of first money (yet another service for which the studios charged a fee). When such a package deal was agreed, the studio would usually rent its facilities to the production company set up to make the movie. It would also take on distribution. This part of the deal was almost essential to the film's success, since only the majors had the sure market penetration to give movies they backed the probability of general release.[5]

It has been argued that, through the mechanism of the package, agents became one of the few sources of innovation in the American cinema of the 1950s and 1960s. As Sklar remarks, if either the agency or a star on its books wanted to do a particular script, it was sometimes possible to put together an attractive package that would convince a studio (perhaps because of the presence of a star) it could make money from a movie which, left to its own devices, it would probably never have approved.[6] To this extent innovation was possible, and even in the 1970s and 1980s some stars (for instance Jane Fonda, Paul Newman, Gene Hackman) have lent their names to projects that would not otherwise have been realised. In general, however, the agent-originated package, like all independent projects, was not inherently different from the studios' own productions: where the studios took a share of the action they usually made sure the film would conform to their idea of what was likely to attract an audience – and their inherent conservatism in these matters was not magically dissipated with divorcement.

All the same there were changes in the kinds of material that reached the screen. In the years before divorcement around two-thirds of films had been based on original screenplays, only 5 or 6 per cent on stage plays, and between 15 and 20 per cent on published novels.[7] This situation had obtained partly because, with the cinema business prospering in America during the war, the studios did not need to market special attractions to bring people through the turnstiles. And studios found servicing continuous production with screenplays prepared by their own scriptwriting departments both cheaper and more reliable than buying in literary or theatrical properties. They had scriptwriters on their staffs and needed to make use of them. But with the sharp reduction in film production that occurred as the factory era came to an end, such departments ceased to be cost effective, and the contracts of scriptwriters, like those of so many talented people, were not renewed. By 1954 only about 30 remained on the studios' books; and by 1958 very few indeed.[8]

Facing the decline in automatic film-going, many studio executives decided they had a better chance of attracting audiences to films which they already knew something about. They knew that advance interest in most films is minimal (an observed fact which remains true even after pre-release publicity for most films other than those whose titles have long been public knowledge).[9] Accordingly the concept of the pre-sold movie found favour once again. As before, such a movie would be one which either had enjoyed success as a popular novel or a hit play, or had the cachet of a famous name (perhaps its writer or star performer) associated with it. Now successful television plays also occasionally provided the original text for adaptation: *Marty* (UA, 1955) was the first such feature. As McLaughlin shows, the proportion of screenplays written originally for the cinema declined sharply during the period 1953–6 to less than 30 per cent of the total. Although this was the low point from which there was later a recovery, Hollywood's interest in literary and theatrical properties remained intense through the 1960s. Inevitably the prices of desirable properties rose, as Hollywood companies redoubled their efforts to secure the rights to stage plays by making pre-production deals.

On Broadway advance payments for screen rights became an ever more significant investment, so that by the 1960s theatrical producers (faced with the wildly rising cost of mounting theatrical spectaculars) made a regular practice of first seeking a sale for the rights to the movie before agreeing to back a stage production. It is not hard to see why from the mid-1950s, in circumstances in which its money (like that of the record industry) was a prerequisite to launching new Broadway productions, the requirements of the American film industry came to have a profound influence on many theatrical productions.[10]

Similar pre-production deals began to be applied in some cases to literary sales. As Dowdy reports, a public relations man called Ted Loeff set up a company, Literary Projects, to arrange tie-ins between film producers and publishers. His idea was to make possible the mutual exploitation of literary properties whose screen rights were sold before the novel was published. He began to arrange for the co-ordination of print publication and film release, and for the interrelation of the marketing campaigns for the two products so that ads for the film reminded people of the book, and vice versa. One consequence of this trend was that sometimes Hollywood was to pay out money for the screen rights to a novel that hardly yet had shape in the mind of its author, let alone on paper.[11]

As the 1960s passed, these tendencies were to grow more pronounced as the media corporations merged and took over one another to form vast conglomerates, the several arms of which would market books, records, videotapes, toys and a host of other products all related to the same fiction. Thus the 1950s saw the beginnings of a major process of restructuring in Hollywood that was to have large consequences for the ways narrative fictions were constructed and marketed in the Western world.

One of the first corporations to involve itself in the pattern of merger and take-over that eventually led to the establishment of a cross-media culture industry began its existence as an agency. The increasing power and profitability of the agent's role contributed to its emergence in the 1950s as a major force in the film industry. The Music Corporation of America (always known as MCA) had been founded by Jules Stein to manage bands and book them into hotels and dance halls. As Pye records, having by 1938 built the biggest agency in the dance band business, Stein decided to move into a new sphere and represent movie actors. He used a variety of techniques to add to his lists, persuading some actors to sign with him; buying up the contracts that bound others to older agencies; or all else failing, buying up the agencies themselves. MCA was soon big enough to go for larger acquisitions. It took over the agency interests of CBS, and in 1945 bought up the firm that was representing Boris Karloff, Greta Garbo, Henry Fonda, Fred Astaire, James Stewart, Gene Kelly and Frederic March.[12]

Now its substantial size made it possible for it to innovate where smaller companies would have held back. Since an agency's income increases with its clients', the company tried what is usually described as a new way of maximising the income of one of its stars. When in 1949 Universal sought James Stewart for the lead role in *Winchester 73*, MCA refused to let him sign unless he was paid a percentage of profits rather than a flat fee. He got 50 per cent – a deal which netted the agency 10 per cent of the $600 000 Stewart eventually made.[13]

Although MCA did not in this invent the profit-sharing deal (Universal had signed profit-sharing contracts with Bing Crosby and W. C. Fields after the company's 1938 reorganisation), it did innovate what soon became an established pattern of business. For, as Staiger argues, the package-unit system of film production intensified the need to differentiate every film on the basis both of its novelty, its story, its director and stars. Since the name of the studio no longer had much importance, names of individuals involved were marketed as part of the 'uniqueness' of each feature film.[14] Thus the profit-sharing deal initiated an explosion of costs as stars (and later producers and directors) discovered that once again they seemed to be essential to films' profitability. Not only did the incomes of such individuals soar, but they began on occasion to act as shareholders in the projects on which they worked, for as corporations they could convert current income to capital gains and reduce their tax liability (see Chapter 10).[15]

As Barry King observes, the changed basis of stars' contractual obligations whereby they now usually signed up for one film at a time rather than for a seven-year period, tended to produce alterations in the nature of the star image. As virtual proprietors of their own images, some stars learned to distance themselves from them, and ceased to project a simple, unified personality. Now they might present themselves in radio and television interviews as thoughtful actors concerned with the responsibilities of their craft. Such a persona could be useful in two ways: it allowed the modern star to venture his or her image in more diverse character roles than their studio forebears had been able to take on; and it distanced the star's image from films that failed.[16]

It was thus, as owners of medium-sized businesses, that key stars, producers and directors could sometimes afford, if they could find a distributor, to put together and back projects which no studio would otherwise make. This was the main source of aesthetic innovation arising from independent production. All the same the main effect of the package system was not to infuse the movies with new ideas but to inflate beyond all recognition 'above the line costs' (the costs of named talent and rights to the story) even of small movies. This inflation continued virtually unchecked on into the early 1980s.

For its part MCA continued to grow spectacularly. It entered television production in the early 1950s, and this side of its business grew so fast that in 1959 the company bought Universal's production facilities. This deal at one stroke gave MCA's TV subsidiary Revue an ideal studio facility on a 400-acre site, and the opportunity to make an immediate return on its investment as it promptly rented studio space back to Universal for its own productions. However, MCA's circumstances were now altering fast. It now faced the threat of anti-trust action from the Justice Department, which required it to discontinue its dual role as both employer (as Revue Productions) and agent for many individuals.

Its executives took advantage of what they knew about the financial weakness of Universal-International: this company, now a subsidiary of Decca Records, was losing enough money for rumours to be circulating in the industry to the effect that the film business might be wound up altogether to save the record business. After a prolonged period of negotiation, MCA sold off its agency and took over control of more than 50 per cent of shares in Decca and Universal.[17] Thus, although the company had to divorce itself from its original agency business, in its new form (as owner of a television production company, a large studio facility, one of the major distributors and an important record label) it constituted a formidable and diversified organisation, well positioned to take advantage of the cross-media dealing which was to pick up pace from the later 1960s.

The size of an organisation like MCA mattered for what followed. The accumulation of vast capital resources around the majors was matched by increments in the scale of the biggest blockbuster movies. For in fact, despite the dominance of independent films in the new Hollywood, studio production had not altogether died. What had been killed off was routine 'factory floor' production on a continuous conveyor belt. However, with the tendency we have already remarked for the industry to release fewer pictures, the majors needed some of them to be big movies. Their massive shareholdings and long-term corporate debts had to be serviced by profits correspondingly large. Whereas in pre-divorcement days the routine release of numbers of successful small films deployed capital on a regular reinvestment cycle and returned fairly steady profit, the much reduced release pattern of the 1950s and after could only provide the same profits if some films made very big returns indeed. As we have seen (in Chapter 11) studio heads had demonstrated to their own satisfaction that truly massive returns came only from films in which they had made heavy investment – an investment that increasingly concentrated on marketing. However, the big film was a risk most independents could not afford to venture. Only the majors were adequately capitalised to be able to survive the possible failure of a blockbuster, and even they were to face severe difficulties as notions of what 'big' meant grew relentlessly over the next thirty years.

For this reason the majors kept an interest in production. Needing their bonanza profits, they initiated and retained control of most blockbuster productions. As before, but now with growing emphasis as the size of the gamble with each giant production increased, they did everything they could to lessen the risk. No longer, for instance, was it enough merely to feature one or a number of supposedly sure-thing stars in the cast list. By the 1950s producers had become aware that different stars had followings in different strata of society. Gallup's Audience Research Bureau reckoned that a film featuring a number of stars admired by the same section of the public would not appreciably improve box-office turnover. But a film that linked stars admired by, say, different age groups would attract both younger and older spectators.[18] Thus casting was implicated in the new sophistication of marketing. Warner Brothers' Western *Rio Bravo* (1959) sought to extend the age range of its audience in this way by starring John Wayne (52), Dean Martin (42), and Ricky Nelson. Nelson, then 19, was a popular figure with teenage audiences through his work as a pop singer and as an actor in television sitcoms.

One consequence of increased investment in individual movies was that the overseas market became ever more important to Hollywood. Even as early as 1950 few movies (perhaps only one in ten) returned their costs in the American market alone. That compared with about eight out of ten that had done so before the war.[19] Big movies therefore had to draw an overseas audience, for which reason producers often tried to give them universal appeal. This might be done by choice of theme – biblical epics and sex comedies of the kind favoured with the introduction of widescreen were thought to have such appeal. Internationally pre-sold subjects like *The Glenn Miller Story* (Universal-International, 1954) were also favoured; as were stars with worldwide reputations. Numbers of films began to be made in Europe, in Britain, and in other exotic places because authentic locale was thought to be as effective as stars in adding production value – *Three Coins in the Fountain* (Twentieth Century-Fox, 1954) was an early example. Location shooting may have slightly enhanced European goodwill by defusing long-standing objections to Hollywood art departments' impressionist renderings of places well-known to overseas audiences.[20] On the other hand, while actual places were now seen, American productions continued to create often wildly impressionist renderings of foreign societies.

American production overseas was also motivated by other significant economic considerations. It will be recalled (from Chapter 10) that after the war overseas governments had restricted the amount of currency the majors could repatriate from their film rentals. This action, taken to protect national economies and domestic film industries from American invasion, now proved to be the stimulus to what became known as runaway production. Initially this mostly entailed shooting films overseas as the Hollywood majors attempted to put their frozen funds to use; and this practice brought them further advantages. In the first instance, runaway production was concentrated on a number of big pictures, so it proved to be another way of distinguishing movies from television, which could not afford this luxury.[21] Secondly, overseas production charges (particularly for the hire of skilled technicians and of extras) cost less than in California. Since the majors preferred to invest in runaway production where they could find efficient labour, not all overseas countries were equally favoured.[22] Finally there were US tax benefits too because the majors only incurred liability on funds blocked overseas when they converted them into dollars.[23]

Runaway production had considerable impact, soaring from 19 films in 1949 to 183 twenty years later. The foreign earnings of the American industry had amounted to some 40 per cent of theatrical revenue in the 1950s, and increased to about 53 per cent in the early 1960s. Europe returned about 80 per cent of those overseas rentals. Absentee production of this kind substantially worsened employment opportunities in California, and the Hollywood trade unions witnessed a rapid decline in the workforce from an average of about

22 000 in 1949 to about 12 500 in 1956. They lobbied hard against it, and a Congressional inquiry was held in 1961–2.[24] By this time, however, the activities of the American majors abroad were changing, and although runaway production continued, it did so in a new form which offered them even greater financial incentives.

The majors were discovering that without much difficulty they could take discreet advantage of the subsidy schemes that several European governments had established precisely to protect their national film industries from unequal American competition.[25] These schemes were designed to compensate – among others – British, French and Italian producers for the advantage Hollywood majors had long enjoyed in undercutting local product by firstly being able to amortise their costs in their vast home market, and secondly from having US government authority to act overseas as a cartel. In practice, however, it proved virtually impossible to define a British, French or Italian film in such a way as to exclude finance which (though it might be routed through a chain of European subsidiaries) ultimately had its source in American-owned capital. Thus films in every other way European might be American funded, and return profits to an American major. What could be more French than the middle period films of François Truffaut – scripted, directed and crewed by French talent? Yet from 1967 many of his films including *La Mariée Etait en Noir*, *Baisers Volés*, *L'Enfant Sauvage*, and *L'Histoire d'Adèle H* were jointly produced by Truffaut's own company Les Films du Carrosse with another French company Les Artistes Associés. The latter is a subsidiary of United Artists, and the American parent company distributed the films.

Co-production of this kind has the advantage for European producers and directors of opening to them the crucial American market. For the Hollywood majors it often meant almost unbelievable cost reductions in the making of a film. Guback shows that in Britain, where subsidies seem to have run at roughly four times the level of French assistance, only about 10 per cent of monies available actually went to British production companies in the mid-1960s. If an American major managed to invest in a co-production deal it might be eligible for subsidies to as much as 80 per cent of production costs. Understandably by the end of the decade the volume of American films financed abroad rose to about 60 per cent of the total output of US producers.[26] For Guback, subsidy schemes have been a means whereby the American majors have been paid to annex European motion picture industries. In this respect the movement of capital in the film industry has presented a microcosm, admittedly exaggerated, of American capital expansion into overseas markets, which multiplied ninefold in the period 1950 to 1973.[27]

Guback has warned repeatedly (warnings he now repeats in the context of American cross-media interests in the new technologies) that the effect of this imported investment is potentially dangerous for Europe's film industries. If some directors like Truffaut have sufficient market strength to resist change (there could hardly be a less American film than *L'Enfant Sauvage*), others have to accept tampering with their projects. Many films made in Europe with international finance either defy any cultural attribution, or may, like the series of James Bond films made from Britain, look as American as the real thing. The worst risk is that the majors can shrink or destroy many European production facilities as readily as they can expand them, simply in response to considerations relating to their American operations, and without regard for European conditions.[28]

Meanwhile the American majors, not content with enhancing their overseas production, consolidated their distribution operations abroad. In this too their continuing success was considerable, except only that as European countries introduced television, here too the cinema audience shrank. By the early 1970s American majors were taking as much as 84 per cent of film rentals in the United Kingdom, and over 40 per cent in France.[29]

During the 1950s and 1960s the film industry's relations with television shifted. If the period to about 1955 can be described as one of uncertainty tending in the case of many of the actions of the majors towards resistance, thereafter a new, lasting symbiosis formed.[30] An early example of changing attitudes is illustrated by the case history of the Walt Disney studio.[31] If we look back at the time of its great expansion in the 1950s we see another instance in which (as opposed to invention) innovation of a new technique appears to have been used to enable a company to do what others had done before. Disney, like Warner Brothers and Fox innovating sound, sought to push through from the ranks of relatively minor producers to take a more dominant share of the profit, capital and control of the entertainment industry market. In making its bid to become the eighth movie major (and take the place of RKO which effectively ceased to produce or distribute in 1955), Disney, like Warner Brothers and Fox before it, deployed a complex market strategy. It too concentrated on more than one aspect of corporate policy in transforming the business affairs and capital structure of the Disney group of companies. It set up its own distribution company, innovated an integrated policy for television production, and diversified corporate activities into new kinds of entertainment business. Each of these developments fed the others. The company's commitment to television would not have been of much fiscal importance to it had it not also distributed its own films and built its first amusement park.

As Schickel records, the first step was the creation of a distribution organisation, Buena Vista. The company took this step partly because the Disney brothers were irritated by the lack of enthusiasm with which RKO, hitherto their distributor, was selling their first live-action movie *The Living Desert* (1953). But now that Disney's output had accumulated (it differed from the product of other studios in that animated features and shorts had very long lives in the cinema and could be released to successive generations of children over a number of decades) it had enough product to set up a viable distribution arm, and in doing so it would save expense. Although RKO's rates (30 per cent of rental income) were at the lower end of the majors' scales, running its own distribution subsidiary would enable Disney to keep more of its takings within the group – which would help it build capital reserves more rapidly.[32] And it would do more, for RKO used the same inefficient system of domestic distribution which each of the other majors operated at this date. Each ran its own local exchanges in 32 American cities, and used them both as centres from which to sell the films to cinemas and for the physical handling of prints. None of the majors would contemplate employing their rivals' services, and as a consequence they duplicated each other's facilities – in many cities there existed a street or even a single building in which they all had offices.[33]

Buena Vista streamlined this system so that it functioned simply as a sales organisation operating through eight district offices and fifteen branches. The prints of films were handed over to an independent courier service which charged a delivery fee. This mechanism enabled Disney to reduce its distribution costs substantially, certainly to less than 25 per cent, and according to one estimate (which presumably excludes the courier's fee) down to 15 per cent of gross rentals.[34] Owning its distribution arm had the further advantage that it enabled the company to control its releases.

It could now package complete programmes comprising, for instance, an animated feature, a short, and a nature film. In particular it would advertise heavily on television in those seasons of the year when viewing was at a peak, releasing films to cinemas in co-ordination with these campaigns.[35] This practice reversed current orthodoxies, for the greater part of the film industry then believed that the best time to get audiences into cinemas was during the seasons when television was least attractive.

However, Disney had an altogether more pressing need to use television effectively than simply to advertise cinema releases. For this was the period when the company, which had been carrying out detailed research into proposals for Disneyland, began to attempt to raise capital for its vast amusement park. Needing more than it could readily generate, Disney turned to a new partner, ABC-TV.[36] At this time ABC was the smallest of the three American television networks. Formerly one of two radio networks owned by NBC, it had been divorced from the other channel by an anti-trust verdict of the Supreme Court in 1943.[37] Although it was well placed at the start of the 1950s to take advantage of the swift growth of the TV industry, it lacked the capital to make the best of its opportunity. In 1951 it merged with a partner of complementary characteristics, United Paramount Theatres, which of course also had been created through divorcement. As a newly independent theatre chain it found itself in command of plentiful capital, but facing an uncertain future as audiences continued to dwindle. The merger gave ABC-Paramount Theatres both capital and prospects of new, large profits from television.[38]

Disney concluded a deal with this new corporation to their mutual benefit. Still very much the third network, ABC needed Disney's name and skills to attain higher ratings as the means to produce higher advertising revenues. Disney for its part required capital. In return for the agreement to produce a weekly television show for seven years, ABC-Paramount Theatres bought nearly 35 per cent of the shares in Disneyland. The new show took the air in autumn 1954 and at once produced the improved ratings required – but for the Disney group it did a great deal more.[39]

The television show gave Disney the opportunity to take advantage of the fact that it was marketing a homogenised product with few lines. The amusement park was to be people with characters from the films: the show featured them too. Nature films were sent to cinemas, and could be pre-echoed on television. And the company took the opportunity to advertise Disneyland for a year before it opened.[40] The kind of thing the TV programme could do for the rest of the Disney product line (and it should not be forgotten that the group was still market leader in merchandising linked products such as Mickey Mouse watches) was soon revelaed. In its first year on television Disney won an Emmy for *Underseas Adventure*, according to Schickel hardly more than a promotion piece for their most expensive live-action movie yet, *Twenty Thousand Leagues Under The Sea*. The advantage of this kind of sales pitch showed in its theatrical grosses, the highest then for any Disney live-action film at $6.8 million on first release.[41]

Thus the television show, which accounted for only 8 per cent of Disney's gross income, and which in its own right did little more than break even, actually became the key element in the corporation's promotional campaigns. It succeeded in carrying messages to the family, the very audience which the other majors had to watch withdrawing from the cinema to the television room, and drew it back to the cinemas and into its amusement park. It did all this in effect at no cost to the company.[42] If in the end Disney never attained the stature of a major it is not because these manoeuvres failed but because one of its new ventures did so well that it led to further growth in the amusement park business, the sector of its investment which soon made the company more profit than either film or television.

If Columbia with the setting up of its subsidiary Screen Gems had the best claim to have invented production for television by the movie industry, Disney innovated by integrating television production into an overall strategy to the advantage of many aspects of its business. In turn, attempts to exploit the new practice followed swiftly. In 1955 Warner Brothers began to produce its own weekly show for ABC, consisting of hour-long dramatic episodes inspired by its movie classics.[43] Twentieth Century-Fox and MGM then produced their own weekly shows. But Disney's emulators did not do the job as skilfully, in that their programmes looked like commercials from end to end, not just in the designated slots.[44] Indeed there is some evidence to suggest that they were counterproductive, and in areas where they were broadcast cinema audiences diminished.[45] The other studios also had the disadvantage that, as distributors of independent productions, they were not marketing a homogenous, factory-line succession of films. Disney on the other hand did put out such a product, refused to fund or distribute the films of independents, and sought to keep things that way.

The studios themselves made television a more effective competitor with cinemas when in 1955 the dam broke and several of the majors did the thing they had earlier refused by releasing their older films (largely pre-1949) to the new medium. At this point things moved fast. Upon its dissolution RKO sold 740 features and 1000 shorts outright to General Teleradio, the entertainment subsidiary of General Tire and Rubber – which promptly syndicated them, earning an estimated $25 million from them by 1957. Columbia Pictures released 100 films through Screen Gems; in March 1956 Warner Brothers sold outright 850 features and 1500 shorts for $21 million. But in June MGM, foreseeing that television would develop a gargantuan appetite, contracted to lease 750 features and 900 shorts, rightly deciding it could rent them out again and again. And indeed rental soon became the regular method of releasing movies to television as the majors recognised that they were too valuable to sell. By 1958 Twentieth Century-Fox, Universal and Paramount had all done deals with the small screen, thereby producing new and 'free' profit for their distribution arms.[46] In the same year an estimated 9500 Hollywood features were available to the small screen. They occupied about 25 per cent of all sponsored television time.[47]

The effects of this switch in policy showed itself in cinema revenues as early as 1956–7, and the further sharp drop in theatrical receipts also affected distributors' rentals on new product. While the latter had the consolation of their new source of income, exhibitors felt badly the latest downturn in business. Neither widescreen, colour, nor the epic were stopping the slow leeching away of the regular weekly audience. The already tenuous existence of large numbers of cinemas was worsening. Their owners complained that distributors now acted as their rivals in business and charged anything from 50 per cent to 70 per cent on popular films while having increased their average rentals to 36 per cent of gross admissions by 1955. Though the distributors argued that average rentals were not that high, and that (through what became known as the 'look') theatre operators had made a convention of renegotiating the rental contracts of films that did not perform as well as expected, nothing could disguise the fact that since divorcement the balance of power in the industry had altered dramatically.[48] It has been estimated, for instance, that immediately before divorcement the theatres controlled 92 per cent of the motion picture industry's capital assets, and received for their own retention 46 per cent of its total receipts. By 1962–3 they controlled no more than 59 per cent of capital assets, and received slightly less than 29 per cent of total receipts.[49]

Not all theatres were entirely defenceless. Good programming could sustain audience interest for the small, independent exhibitor. The chains had other recourses, and could sometimes force preferential programming and advantageous rental terms from distributors. Diversification was an option some took. We have mentioned the merger of United Paramount Theatres with ABC TV; and in 1956 the merged corporation began through a subsidiary to produce movies for theatrical release. Balio reports that in 1959 National Theatres Inc. (the divorced chain formerly part of Twentieth Century-Fox) bought National Telefilms Associates, a nationwide television-film distribution network. And other theatre circuits (let alone major producers) acquired TV stations. As Balio, Conant and others have remarked, all these acquisitions and mergers violated the spirit if not the letter of the *Paramount* decision, opening up a new range of monopolistic possibilities. But they did offer some of the stronger theatre groups protection against the inroads of the new medium.[50]

The great popularity of television (by 1959 around 90 per cent of American homes had sets) affected the motion picture industry. Firstly, whatever kinds of show it produced in bulk were usually lost to the cinema, and we have already mentioned how it took over serials, series and a large part of family programming. It is also said to have contributed to changes in the musical, which had gained new life from the advent of widescreen cinema. A few years later rising costs within the industry combined with television's regular provision of spectacular entertainment to produce a shift of emphasis in movie musicals away from large-scale, extravagant dance routines to definitive versions of pre-sold Broadway scores.[51]

Occasionally even in these comparatively early days, the older industry benefited from a profitable television spin-off. For example, as TV moved from live, adventurous production to an altogether more cautious, ratings-conscious approach (which it did rapidly in the mid-1950s), the cinema inherited a number of projects which by Hollywood's conservative standards were experimental. Most famous of these was writer Paddy Chayefsky's small film *Marty* (UA, 1955), a low-key story about unglamorous people living in the Bronx.

Other well-known borrowings included Reginald Rose's *Crime in the Streets* (Allied Artists, 1956) and the same writer's *Twelve Angry Men* (UA, 1957). It is sometimes said of them that they reveal their origins through not only their thematic seriousness, but also their restricted *mise-en-scène*.[52]

We have already noted the impact television made on the film industry when from 1965 it started a major drive to convert fully to colour. Thereafter almost all films for cinema release had to be produced in colour for fear they might look drab. And at least in the early years after conversion, while viewers remained conscious of the new phenomenon, it was difficult to rent black and white movies to television. There were, however, advantages for the film industry in making the change to near 100 per cent colour production.

Balio records a rise in the rental prices of features in the 1960s. The RKO package of 1955 had sold for an average price of $10 000 per film. In the early 1960s rental for run-of-the-mill features rose to $150 000 as the studios began to release post-1948 product. That price jumped to $400 000 in 1965, and in the following year took an extraordinary leap to $2 million which ABC paid to Columbia for screening rights to the nine-year-old film *Bridge on the River Kwai*. Although Balio remarks that this was an exceptional deal, it presumably satisfied the sole sponsor, the Ford Motor Company, which used it as the occasion to launch its 1967 product line: it reached an estimated audience of 60 million people, and sharply reduced the ratings of *The Ed Sullivan Show* and *Bonanza* on the rival channels.[53] Though Balio regards this as having been an exceptional deal, the underlying price trend continued up, and from 1966 rental charges had moved up to $800 000 for two showings. Hits and blockbusters cost more.

Soon movies were being aired at prime time, every night of the week. Equally significant, the networks were making large deals to hire packages of movies from the studios.[54] Two factors seem to have underpinned this intense demand for product. Viewers seem to have responded well to colour films and big features now that they could be televised; and the networks, believing such product to be scarce, rushed to buy while they could. This boom further improved the health of the movie industry's distribution arm.[55]

Nor was this all. In the rush for new colour programmes, one network inaugurated the 'TV movie'. NBC signed a contract with MCA's Universal to co-finance a series of two-hour feature films for release first to television and then to theatres. As Balio says, this contract set the seal on what now became a partnership between the broadcasting and film industries, with most of the movie majors now operating a division for television production.[56]

TV movies were budgeted at a cost considerably lower than theatrical features, and were brought in with much tighter shooting schedules. In the later 1960s, typical costs were $435 000 for a 90-minute movie, and $700 000 for one of two hours. As Champlin speculated acutely, what was reappearing was the B picture. Not usually particularly imaginative, except in finding ingenious ways around budget limitations, the TV movie employed familiar, but not top-price actors and actresses. Often it would further reveal its television derivation by relying heavily on established genres without the least innovation. When it did open in cinemas after TV screening, these would not be the better venues.[57] But just how important the new format was to both industries can be measured by the fact that in 1974 the networks screened 130 new TV movies in prime time, compared with 118 theatrical features broadcast for the first time. TV movies proved safer in sustaining ratings than theatrical features, some of which were considered to be too specialised or too offensive for the TV audience.[58]

However, for a number of reasons television did not prove to be the ceaseless cornucopia for the movie industry that might at this moment have appeared likely. In the first place the rush to secure product could not proceed indefinitely at the pace of 1966, simply because the networks soon bought enough films to last them several years. The boom had ended late in 1968. In addition their need for TV movies and series (which some movie majors also produced for the networks) declined as repeats became a regular feature of the programming schedule. Stanley reports that in the earlier years of television the annual cycle for every network series had run to 39 originals and 13 repeats, which were played in summer. By the late 1960s summer began in March; and by 1978 the average TV series was to have only about 22 original episodes each year – a shrinkage which entailed a considerable reduction in revenue for programme makers.[59]

There were other difficulties. Not every sale was guaranteed – for example in 1966 the networks killed off a third of the season's series at great cost to their producers.[60] And the networks began to co-operate with each other on pricing policy so that although TV movies went into profit after their second airing, successful series became extremely slow to pay returns to their producers. With such series, the networks signed up renewal rights well into the future, pre-setting the fees payable for both first and repeat airings so that the typical programme supplier could not expect to move into profit unless the show ran four or five years and went into syndication. This co-ordinated action was blatant enough for the Justice Department to commence anti-trust action against the networks in 1970. But until 1980, when the case was concluded with the networks consenting to alter their practices, very low returns indeed were payble to any TV series production company honest enough to resist the common Hollywood practice of 'creative accounting'.[61]

Incidentally, allegations of creative accounting were to be made of virtually all the majors from the 1960s on, and by people very well placed to know what was going on. Hollywood was never well known for its scrupulous approach to either accountancy or the observance of contractual obligations; but as investment in individual productions grew ever larger, so did the urgency with which many of the big companies used whatever means they could command to manipulate business to their best advantage.[62] It has been alleged, for instance, that in the 1960s MCA actually made about $5500 on a typical episode of each series it produced. However, it is said to have been able to demonstrate to any actor who might have signed up with a profit-sharing deal that in fact it had made nothing whatever.[63]

After the sale to television of *Bridge on the River Kwai*, no film could be made for the cinema without its producers keeping TV rental in mind. This did more than merely ensure that movies would now be made in colour. Television, in taking over the majority audience, had also taken on the burden of inherent caution required of those companies that mean to keep huge audiences. TV executives soon learnt to concentrate on securing good ratings for the solid advertising returns they implied. For theatrical movies made with eventual prime-time networking in mind, the caution of the networks reinforced in the film majors a tendency towards which they always swerved in times of nervousness. Then, as Champlin remarks, they mostly produce technically competent, handsome films – but films which do not innovate, and which certainly do not arouse controversy in ways which might alarm a network buyer.[64] Not all movies would admit to these requirements, happily, but a great number did.

It was not long before the networks became sophisticated in their rental policies in a way they had not been in 1966. They soon learned to couple a film's earnings on theatrical release with the rentals they offered for broadcast rights. Thereafter only films which had done exceptionally well in the cinema earned the exceptional rentals to which we have referred. TV rentals did not help most theatrical movies do more than break even. Thus the costly film which failed in the cinema (and there were plenty in the late 1960s) would fail doubly since it would not sell well to television.[65] Nevertheless television rental had become a hedge against loss for most competent movies.

In summary, the development of a thriving partnership between the two industries substantially benefited the studios as distributors, and as renters of facilities and services. Producers did less well. Though many got extra work for TV much of it was at a low level of profitability. For the television arms of the movie majors this was not necessarily unacceptable. Since regular income from TV helped them amortise fixed overheads such as rates, depreciation and administration expenses, they would look to take real profit from other production activities. For small independent producers, however, the low profitability of TV series was a marked deterrent from undertaking such work. For the cinema operator, television brought little but anxiety except in those rare instances when it was used to publicise theatrical releases. Disney aside, such promotions did not develop into routine practice until the 1970s.

13 Conglomerates and Diversification, 1965–86

Near the end of the 1960s the motion picture industry met the crisis towards which it had been moving for some years. For the habit of thinking big, acquired during the 1950s, had stuck with studio executives. Since the history of Hollywood had accustomed those who spent their working lives in its ethos to thinking of the truly big as that which exceeded the grandeur or cost of what had already been made, it follows that, in thinking big, executive producers actually often thought bigger.

During the 1960s the extravaganza became the norm as studio production heads continued to go for big hits. The most successful did return ever-increasing box-office income; but there were fewer such films, and in the search for them studios spawned greater numbers of flops. An incidental consequence was that production executives tended not to stay long with individual studios. More than this, the constantly rising cost of producing ever bigger blockbusters was by the late 1960s placing in jeopardy the survival of the major film corporations. Although in the long view it appears there was a cycle to the fortunes of most of the majors, financiers cannot wait for the wheel to turn from its downpoint, and a succession of flops could change the fate of both studios and the individuals in charge of them.

For example, after the catastrophic failure of *Cleopatra* (1963) when Twentieth Century-Fox lost almost $40 million, Spyros Skouras was replaced by Darryl Zanuck and his son Richard. Although they began by cutting the studio's overheads heavily, they plainly saw that small films would not return profits large enough to service the corporation's capital. Relatively early they produced in *The Sound of Music* (1965) (costing $10 million, but grossing nearer $100 million in rentals) a hit colossal enough to make back all that had been lost on *Cleopatra*, and sufficient besides to stabilise the· company's finances. Then they tried to reduplicate that success through a number of gigantic movies mostly aimed at the same market; but *Dr Dolittle* (1967), *Star!* (1968), and *Hello Dolly!* (1969) all lost money. Only *Patton* (1969), which cost $11 million, made profits.

The spiralling costs incurred by productions of this kind carried their own warning: *Dr Dolittle* cost $18 million to produce, and (one of the marks of the blockbuster) another small fortune at almost $10 million to market and distribute. Interest accumulating on such a debt would make it even harder for movies turned out at this kind of cost to return profit. The industry reckons, as an approximate guide, that a film must take at box office 2.5 times the cost of production before it breaks even: *Dolittle* would have had to gross some $70 million to reach this point. As we shall see, simple arithmetic of this kind led at the end of the 1960s to some very uncomfortable conclusions.

For the Zanucks these failures had the inevitable consequence, and they were fired. Although Darryl retired, Richard had no difficulty obtaining another senior position. He was first hired by Warners, and later by Universal where he produced *The Sting* (1973) and *Jaws* (1975).[1] This too became a recurring pattern in the 1970s and 1980s, with the studios so desperate to hire as senior executives people who had tasted success and to fire those who had failed with them, that an elite corps circulated none too slowly around the majors. In the case of one individual, conviction on charges of embezzlement in one major did not discourage another from employing him as its president. Confidence, or the talent for arousing it in others, is a saleable commodity in Hollywood.

For Twentieth Century-Fox the consequence was another financial crisis. Holding an inventory of movies costing $238 million in 1968, the corporation lost $65 million in 1969 and $81 million the following year. From 1971 its new management took urgent remedial action. it reduced inventory (i.e., cut production) to $65 million in 1973. To raise cash it had to sell land and buildings. And it ensured that the group's other activities made money – in television production, its film laboratories, its three TV stations, and the Hoyt theatre chain in Australia and New Zealand. Then it began to take profit from a number of very successful films including *The Poseidon Adventure* (1972) and *The Towering Inferno* (co-produced with Warners, 1974). The seal was set on the return to profitability with the huge profits accruing from *Star Wars* (1977).[2] Thereafter the company continued in financial health until it fell into the hands of Marvin Davis in the early 1980s.

The stability of the market was disturbed not only by the production of grandiose movies but also by the release of too many films. This surge in output was largely caused by the creation in the late 1960s of three new production–distribution companies which were set up to force their way into the old oligopoly as 'instant majors'. Two of them were subsidiaries of the TV networks CBS and ABC, seeking to produce theatrical films which they could rent after cinema release to their parent channels. Each of the three produced about ten feature films a year, and spent heavily in doing so. They sought to persuade exhibitors to take their product by undercutting the rental terms offered by the old majors. In the event the majors matched their terms and drew on their capital reserves to cover their losses. They succeeded in driving the newcomers out of the business by 1972, but at a considerable cost to themselves. And the new entrants lost $80 million between them.[3]

Perhaps the most trenchant account of the problems of the industry in the 1960s was advanced by a banker. A. H. Howe of the Bank of America argued the simple thesis that the size of the industry's investment put it inevitably in a position where it must make a loss on production. And although later writers gave different figures, they echoed his conclusion.[4] He reckoned that worldwide box office revenue for film was in the order of $2000 million. Of that sum the cinemas kept $1400 million and passed the rest to the distributors. They in turn would deduct about $180 million for their fees, and a further $180 million for their costs, including advertising, making prints and despatching them to exhibitors. This left a notional $240 million (which Howe thought was in fact nearer $200 million) to pay the cost of production. However:

> During most of the 1960s, seven major American motion picture companies assumed production risks each year exceeding $50 million each, and all other US companies and risk-takers probably totalled another $50 million, a total of about $400 million. Thus, the expense of making the product exceeded the market return by something like two to one, and something had to give.[5]

Howe of course knew that the industry had another major source of revenue in rentals to television; but the networks had over-purchased by late 1968 and had already filled their needs for the 1969–72 seasons. Thus this market had temporarily collapsed.[6] He also knew that with their own movies the studios collected twice, so that what they made as distributors they could offset against their losses as producers. But even with this modification his is a gloomy picture of an industry the earnings ratio of which had gone so wildly awry that it threatened the capital structure of the majors. For good measure he challenged two of the industry's most cherished orthodoxies. He argued firstly that stars were not bankable, that the films in which they appeared at great expense could not be guaranteed to make money, and secondly that there appeared to be no correlation between the cost of a picture and the money it took. The industry could reduce its risk by cutting investment both in total and by putting less into individual pictures.[7]

The industry continued to debate these ideas long after Howe's papers had been forgotten; but in the event it did not take his simple prescription in the terms he meant it, except in one respect. The studios did cut their overall production investment after the cash crisis of the late 1960s, and Hollywood's annual releases, having risen from around 130 in the early 1960s to 180 in 1968, now declined to about 120 by 1975.[8] Although small movies were made, some without stars, this was done mainly because theatres, as we have already remarked, still needed to keep movies on their screens the whole year round. But after *The Godfather* (Parmount, 1971) took record receipts the industry continued to make blockbusters, and its investment in individual pictures kept climbing.[9]

From the mid-1960s no responsible businessman could watch untroubled as a state of affairs continued in which the production of enormously costly films jeopardised the future of major film corporations. But as most of the studios seemed unable to extricate themselves from their problems, it was left to outsiders to take action. Two groups in particular did so. First were the bankers because they frequently had to finance the losses of the majors. It was they who forced the companies to streamline their operations, reduce overheads, to share some facilities (in particular overseas distribution networks) with their competitors, and to hold off making blockbusters at least for a couple of years.[10] Second were the chief executives of other corporations who recognised that the unhealthy balance sheets of the majors gave them the chance inexpensively to take over assets that could be well worth acquiring.

In what amounted to changes as marked as the passage from one generation to another, some of the movie majors were taken over by or merged with other corporations, others were refinanced, and all were encouraged further to diversify their activities into other markets than the cinema. The process of transformation this entailed (which began for most of the studios with the crisis of the 1960s) continues to this day. It has transformed most of them into units located within multi-media conglomerates; and it has made theatrical film distribution and exhibition no more than one way of several in which a narrative fiction (the term 'software' is now sometimes used) may be released and marketed.

During the 1960s a number of the majors became targets for take-over bids. They were attractive for a variety of reasons. Despite the trading losses they had recorded, most of them possessed substantial assets, some of which were undervalued. Thus the shares of some of the majors (Paramount was an instance) could be bought in 1965 at a price well below their true worth.[11] It follows that one attraction of the majors for a predator company was the chance to make a quick capital profit. If, however, this had been their only motivation, many predators would have sold the studios early and taken their profit. This the Australian-based Alan Bond Corporation did in 1986, selling Screen Entertainment, a British multi-media company, to Cannon International within days of its purchase from Thorn-EMI. In fact such resales were not common.

The assets of the old studios included land and buildings. Sometimes property was sold, either to help refinance the company (Twentieth Century-Fox), or to help pay off the massive loans which the new owner had incurred in buying the studio (the motivation for Kirk Kerkorian's sale of MGM land and studio props after his purchase in 1969).[12] However, these assets, which could be sold off without killing the studios' activities either as producers or distributors of film and television programmes, were not substantially undervalued. Their sale was often a part of wider rationalisation, as at MGM where within six months of Kerkorian's take-over his new director of production James Aubrey cut a number of agreed film projects, fired 40 per cent of the labour force, arranged to move the company's headquarters to California from New York, closed two-thirds of the thirty-two domestic sales offices, and set up the next season's production run of twenty films.[13]

It will be recalled that in the mid-1960s demand from the television networks rapidly pushed up the rental price of feature films. One consequence was that the value of the majors' libraries increased rapidly by two to threefold; but in the companies' books (and in their share values) they figured at a sum lower than their realisable value. Here big capital profits could be made, and this was a lure that attracted many take-over bids. What made the film library an even more attractive proposition for the new parent company intending to keep its acquisition was the belief that television, unlike theatrical rentals, would return relatively constant profits.[14]

Ownership of the movie majors had other attractions for the large corporations that sought to acquire them. It could provide a conglomerate (as Paramount did for Gulf & Western, and Warner Brothers for Kinney National Services respectively) with a position of dual control in both the film and television industries. From such a base it was possible to extend through a chain of subsidiaries into strategic positions within the total entertainment market – linking with, for example, hotels and travel, sports, or the other media.

Possession of a Hollywood studio might also boost the value of shares in the holding company. Bach says the Transamerica Corporation hoped for such a result when it bought United Artists in 1967, believing that owning a glamorous subsidiary would make its stock more appealing to investors. It was to be disappointed. In addition the directors of some conglomerates thought that the huge windfall profits generated by successful blockbusters should boost dividends in the holding company nicely. This did happen, but there were also years in which the studios plunged into deficit. United Artists, having earned Transamerica $20 million profit in 1968, reported a deficit of $45 million in 1970. When, as on this occasion, a number of other subsidiaries of a conglomerate were in difficulty, the effects could be serious. Transamerica's stock slid in six months from $27 to $11 per share; eight years later it stood no higher than $15. Ultimately, then, conglomerates found they were not invulnerable; and in the late 1970s and 1980s some sold all or part of their holdings. Transamerica sold United Artists to MGM in 1981 in the wake of the debacle with *Heaven's Gate* (which the studio had to write off at a net cost of $44 million). It turned out to be a good way to recover the loss, since the former parent is estimated to have made a healthy profit of perhaps $100 million over the company's book value.[15]

For the studios there were in most cases considerable advantages in becoming subsidiaries within conglomerates. In general they were stabilised by the massive capital backing afforded by these financial empires. If the conglomerate benefited from windfall profits in good years, the movie major could look for security in bad seasons. And there were routine benefits too.

If, for example, the group found it had on its hands spare capital, it could invest funds in film production. This facility became of acute importance when from the mid-1970s interest rates rose, to be sustained at high levels through to the mid-1980s by the fiscal policies of the Reagan administration. To be sure, the majors continued to raise funds from banks – with production costs averaging $11.3 million and publicity adding a further $7–9 million per movie by 1981, they had use for both production loans against specific pictures and general corporate funding.[16] As Quart and Auster remark, since the lifeblood of Hollywood is borrowed capital, high interest rates tend to force the studios to cut back on the number of films they put out.[17] They also exert pressure on producers to release films immediately they are complete. In these circumstances the investment of funds from within a group might provide capital at a cost lower than that raised on the open market; and at whatever rate funds were provided, internal investment kept profits within the group.

The idea of keeping money within the conglomerate helped shape the strategy of merger and take-over of several groups with media interests. This is true of Gulf and Western (with Paramount), Kinney Services (later Warner Communications), and Rupert Murdoch's News Corporation, with its global media interests (including Fox). All of them might be described in Gustafson's terms as being:

> organized according to the principle of multiple profit centers which reinforce each other in an interlocking and financially conservative pattern that is designed not only to generate revenue and profits, but to keep such monies within the corporation.[18]

To give an example, by the early 1980s the old Warner Brothers was merely one firm in a large nest which included many other companies, some representing heavy new investment (like Atari and Warner Amex Cable Communications). The list included subsidiaries concerned with music publishing, record production and distribution both at home and abroad (for four labels – Warner, Atlantic, Elektra and Nonesuch); film, television and home videotape production and distribution; merchandising of toys and ancillary rights; production for the legitimate stage; manufacture of Panavision equipment; publication of paperback books, comics and magazines; controlling interests in Atari home computers, video games and associated electronic toys; New York Cosmos soccer team; Warner Cosmetics; the Franklin Mint; and a 50 per cent interest jointly with American Express in the country's second largest cable and satellite operation. And these operations represented only the entertainments division of the corporation – National Kinney having entirely distinct interests in building, running parking lots, funeral parlours, and car rental.[19]

These holdings were in 1984 sharply reduced in a way which illustrates both the weakness and strength of the conglomerate. In 1983 Atari swung from what had been enormous profitability to reporting a loss of $536 million.[20] The following year Warner Communications suspended Qube (its experimental interactive cable network); it sold off its interests in Panavision, the New York Cosmos and the Franklin Mint, and renegotiated its corporate position with its bankers. However, although it had to sacrifice these activities, the conglomerate appears to have protected most of its operations successfully. The film arm, which had consistently improved its profits through the previous decade from less than $10 million to more than $110 million in 1979, continued to thrive with solid profits from *Gremlins*, *Police Academy* (both 1984), and Clint Eastwood's films.[21]

The practice of protecting corporate interests via multiple profit centres was also practised by those Hollywood majors that did not belong to conglomerates. During the 1970s, they diversified their activities as widely as they could, often encouraged by their bankers to reinvest their windfall profits in this way, setting up new subsidiaries to engage in related fields of entertainment. TV stations, video companies, a pinball machine manufacturer, and holiday resorts were among the targets for diversification. Some, like Fox, Universal and Warners, bought into Coca-Cola bottling companies.[22] Where they could not afford wholly to own a laterally connected concern, they co-operated with other companies in joint ventures. Some studios shared studio facilities. Others entered co-production deals (*The Towering Inferno* (1974), *1941*, and *All That Jazz* (both 1979) were examples). And it became common practice to share overseas distribution facilities, an activity which anti-trust provision forbade at home. Paramount and Universal joined forces in the Cinema International Corporation which claimed about a third of the market in 1977. In 1981 this operation grew to take in MGM–UA's overseas business, and changed its name to United International Pictures (UIP).[23]

What resulted was both the preservation of the oligopoly and its extension through a network of multinational companies. Characteristic of these companies was that they would possess interests extending across a number of entertainment and information media, and/or would have formal links with other corporations to give them further reach and breadth to their media-related activities.[24] As new media technologies were innovated these corporations positioned themselves so as to exploit them, and in so doing they often implicated the Hollywood majors.

For example, by the early 1980s Pay or Cable Television was emerging as a market force formidable enough to have an impact on American film production. It returned in 1982 over 17 per cent of total movie revenues, exceeding for the first time film rentals abroad. In particular HBO (Home Box Office), the most powerful movie channel and a subsidiary of the publishing company Time Inc., began to invest massively in Pay TV rights to new feature films. In January 1983 it bought, in many cases before they were ready for production, exclusive rights to 37 of the 106 features then scheduled for release by the movie majors. Coca-Cola, which had purchased Columbia Pictures a year earlier, quickly saw that Pay TV needed more new releases than it could get. In 1983 Columbia jointly with HBO and CBS established a new studio, Tri-Star, to produce feature films for cinema, network TV and Pay TV.[25] Two years later Rupert Murdoch's News Corporation bought Twentieth Century-Fox, and placed it so that its film library and its film and television production could feed both the conglomerate's nascent fourth TV network and its European satellite Sky Channel.[26]

The impact of the movement of the media majors into the new technologies was such that by the start of the 1980s it was possible for more than one observer to remark that the oligopoly which anti-trust action had split apart in the late 1940s was now being put together again through openings particularly in cable and satellite. The economic reasons for this interest are not hard to find. While the studios could not anticipate significant increases in their share of the rental from cinematic exhibition without destroying that business, they could anticipate altogether greater returns if they or companies in their group owned the concerns that would deliver their films into patrons' living-rooms. If they merely hired out their films they would receive only 20 per cent of the cable companies' revenue as rental.[27]

During the 1970s the majors, assisted by the programme of diversification which we have described, were restabilised. Having reduced the total number of films they put out they kept a careful watch on this limit (until the arrival of Pay TV as a major force in the 1980s). An informal indication of the change is found in the industry estimate that while at the end of the 1960s only one picture in ten had made a profit, by the end of the 1970s that figure had risen to about three in ten. In 1985 *Variety* claimed that the earning capacity of big budget films having negative costs above $14 million had improved in the three years ending in 1984. Now every second such film achieved box-office success.[28] During the 1960s only 5 movies made over $40 million in rentals; 29 did so in the 1970s, and to Laskos this indicates that profitability was increasing about four times faster than inflation.[29] However, these advances should not be allowed to disguise the fact that the audience was not growing in numbers.

The day-by-day observer of Hollywood can easily be forgiven for imagining that the flow of people going through the turnstiles fluctuates in wild swoops, so nervy is the industry's reaction to every alteration. The longer view, however, shows that the domestic audience remained roughly constant, at 1 billion admissions per annum with variations no greater than 20 per cent up or down, from 1961 to the mid-1980s. Above-average periods alternate around this norm with below-average seasons in a cycle that usually repeats itself every four to five years.[30] Although the box-office ceiling moved up substantially it did so primarily because ticket prices rose. Gross domestic box office takings passed the $1 billion mark in 1968, reached $2 billion in the mid-1970s, and hit $4 billion in 1984. In the same period average admission prices rose from $1.31 in 1968 to $3.40 in 1984.[31]

All this means that a great deal more cash rides on the feature that manages to mobilise a very large audience. Conversely, since the overall audience size remains constant, proportionately less goes to small films. The kinds of figure that Gordon gives for 1977 were reported year after year through the 1970s and 1980s. He analysed films reported to have returned gross rentals from the North American market in excess of $1 million. In that year the top 6 films accounted for one-third of the rentals received by distributors; the top 13 films accounted for half; only the top 28 films grossed more than $10 million, and between them they accounted for three-quarters of the total receipts. Yet these 28 films represented less than a quarter of the 119 films analysed.

Twelve of the thirteen top pictures were distributed by the majors, a typical statistic, and one which underlines their continuing dominance. They continued to be virtually the only organisations with the skills and the international sales force necessary to place films regularly and profitably. No other distributors had the cash flow that allowed them to set off their inevitable losses against the much rarer successes – long their routine practice. Although this was a constant source of outrage to successful producers, they had very few alternatives but to use their services.[32]

Figures like these show why the majors concentrated so intensively on the films that during the 1970s swelled beyond even the grandeur of blockbusters, and began to be known as 'event movies'. For the massive capital backing which the conglomerates made available to the movie majors carried with it obligations. Shareholders will not invest in stock that fails to produce profits or enhanced capital value at a rate comparable to that of other investment opportunities – and corporations require from time to time to raise capital in order to enter new markets with new products. The inexpensive film, even if as a sleeper it returned unexpected millions on a small investment (as *Easy Rider* (Columbia, 1969) and *Breaking Away* (Twentieth Century-Fox, 1979) did), could not service a major's capital account, though it could provide a pleasant gloss to its accounts. The motion picture industry discovered that its success in raising new capital from the conglomerates meant that the 'event movie' had become an essential part of its profit-making programme, for it returned profits of a different order of magnitude.[33] The key to understanding why this should be so (and why such films developed certain typical characteristics) lies in two linked factors – audience behaviour and marketing practice.

As the film industry had known since the early 1950s, about 70–75 per cent of its audience was aged under 30, with the greater part coming from the age range 14–25 years, a pattern which did not alter during the next thirty-five years. However, the Broadcasting Research Unit of the British Film Institute argues that the tendency to concentrate on it exclusively ignores the fact that the family audience continued to be an extremely important component in a healthy cinema. The broad pattern of their findings seems to match American movie-going behaviour, although their data derive from a December 1984 survey of the British cinema-going audience. They note that families might attend the cinema only a couple of times a year, but that they swell the numbers for event movies (and introduce children to the cinema). However, their attendance is cyclical, and is best seen in relation to the calendar of domestic life rather than the films on offer. This is readily understood if one sees the audience as subject to both push and pull factors. For the family audience a major push factor is the need to find something to do which gets children out of the house during their holidays. The range of leisure opportunities available are the pull factors. They include many other activities besides film-going.

Thus there has for some time been a strong seasonal weighting in cinema attendance. As the majors know, the peak periods fall in the Christmas and summer holidays, with the Easter break a little less busy.[34] American domestic rentals for films released in the Christmas holidays between 1972 and 1979 averaged, when all other factors were constant, $3.2 million higher than for releases at other times of the year.[35] But if these are potentially the best weeks for the cinema, they are also the most unpredictable precisely because they depend on the irregular audience. The difference between a good and a poor year for the cinema largely turns on the handful of big movies that attract the greater part of that irregular audience – those who go to the cinema between one and three times a year. At these periods when push factors operate to create an intense demand for leisure activities, pull factors exert their influence. In short, only if the few films on offer in the holiday period are attractive enough do cinemas enjoy a good year.

The Broadcasting Research Unit observed one other factor – that the film-goer's choice of which film to see is shaped by the reasons for going to it. If a family goes out to amuse the children, then it is likely to look for a film which meets their preferences.[36] This explains why so many event movies made since the mid-1970s suit children. Robots, cuddly toys, nasty little creatures and children abound as in the *Star Wars* trilogy (Twentieth Century-Fox, 1977–83), *ET* (Universal, 1982), and *Gremlins* (Warner, 1984)). Many of these films, however, offer pleasures that a child presumably cannot enjoy, which suggests the studios also work at making parents' visits to the cinema enjoyable. A movie may offer to the child an exhilarating, uncomplicated adventure, the stuff of heroic myths. For the adult, however, it may provide more sophisticated pleasures – the chance to enjoy supercilious amusement stimulated by the arch gaucherie of character byplay (the *Superman* trilogy (Warner, 1978–83)); or space for wry nostalgia, perhaps aroused by resemblances to star performances of genre films of earlier decades (*Indiana Jones and the Temple of Doom* (Paramount, 1984), and *Back to the Future* (Universal, 1985)).

The predominance among these big releases of action-adventure movies and of comedies can of course be attributed to the industry's concern also to cater for its regular audience of young people, 14 to 25 years old. By the mid-1980s, six of the top grossing films of all time belonged to the action-adventure category, a fact which made it certain that Hollywood would perceive its immediate future lay with the big-budget spectacular.[37] And all these factors made it inevitable that the majors would continue to concentrate on augmenting the pull factor in every way they could through marketing.

Marketing developed, as far as the film industry was concerned, after the success of Paramount in promoting *The Godfather* in 1971. It differs from publicity, which the studios continued to employ, for instance by writing stories about a production to place in the columns of the popular press. It also differs from advertising. Marketing usually commences before the film has been scripted, with detailed interviews with potential members of the audience. These are meant to discover what elements of the project (from its title to its 'concept') will appeal to which people (by age, sex, class, liking for particular stars or genres). The kind of information that Litman discovered by analysing selected theatrical rentals for the period 1972–9 would be familiar to the marketing agent. In that period the science fiction film, other things being equal, would generate $6.3 million more domestic rentals than films in other categories, horror films would yield an extra $3.8 million, and comedies $3 million.[38] A crucial guideline is that if a film aims only for a narrow segment of the audience, it is unlikely to appeal to a broader audience. Conversely if a project broadens its appeal, the narrow audience will still be attracted.[39] Paramount was convinced it had the right subject for *The Godfather* because it had 'emotion, a structured story, jeopardy, romance, and action'.[40] As some have argued this can be the recipe for an inoffensive but bland product, with huge expense and considerable talent lavished on saying as little as possible.[41] This is not, however, a new phenomenon in Hollywood. In the factory era, family-oriented features were celebrated for their power to entertain and amuse, not for their authority as significant documents.

The marketed film is launched with a tailor-made campaign

designed to highlight its saleable aspects, and to disguise those that seem unattractive to the majority of people. Expertly done, an effective campaign can be put together without much help from the movie itself, as the case of *The Deep* (Columbia, 1977) suggests. Since market research has already indicated the characteristics of the film's potential audience, it becomes possible to decide through which media to reach it and, taking advantage of the majors' corporate relations, through what other lines to spread the product. To give them immediate visual identity, promotional materials for book covers, film, television, video, record album and merchandise usually feature co-ordinated artwork and logos.[42] Thus, by reaching audiences through as many channels as possible, the majors seek to build their blockbusters into events of which most people would be aware.

As an event, *The Deep* began with Bantam's publication of Peter Benchley's novel: Columbia had a royalty sharing arrangement with the publisher. The novel itself was a follow-up to *Jaws*, and thus typified another marketing strategy of the 1970s and 1980s: insistent pre-selling through every channel possible. Often this led to replicating movies in a cycle in which later films were commonly sequels to the first. Invariably a repeat experience was promised: studios sometimes simply numbered a succession of films (*Rocky I* to *IV* (UA, 1979–85)). Where a film was based on an original screenplay, the studios might hire writers to draft a 'novelisation' of it, for publication to coincide with theatrical release.

The studio has to decide what release pattern to use with each film. It may be given saturation booking, in which case it will open on anything from 800 to 1000 screens – and this was the case with *The Deep*. Such a release will be prepared by a massive national advertising campaign in those media that marketing research suggests will most likely reach the target audience. Columbia spent a $3 million advertising budget. Any or all of newspapers, selected magazines, billboards, radio and television may be used; and other methods of drawing attention to such an event include the production of television featurettes, and of behind-the-scenes documentaries (both part of advance marketing for this film). In addition special interest audiences are sought out – in this case, boat shows were covered.

The Deep opened in mid-June, two days after payday. Two days before its launch its producer published a behind-the-scenes book. The film's director and stars did the rounds of TV chat shows.

Supermarkets were saturated with T-shirts, soundtrack record albums, and other merchandise and competitions. These means of marketing, that make money in their own right, are particularly attractive – the ancillary market for *The Deep* was very profitable to the studio. (As Nic Roeg once asked, is it the fate of the successful Hollywood director to become a manufacturer of toys?)

The company's research showed that by the time the film opened, this target audience should have been exposed to fifteen different media pitches. And despite adverse reviews Columbia made good money on a fairly weak film, just as its market plan had proposed. For the saturation method of release is designed to get the audience into the theatres as soon as the film is launched and to take profit before bad word-of-mouth reports get about.[43]

Not all films 'open broad' like this. Some will be opened with preview screenings to test audience reaction. Such a film may be released in a selected territory (a part of the country with an audience whose interest the film is likely to engage), with advertising confined to that region. Others commence in the largest cities, and the marketing attempts to build an audience for what may be perceived as a difficult film. Yet other films (Gustafson names *Blade Runner* (Warner, 1982)) do poor business in the cinema. They may be pulled quickly for re-release through cable television and videocassette. Finally, if the distributor can see no prospect of selling a movie, it may decide not to release it in any format.[44]

The question of re-release, or sequential marketing, has become of great significance, since a movie's commercial life is no more than begun in the cinema. But even in that one segment of the market, it has become common practice since *Star Wars* (1977) for the majors to withdraw event movies from cinemas when they calculate that a theatrical re-release, linked with a new advertising campaign stressing previously unremarked facets of the product, will stimulate business. *Star Wars*' first weekend back in the cinemas in July 1978 generated over $10 million at the box office.[45] But theatrical release is simply one stage in a sequence which includes sales to the movie channels for cable TV screening, sales and rentals on home videocassettes, marketing to non-theatrical outlets (the airlines principal among them), network broadcast and syndicated release through local TV stations.[46]

The marketing agent has, as Litman says, to estimate all the interlocking markets in advance, deciding when and in which order to go to each medium. This is done with some care on the basis of as much information as can be discovered about the current state of the market.[47] This calculation was agreeably more difficult when from the late 1970s the demand of the new outlets for product stimulated the networks to offer soaring rentals for box-office hits. *The Deep* collected $7.5 million, and ABC paid over $6 million for three runs of *American Gigolo* (Paramount, 1980). Clint Eastwood and Burt Reynolds films earn from this source alone $10–$13 million each.[48]

With the marketing of the event movie to television a delicate paradox arose. For while the economics of the industry dictated that the more costly the movie the better it must sell to TV, such a film by its very nature had to offer more to its theatrical audience than the standard small-screen fare.[49] To this end spectacle became an integral part of the event movie, which special effects and animation techniques played a big role in creating. By the mid-1980s some described these techniques as the new stars of event movies like *Indiana Jones* for their intricacy, cost and drawing power. Their effects, of course, barely register on television, so TV screenings were reduced for many viewers to prompts that recalled the fuller experience offered by the big screen.

Cross-media marketing has since *Saturday Night Fever* and *Grease* (Paramount, 1977 and 1978) worked particularly well where music is the selling feature of the film. In the former case a single 'How deep is your love?' was first released, and this quickly became a hit. Then a double album was marketed at a high price, and disc jockeys gave repeated air time to the track 'Staying Alive'. By the time the movie opened six weeks later it had received almost endless free publicity.[50] These films took advantage of new systems which could reproduce sound to much higher specifications than before, with an attack the domestic television receiver could not equal.[51] In the 1980s, cross-media marketing of music has concentrated on music videos – an oblique tribute to the success of MTV (Warner Communications' music channel) in winning an audience of young people. Films such as *Flashdance* and *Footloose* (Paramount, 1983 and 1984) are preceded by music videos of songs that are marketed to become hits with a view to implanting both a sound and an image of the film in the minds of the right audience before the movie opens.[52]

If such films can be described as illustrated soundtracks, a further development in the mid-1980s was the movie designed as part of the marketing campaign for cuddly toys. *The Care Bears Movies I* and *II* (1985 and 1986) and *My Little Pony* (1986) exploited the holiday market for very young children. The films differed from Disney's in that here the toys preceded the films, the characters were limited in range, and the sentimentality has been described as making Disney animation look austere by comparison.[53]

The marketing machine at its most effective should give the majors security. While not every film will turn huge profits, the opportunities to lay off costs and to explore a number of interlinked markets should have given the studios safeguards against heavy losses. On paper the risk of huge flops seemed to have been removed. In practice this was not the case. At least four factors made it possible for marketing campaigns to fail:

1. The cost of television advertising rose at a phenomenal speed through the 1970s, a large extra on-cost item.
2. The cinema audience remained difficult to predict and to mobilise.
3. Word-of-mouth report on bad films could still spread fast enough to sabotage all that marketing sophistication – and there were still plenty of feeble blockbusters in release.
4. The majors in the late 1970s and early 1980s once again became complacent in their production scheduling, and sometimes downright impotent in their attempts to control costs. Few people appear to have heard of *Sorcerer* (Universal/Paramount, 1977), *Hurricane* (Paramount, 1979) or *The Island* (Universal, 1980). Yet each cost $22 million, and returned in domestic rentals only $5.9, $4.5 and $9.6 million respectively.[54]

In 1966 the MPAA capitulated to strong pressure (since many films were reaching American screens without its authorisation), and withdrew the old Production Code that had imposed pre-censorship on the industry. It replaced it with a system that rated films according to their suitability for specified age groups. This arrangement allowed rating criteria (unlike those of the Production Code) to shift in response to social change and industry pressure. For this reason two important religious groups (one Catholic, the other representing Protestant Churches) withdrew their support for it in 1971, seeing it as licensing permissiveness. Local censorship emerged in some communities which could not accept the changing standards of the MPAA's Ratings Board: effective campaigns were mounted to keep off the screens of some towns movies regarded as offensive.[55]

After some changes in the first years, ratings categories were:

G   General audiences – all admitted.
PG Parental Guidance advised for children – but all admitted.
R   Restricted entry – children under 17 admitted only in the company of a parent.
X   Banned to all children under 17.
Films not submitted for rating could be screened, but must carry an X rating.

In practice the new system generally worked quite well. For good economic reasons most films (whether of American or overseas origin) were submitted for rating. Randall estimates that about 98 per cent of the American movie-going audience on any given day would be viewing rated films. It was this effective because much of the industry believed (a supposition supported by research) that the X-rated film (except for the brief period in the early 1970s when hardcore porn caught popular fancy) would either close out or deter a large part of its audience.[56] It was generally believed that a G rating would lead adults to expect kids' fare; and that PG and R rated films were most likely to do well at the box office. For these reasons producers and marketing experts stipulated carefully, when signing contracts for the production of blockbusters, the MPAA rating they required. Most would be aimed at the PG category.

A retrospective survey of films released between 1969 and 1979 does show that more were in the R (2037) and PG (1836) categories than X (341) or G (720). In other words, the industry acted according to its perception of the market. However, in terms of profitability the important categories were PG and G, with approximately a quarter of their releases taking $1 million or more in domestic rentals. By contrast only about 14 per cent of R-rated and 5 per cent of X-rated films did that well.[57] The actual performance of the market, rather than its supposed behaviour, confirms the continuing significance of the family audience.

While the blockbuster movie was oriented within the paradigms described above, the industry completed its schedules with 'small' films; and these, the majority of releases, and often by the 1980s quite costly films, continued largely to be made by independent production companies. They can be identified by their having been directed at specific sectors of the fragmented audience. Such audiences make themselves known to the industry (it is a circular pattern) by going to see cycles of films which may eventually come to resemble short-lived genres. Thus in the early 1970s a large audience became interested in hardcore porn; but this genre appears to have exhausted its appeal quickly as its novelty passed.[58]

In the late 1960s the studios belatedly discovered that black people would turn out in number for films which featured black heroes and heroines, and were vigorously spiced with sex and violence. Blacks were estimated to be contributing about 10 per cent of the domestic box-office takings; and between 1970 and 1972 some fifty features were released specifically for this audience.[59] From the mid-1970s the supply of black movies dwindled to a trickle, even though the success of *Carwash* (Universal, 1976) showed the market had not disappeared. Monaco speculates that the studios decided that black and white audiences wanted similar fare – action, sex and violence in urban-cop, drug, and caper movies. It may have seemed easier and more safely profitable to replace the black film with the 'crossover' film (like *Sounder* (Twentieth Century-Fox, 1972) and *Lady Sings the Blues* (Paramount, 1972)) in which black themes and roles are filtered through white sensibilities so that the movies can be marketed to white as well as black audiences.[60]

Features intended primarily for adolescents continued to find an audience. From time to time they emerged as among the most profitable of the 'small' movies; and following the success of *Easy Rider* (Columbia, 1969) the music-based movie became, as we have remarked, a sub-genre in its own right. Police, suspense, horror and caper movies were also marketed at this age group through the 1970s and into the 1980s.

During the seventies a successor developed to this market, popular at drive-ins. This was a wide category, including country and road movies. They had plenty of action, often lighthearted violence, and endless conflict between working people (the target audience) and cops, usually in a rural or small-town setting. Monaco sees them as inheriting much of the ethos of AIP's B movies, though they screened as single features. They were characterised by being financed and produced in regions not much exploited by Hollywood – Georgia, Texas and Nebraska. Though about twenty independents worked in this field, they were largely ignored by the studios and reviewers alike. Only after a road movie, *Smokey and the Bandit* (Universal, 1977), earned almost $40 million in rentals did the studios take notice, EMI releasing *Convoy* in 1978 in four-wall theatres.[61]

The art movie of the 1950s and 1960s did continue, often via

imports, for specialist audiences. However, Hollywood colonised
this 'genre' and adapted some of its elements into what became from
the late 1970s a loose grouping of films concerned with 'serious'
issues. Typically they were intimate dramas (often domestic
comedies) that allowed the studios to address those social issues
which, despite their characteristically conservative delay in getting
round to them, would not go away. Many of these 'small' films
served what had been the young audience of the 1960s. In so far as
they dealt with social topics, they usually did so via the personal
lives of a handful of protagonists on whom the plot focused: some
things did not change. Nonetheless some of the social relations
which these films considered came relatively fresh to the American
screen. Some movies responded belatedly to the women's movement
(*An Unmarried Woman* (Twentieth Century-Fox, 1978)); some
centred on marital problems (*Kramer vs Kramer* (Columbia, 1979));
others on growing older and death (*The Big Chill* (Columbia,
1983)).

Over a period of time, the studios discovered that they could
occasionally distribute movies which ran counter to the interests of
American corporate or political power, without damaging their
standing, and to the advantage of their balance sheets. Universal
released two social consciousness films with *Carwash* and *Blue Collar*
(both 1978). And as Talbot and Zheutlin show, in *Godfather II*
(1974) Paramount distributed a film which by implication attacks the
wheeling and dealing of American companies slicing up Cuban
resources. Yet Gulf and Western, Paramount's holding company,
was itself a symbol of US imperial power in the Dominican Republic
(where Coppola's sequences were shot). It owned there a vast sugar
cane operation, a major tourist complex and a local film company.
Paramount presumably decided to distribute the film because it
promised very good profits, and because, especially in the United
States, narrative cinema does not have a record of rousing its
audiences to political activity.[62]

The studios' willingness to sanction in some movies the adoption
of an approximately European seriousness and manner reflected not
only a change in American middle-class values, but also the
continuing deep involvement of the American industry in its overseas
operations. The majors would have counted on giving these
comparatively 'difficult' films the chance of earning well in the
continent which still dominated their export market even though
Japan became the largest single importer of American films in

1984.[63] Although the percentage of the majors' revenues taken abroad declined, that shift was largely caused by the healthy increase in domestic box office takings. And it was more than compensated for by increased penetration in video and ancillary markets.

In general the nature of the industry's commitment to its overseas markets did not change from its state at the end of the 1960s. Runaway production continued – not only abroad, but also in states other than California (New York, Texas, Nebraska and Florida among them), where production companies could pay less than union rates for labour. From the second half of the 1970s this tendency for productions to runaway inland became a distinctive feature of American film and television production. Both state and municipal authorities began to recognise the economic benefits imported with production crews – short-term local employment; a boost to the regional economy, with anything between a quarter and a third of the budget being spent locally; and publicity which might increase both an area's prestige and its tourist potential. By the mid-1980s all fifty states and more than forty major metropolitan centres had set up their own film bureaux. These offices try to attract producers to locations in their territories with offers of a wide range of support services. Such offers can include part-financing of the production; provision of free transport (often by helicopter) to aid the producer reconnoitre locations; assistance with administration; the arrangement of advantageous contracts for lodging, feeding and transporting the company; even the casting of small parts and extras' roles. With the more active bureaux having contacts with skilled local technicians in every trade, visiting production companies began to find there were few disadvantages (and sometimes large savings) in working away from California. Having found the rest of the world in the 1960s, Hollywood appeared to be rediscovering America in the 1970s and 1980s.[64]

As before it remained very difficult for overseas distributors to penetrate the American market. Two large British media groups, EMI and ITC, jointly formed a subsidiary, Associated Film Distributors, in 1979; but the operation was closed down after only a couple of years' trying to equal the American majors on their own territory. Also as before, it continued to be difficult for overseas producers to gain entry to the American market unless via a distribution deal with one of the majors – and such deals were usually arranged, both commercially and artistically, in terms which suited the majors. More often than not this meant that such productions took on an American appearance.[65]

The 1970s and 1980s saw an intensification of the war that had begun after divorcement between the exhibition and distribution arms of the industry. Conant and others report recurrent litigation initiated by distributors against theatres, and vice versa.[66] Yet each side continued to have need of the other. Although exhibitors' dependence on distribution could hardly be missed, it was only in the mid-1980s that the majors began publicly to recognise that, despite the growth in the value to them of outlets in network TV and the newer technologies, they still needed first-run theatrical release as a showcase for product which would probably earn substantial profits outside the cinemas only if it had enjoyed a successful run in them first.

During the 1970s and 1980s distributors sought to maximise their returns from theatres, arguing that this was necessary to counter the increasing risks of the business as costs climbed but admissions did not. We have already seen that they tried to reduce those risks by accepting advances at an early stage against specific productions from the TV networks, and latterly from Pay TV.[67] Now they began to require from exhibitors guaranteed minimum sums, and payment of advances for films which they said would do exceptional business – especially for those to be released during the holidays. Such guarantees would also fix the distributor/exhibitor split and specify a number of additional obligations upon the cinema. During the holidays they would enforce a minimum period of run, which entailed an undertaking to pay for the whole period even if a film was not screened throughout it. For event movies the minimum run could be 12 weeks, which was fine if the film in question was *Jaws* (Universal, 1975) but a catastrophe for the theatre if it was *1941*. Finally, these terms might be enforced as much as a year in advance; and rental contracts often contained a clause prohibiting exhibitors from reviewing terms in the light of the film's performance, a practice which had become almost routine since the 1950s.[68]

As we have seen, in order to limit interest charges on the debts incurred in production and marketing, release now followed quickly upon a feature's completion. Thus exhibitors' guarantees were usually signed without sight of the product. Indeed in 1979 the President of the National Association of Theatre Operators claimed the majors were blind-bidding at least 90 per cent of their movies. Distributors said it was not more than 60–70 per cent.[69] Certainly this was a manipulation of the market that many exhibitors claimed was prejudicial to their interests. In their anger they formed lobbies powerful enough to persuade legislatures in a number of states to outlaw the practice. Distributors responded by grudgingly arranging advance screenings in those states where takings from new releases were buoyant; but they simply boycotted those (mostly in the South) with a relatively modest share of first-run box-office revenue.[70]

Blind-bidding was not, however, as totally dominant a practice as Edgerton's statistic implies because by no means every cinema operator found it necessary to bid for product. A true bid would require unrestricted competition in each area, contracts being agreed with those who offered the best terms. Those terms had to include not only the contractual points mentioned above, but also the vital matter of the split. Three factors inhibited the practice of bidding, whether blind or unrestricted.

Firstly the bargaining power of the theatre circuits, which had grown so strong that they divided the cities between them, enabled them to enforce on distributors negotiated terms of rental. Not only would they obtain a preferential split to those offered to independent exhibitors, but they could demand favourable clearances, often of as much as twenty-five miles. In Edgerton's opinion circuits had not wielded so much power since divorcement.[71] Their strength made it difficult for independent operators to keep in business.

The second mechanism that undermined bidding occurred where a theatre had an arrangement whereby a particular distributor offered it pictures first, on the understanding it gave them first preference over other movies. Thirdly, in many cities and large towns exhibitors colluded to divide the product of the various distributors among them, an arrangement called a product split. In such cases (not to be confused with the distributor/exhibitor split), exhibitors agreed to bid in turn without competing against each other for future releases – and by this means they divided up the majors' output and tried to reduce the terms the distributor could demand.[72] Thus the circuits and operators in urban areas were by no means impotent in the face of distributor demands.

The terms sought by distributors standardised at a 90–10 split for event movies, and altered in favour of the cinema the longer a film ran, when the volume of admissions would be expected to decrease. Such a split would be made after the exhibitor had deducted from the cinema's gross takings an agreed sum for house overheads – known as the 'house nut'. (Typically rental contracts would specify that the distributor should meet a proportion of local advertising costs equivalent to its share in the split.) But after about 1975, distributors began with major films further to harden their terms, demanding that regardless of the agreed split they must be paid 70 per cent of gross takings before deduction of the 'nut'. In such a case, if business happened to be poor the exhibitor might not even get his expenses.[73] Beyond this, they did what they could to insist that cinema operators lifted their admission prices, regardless of circumstances obtaining in the exhibitor's market.

One effect of the product dearth of the 1970s was to return cinemas to a position in which they had been before: it was estimated that in 1978 only 1.5 per cent of their profits came from the admission price; 60 per cent was made from 'concessions': that is, from food, drink, posters, prints, T-shirts, and pinball machines. Theatres had long since discovered that with the audience to all intents and purposes locked in, a person who is going to buy a drink or an ice cream will do so no matter whether it costs twice its selling price on the high street.[74] As we shall see, theatre architecture began to take account of this fact, with foyers being designed to encourage people to spend.

If most of these circumstances imply that the balance of the market had swung heavily in favour of distributors, it has to be added that they could not enforce high returns or blind-bidding while theatres had a wide choice of pictures. In the first half of the 1980s there were marked swings between glut and dearth of product, so that rental terms tended to shift accordingly. It was in the exhibitors' interest that there should be an abundance of movies; but the studios believed their best interests were served by keeping product in short supply.

Two significant factors show that for the cinema chains things were not totally gloomy despite the familiar complaint that they had felt the burden in reduced admissions of almost every development in the entertainment market. Firstly, the old divorced theatre chains either left the business or continued throughout the 1970s to reduce their theatre holdings and to move into other lines of business. Relative newcomers like General Cinema, incorporated in 1950, and now the largest American circuit, invested heavily and moved into market dominance.[75] Secondly, the number of auditoria rose steadily. In 1963 the number of cinemas had dwindled with the decline in the audience to a low point at 12 652. (Thereafter it becomes appropriate to count screens rather than theatres as the nature of cinema architecture changes.) At the beginning of the 1970s there were about 14 000. By 1984, there were over 20 000 and still more were being constructed.[76] But ever fearful of a glut of product similar to that which led to the crisis of 1968–72, distributors tended to argue that exhibitors were bringing their own troubles on themselves by providing too many seats.[77]

Not only were there more screens by the mid-1980s than twenty years before but, as Edgerton shows, the simple increase in numbers disguises more radical changes. For in the same period many cinemas closed. Drive-in theatres, which reached their greatest number at about 4500 in the mid-1950s, had reduced to about 3500 in 1963 and remained at that number through the 1970s. Their takings, which had peaked at nearly 25 per cent of all domestic revenues in 1967, declined to about 21 per cent in 1976.[78] Often the land on which they stood (sometimes wanted for suburban development) was worth more than the business. But even the steady upward movement in the number of four-wall theatres disguises a quite heavy turnover. For example in 1964 when that movement began, the net increase of 88 new screens for the year hides the fact that, since 450 were opened or under construction during the year, about 360 cinemas would appear to have closed.[79]

As we have said, many of those closing were small operators. Theirs were the theatres most likely to be caught up in the blind-bid, guarantee system. When big pictures failed, they took a share of the loss – a drain which many could not afford. Thus most of the investment pouring into new screens came from the theatre chains, which increasingly consolidated their hold on the business. For example, General Cinema grew from 233 screens in 1970 to over 1000 in 1984, and planned to add a further 125. By 1975 the largest six chains owned 1735 screens, or 12.5 per cent of the national total, and their hold on the market was tightening: in 1980 the top four circuits alone possessed 2719 screens – 16 per cent of the total.[80] In addition to the bargaining power their size gave them, they developed the capital backing to allow them to diversify, or were merged into conglomerates. Stanley Warner was linked to Playtex Bras and Sarong Corsets. General Cinema invested heavily in the 1970s in soft drinks franchises, a cognate business from which they derived about 35 per cent of corporate profits.[81] As such confident capital backing suggests, these were cost-conscious and efficient businesses, committed to maximising their profitability. The way they designed and ran their cinemas confirms the fact.

The growing authority of the circuits continued the old trend of the cinema to urbanisation at the expense of rural areas; but this was urbanisation with the difference that the new cinemas were predominantly not of the old downtown type. Edgerton cites the case of the American Multi-Cinema Corporation to show what happened. The company owed much of its success to its anticipation of changes in the suburban market, for in the 1960s the movement of people to the suburbs continued. Both manufacturing and office employment became available so that more and more people were not only living but also working there. Shopping centres grew up on the back of these developments. Multi-Cinema (and presumably its rivals) commissioned demographic research to study potential growth in cities of more than 100 000 population. It looked at the age, income, education and occupations of citizens; and sought to place its new theatres in growing middle-class areas inhabited by college-educated young people – the core of the movie-going audience.

The new theatres differed from the old. Typically the auditorium would be a lot smaller than its predecessors. The average size dropped from 750 seats in 1950 to 500 seats in 1977. And it would be just one cell in a nest, since the new theatre complex (or multiplex) comprised between two and twelve auditoria grouped around central facilities which served them all. In 1979 Multi-Cinema operated 522 screens on 108 sites.[82] A big chain like this could achieve a high concentration of screens, and new kinds of efficiency.

Frequently sited right in the new suburban shopping malls, the new multiplexes had all the advantages of the old drive-ins (informality, inexpensive admission, easy parking) and more: shops and restaurants close to hand, and a choice of programmes. They could offer their audiences variety and attract people of different tastes. Now the family could go together to the cinema, but split up inside the building to see films that suited the age and taste of each person. And the start time of films could be staggered so that casual movie-goers would not have to wait long for a film to start.

Multiplexes usually comprised auditoria of different sizes, with the largest seating perhaps 500 and the smallest 100 or less. This made it easier for a theatre management to hold over a big attraction until public interest in it was exhausted. As audiences dwindled, it could be moved on to successively smaller screens, leaving the larger halls free to do fresh business. Thus long, guaranteed runs of blockbusters held fewer terrors for multiplexes than for single-screen theatres. And the large multiplex could also use its smaller screens to accommodate minority audiences – whose members would often include regular patrons.

This new kind of theatre also made it possible to reduce costs per screen – of great importance at a time when the underlying trend was for no growth in the audience, and profits were being heavily squeezed by the majors. Projection equipment was so fully automated that only one operator needed to be on duty in many multiplexes. One central concourse with snack bar and an increasing array of entertainments served the entire building. Administration was centralised, in that one managerial, accounting, and box-office staff coped with the requirements of all screens; and in the circuits other management functions could be centralised at company head office.[83]

The design of the multiplex is at the furthest possible remove from the baroque extravagance of the picture palace. The cinemas of one chain are likely to resemble those of any other, no matter where in the States they have been constructed. Edgerton cites an experienced theatre constructor heralding the era of the multiplex. The patron should find:

> an auditorium functional in design, a comfortable seat with plenty of leg room and sufficient lighting to prevent groping and tripping; a lobby and foyer with attractive eye appeal, colors harmoniously blended to sooth and yet be admired and a sales area with a head-on shot and equipment which blends with the architectural design and with no unsightly bulges . . .[84]

Decor is deliberately bland to stay attractive beyond the life of any particular fashion; it is neither too modern nor too old-fashioned, so as to offend neither the old nor the young. The design of the central concourse has but one purpose: to put patrons in the humour (with bright, cheerful colours and comfortable surroundings) to buy, and to direct their attention to the sales area. This as often as not will be highlighted, and will have a circular bar for easy access and to give the impression, since there can be no queuing, that service will be swift. Goods are displayed temptingly. As Edgerton remarks, no longer a dream palace, the movie theatre has become a retail outlet as efficient in making consumption a pleasure as any other retail chain – and as undistinctive.[85] While the entertainment on the screen seeks sometimes honourably, sometimes not, to work on the emotions, the shopping mall multiplex does not engage the imagination. Rather its interior reassures, soothes the senses, and directs them to trivial means of immediate further gratification – which require more spending.

Notes and References

1 Inventions and Patents

1. Robert Sklar, *Movie-Made America* (London: Chappell, 1978) p. 12.
2. A. R. Fulton, 'The Machine', in Tino Balio (ed.), *The American Film Industry*, rev. edn. (London: University of Wisconsin Press, 1985) pp. 35–6.
3. Ibid., pp. 32–3.
4. Sklar, pp. 10, 13.
5. Balio, *The American Film Industry*, rev. edn, p. 10.
6. Garth Jowett, *Film: The Democratic Art* (Boston: Little, Brown, 1976) p. 28.
7. Robert C. Allen, 'The Movies in Vaudeville', in Balio, *The American Film Industry*, pp. 63–71, 81–2.
8. Benjamin B. Hampton, *History of the American Film Industry* (1931) (New York: Dover, 1970) pp. 18–19.
9. Balio, *The American Film Industry*, rev. edn, p. 10.
10. David Bordwell, Janet Staiger and Kristin Thompson, *The Classical Hollywood Cinema* (London: Routledge & Kegan Paul, 1985) p. 114.
11. Balio, *The American Film Industry*, rev. edn, pp. 6–7.
12. Ibid., p. 10; Lewis Jacobs, *The Rise of the American Film* (1939) (New York: Teachers College Press, 1975) p. 4.
13. Bordwell, Staiger and Thompson, p. 159.
14. Robert C. Allen, 'Contra the Chaser Theory', in J. L. Fell (ed.), *Film Before Griffith* (London: University of California Press, 1983) pp. 108ff.
15. Ibid., pp. 109–12.
16. Sklar, pp. 4, 14.
17. Edward Lowry, 'Edwin J. Hadley: Travelling Film Exhibitor', in Fell, *Film Before Griffith*, pp. 131, 142.

2 Nickelodeons and Narrative

1. Jacobs, p. 23.
2. Ibid., p. 25.
3. Ibid., pp. 5–6.
4. Russell Merritt, 'Nickelodeon Theatres 1905–1914: Building an Audience for the Movies', in Balio, *The American Film Industry*, rev. edn, p. 83.
5. Sklar, p. 16.
6. Kevin Brownlow and John Kobal, *Hollywood: The Pioneers* (London: Collins, 1979) p. 46.
7. Sklar, p. 16.
8. Brownlow and Kobal, p. 46.
9. Lary May, *Screening Out the Past* (New York: Oxford UP, 1980) p. 38;

Charlotte Herzog, 'The Archaeology of Cinema Architecture', *Quarterly Review of Film Studies*, 9, 1 (Winter 1984), p. 16.
10. Sklar, p. 24.
11. Merritt, in Balio, *The American Film Industry*, rev. edn, pp. 85–6.
12. Sklar, pp. 29–30; Robert Anderson, 'The Role of the Western Film Genre in Industry Competition, 1907–1911', *Journal of the University Film Association*, 31, 2 (Spring 1979) pp. 21–2.
13. Jowett, pp. 5–7, 11.
14. May, pp. 27–8.
15. Ibid., p. 38.
16. Ibid., pp. 16ff.
17. Ibid., pp. 28–32.
18. Ibid., pp. 36–8.
19. Sklar, p. 41.
20. Merritt, in Balio, *The American Film Industry*, rev. edn, pp. 95–6.
21. Jowett, p. 101.
22. Jacobs, p. 49.
23. Bordwell, Staiger and Thompson, pp. 115–16, citing Robert C. Allen; Balio, *The American Film Industry*, rev. edn, p. 20.
24. Peter Baxter, 'On the History and Ideology of Film Lighting', *Screen*, 16, 3 (Autumn 1975) pp. 90–2.
25. Hampton, pp. 24, 49.
26. Balio, *The American Film Industry*, rev. edn, pp. 16–17.
27. Ibid., p. 17.
28. Jacobs, p. 53.
29. Ibid.

3 The Motion Picture Patents Company

1. Jeanne Thomas Allen, 'The Decay of the Motion Picture Patents Company', in Balio, *The American Film Industry*, 1st edn, p. 120.
2. Sklar, pp. 34–5.
3. Kristin Thompson, *Exporting Entertainment* (London: British Film Institute, 1985) pp. 2–12; Anderson, 'The Role of the Western Film Genre', p. 21.
4. Reese V. Jenkins, *Images and Enterprise* (London: Johns Hopkins UP, 1975) p. 285.
5. Jacobs, p. 82; J. T. Allen, in Balio, *The American Film Industry*, 1st edn, pp. 120–2.
6. J. T. Allen, in Balio, *The American Film Industry*, 1st edn, p. 122.
7. Jenkins, pp. 284–5.
8. J. T. Allen, in Balio, *The American Film Industry*, 1st edn, p. 122.
9. Ibid., pp. 123–6; Ralph Cassady, Jr., 'Monopoly in Motion Picture Production and Distribution: 1908–1915', *Southern California Law Review*, 32 (Summer 1959) pp. 355–8.
10. J. T. Allen, in Balio, *The American Film Industry*, 1st edn, p. 126.
11. Jenkins, p. 285.
12. Cassady, 'Monopoly in Motion Picture Production', p. 360.

13. J. T. Allen, in Balio, *The American Film Industry*, 1st edn, p. 126. Cassady, 'Monopoly in Motion Picture Production', pp. 359–61; Hampton, pp. 70–1.
14. Merritt, in Balio, *The American Film Industry*, rev. edn, p. 86.
15. Cassady, 'Monopoly in Motion Picture Production', pp. 342–3.
16. Sklar, pp. 37–8.
17. Tom Gunning, 'Weaving a Narrative: Style and Economic Background in Griffith's Biograph Films', *Quarterly Review of Film Studies*, 6, 1 (Winter 1981) p. 15.
18. Sklar, pp. 37–8.
19. May, pp. 43–9.
20. Sklar, pp. 31–2.
21. May, p. 63.
22. Sklar, p. 32.
23. May, p. 64.
24. Sklar, p. 29.
25. Jacobs, p. 148.
26. May, p. 63.
27. Jacobs, p. 137.
28. Ibid., pp. 137ff; May, ch. 3.
29. Gunning, p. 15.
30. Jacobs, p. 137.
31. Ibid., pp. 138–41.
32. Gunning, p. 16.
33. Jacobs, pp. 130–2.
34. Bordwell, Staiger and Thompson, pp. 123–4.
35. Sklar, p. 41.
36. J. T. Allen, in Balio, *The American Film Industry*, 1st edn, pp. 126–8.
37. Robert H. Stanley, *The Celluloid Empire* (New York: Hastings House, 1978) p. 12.
38. Robert Anderson, 'The Motion Picture Patents Company: A Re-valuation', in Balio, *The American Film Industry*, rev. edn, pp. 140–1, 145.

4 Independents, Innovation, and the Beginnings of Hollywood

1. Thompson, *Exporting Entertainment*, p. 14.
2. Cassady, 'Monopoly in Motion Picture Production', p. 364.
3. Sklar, pp. 38–9.
4. Jenkins, pp. 287–8.
5. Quoted by Jenkins, p. 286.
6. Cassady, 'Monopoly in Motion Picture Production', p. 367.
7. Brownlow and Kobal, pp. 55–6.
8. Cassady, 'Monopoly in Motion Picture Production', pp. 368–9.
9. Thompson, p. 22.
10. Anthony Slide, *Early American Cinema* (London: A. Zwemmer, 1970) pp. 96–7.
11. Richard Dyer, *Stars* (London: British Film Institute, 1979) p. 10.

12. Mae D. Huettig, *Economic Control of the Motion Picture Industry* (Philadelphia: University of Pennsylvania Press, 1944), p. 25; Gorham Kindem (ed.), *The American Movie Industry* (Carbondale: Southern Illinois UP, 1982) pp. 80–2. Kindem notes that Trust members Vitagraph and Edison imitated Laemmle's initiative quickly; other Trust members held back.
13. Timothy James Lyons, *The Silent Partner* (New York: Arno Press, 1974) p. 30.
14. Cassady, 'Monopoly in Motion Picture Production', pp. 370–2.
15. Lyons, pp. 175–6.
16. Ibid.
17. Ibid., pp. 71–2.
18. Stanley, pp. 14–15.
19. Sklar, p. 37.
20. Lyons, pp. 176–9.
21. Ibid.
22. See for instance Brownlow and Kobal, ch. 6.
23. For example, such a claim was made by Hampton, p. 79.
24. Sklar, p. 67.
25. Brownlow and Kobal, p. 55.
26. Ibid., p. 90.
27. Sklar, pp. 67–8.
28. May, p. 168.
29. Ibid., pp. 184–6.
30. Ibid.
31. Ibid.
32. Cassady, 'Monopoly in Motion Picture Production', p. 374.
33. Merritt, in Balio, *The American Film Industry*, rev. edn, p. 86.
34. Ibid., p. 102.
35. J. Douglas Gomery, 'The Coming of the Talkies: Invention, Innovation, and Diffusion', in Balio, *The American Film Industry*, 1st edn, pp. 193–4; and 'Problems in Film History: How Fox Innovated Sound', *Quarterly Review of Film Studies*, 1, 3 (Aug 1976) p. 316.
36. Balio, *The American Film Industry*, rev. edn, p. 110; Sklar, pp. 42–4.
37. Sklar, p. 50.
38. Hampton, pp. 141–5.
39. Janet Wasko, *Movies and Money* (Norwood, NJ: Ablex Publishing, 1982) p. 9.
40. Cassady, 'Monopoly in Motion Picture Production', p. 377; Balio, *The American Film Industry*, rev. edn, pp. 111–2.
41. Hampton, p. 107.
42. Cassady, 'Monopoly in Motion Picture Production', p. 381.

5 Architecture of the Feature Film

1. May, p. 150.
2. Merritt, in Balio, *The American Film Industry*, rev. edn, p. 99.
3. May, p. 150.

4. Ben M. Hall, *The Golden Age of the Movie Palace* (New York: Clarkson N. Potter, 1961) p. 95.
5. May, pp. 150–1.
6. Ibid., pp. 153, 164.
7. Ibid., pp. 153–4; Herzog, 'The Archaeology of Cinema Architecture', pp. 11–32.
8. Q. David Bowers, *Nickelodeon Theatres and their Music* (Vestal, NY: Vestal Press, 1986) pp. 131ff.
9. Merritt, in Balio, *The American Film Industry*, rev. edn, p. 98, citing Frederic C. Howe.
10. See for instance Merritt's account of changes in Boston, in Balio, *The American Film Industry*, rev. edn, pp. 100–1.
11. Ibid., p. 101.
12. Douglas Gomery, *The Hollywood Studio System* (London: British Film Institute/Macmillan, 1986) p. 17.
13. Merritt, in Balio, *The American Film Industry*, rev. edn, pp. 101–2.
14. May, p. 147.
15. Ibid.
16. Hall, pp. 95–102.
17. Ibid., pp. 106–13.
18. May, p. 156.
19. Douglas Gomery, 'The Picture Palace: Economic Sense or Hollywood Nonsense?', *Quarterly Review of Film Studies*, 3, 1 (Winter 1978) pp. 24–5.
20. Hampton, p. 204.
21. Hall, pp. 20–1; Gomery, 'The Picture Palace', p. 25.
22. Gomery, 'The Picture Palace', p. 25.
23. May, p. 157.
24. Sklar, p. 45.
25. Peter Baxter, 'On the History and Ideology of Film Lighting', pp. 96–7.
26. Charlotte Herzog, 'Movie Palaces and Exhibition', *Film Reader*, 2 (1977) pp. 185–97 gives a full account of these astonishing effects.
27. Peter Baxter, pp. 98–9.
28. Ibid., pp. 102–3.
29. Martin Levin, *Hollywood and the Great Fan Magazines* (New York: Arbor House, 1977) pp. 7–8; Jacobs, p. 282; Cathy Klaprat, 'The Star as Market Strategy', in Balio, *The American Film Industry*, rev. edn, pp. 354–5.
30. Hampton, pp. 97–8; Balio, *The American Film Industry*, rev. edn, pp. 116–7.
31. Sklar, pp. 142–3.
32. Jacobs, p. 160; Balio, *The American Film Industry*, rev. edn, p. 117.
33. Balio, *The American Film Industry*, rev. edn, pp. 117–8.
34. Jacobs, p. 163.
35. Balio, *The American Film Industry*, rev. edn, p. 119.
36. Tino Balio, *United Artists* (London: University of Wisconsin Press, 1976) pp. 35–6.
37. Huettig, p. 22.
38. Balio, *The American Film Industry*, rev. edn, p. 120.

39. Jacobs, p. 289.
40. Ibid., pp. 166, 289.
41. Balio, *The American Film Industry*, rev. edn, p. 163.
42. Balio, *The American Film Industry*, rev. edn, pp. 162–3; and *United Artists*, pp. 11–14.
43. Balio, *The American Film Industry*, rev. edn, p. 121.
44. Hampton, pp. 254–8.
45. Ibid., p. 278.
46. Balio, *The American Film Industry*, rev. edn, p. 121.
47. Wasko, p. 32.
48. Jacobs, p. 288.
49. Huettig, pp. 74–84.
50. Balio, *United Artists*, pp. 63–4.
51. Gomery, 'The Picture Palace', p. 26.
52. Jeanne Allen, 'The Film Viewer as Consumer', *Quarterly Review of Film Studies*, 5, 4 (Fall 1980) p. 484.
53. Douglas Gomery, 'The Movies Become Big Business: Publix Theatres and the Chain Store Strategy', *Cinema Journal*, 18, 2 (Spring 1979) pp. 26–40.
54. Ibid., pp. 31–8.
55. Ibid.
56. Sklar, p. 82; David Robinson, *Hollywood in the Twenties* (London: A. Zwemmer, 1968) pp. 16–19.
57. Hampton, pp. 248–50.

6   Standardising Production and Consumption

1. Richard Dyer, *Stars* (London: British Film Institute, 1979) *passim.*
2. Klaprat, in Balio, *The American Film Industry*, rev. edn, pp. 355, 369–72.
3. I. G. Edmonds, *Big U: Universal in the Silent Days* (London: Thomas Yoseloff, 1977) p. 36.
4. Jacobs, pp. 162–4.
5. Robert McLaughlin, *Broadway and Hollywood* (New York: Arno Press, 1974) pp. 53–65.
6. Bordwell, Staiger and Thompson, p. 99.
7. Huettig, p. 88.
8. Janet Staiger, 'Dividing Labor for Production Control: Thomas Ince and the Rise of the Studio System', in Kindem, pp. 94–103.
9. Ibid., p. 96.
10. Herbert Braverman, *Labor and Monopoly Capital*, cited in Staiger, ibid., p. 97.
11. Staiger, p. 97.
12. Janet Staiger, '"Tame" Authors and the Corporate Laboratory: Stories, Writers, and Scenarios in Hollywood', *Quarterly Review of Film Studies*, 8, 4 (Fall 1983) pp. 37–8.
13. Ibid., pp. 37–41.
14. Jacobs, pp. 295–6.

15. Thompson, pp. 40–1, 89.
16. Sklar, pp. 225–6.
17. Albert E. Smith, *Two Reels and a Crank* (Garden City, NY: Doubleday, 1952) pp. 251–2.
18. Thompson, p. 3.
19. Thomas H. Guback, 'Hollywood's International Market', in Balio, *The American Film Industry*, rev. edn, p. 465.
20. William K. Everson, *American Silent Film* (New York: Oxford UP, 1978) p. 100.
21. Thompson, pp. 30–2.
22. Ibid., pp. 71, 78.
23. Sklar, p. 47.
24. Guback, in Balio, *The American Film Industry*, rev. edn, p. 465.
25. Ibid., pp. 466–7.
26. Ibid., pp. 468–9.
27. Thompson, pp. 117ff.
28. Hampton, pp. 351–2.
29. Jeanne Allen, 'The Film Viewer as Consumer', p. 484.
30. May, p. 167.
31. Hampton, p. 313.
32. May, pp. 109–46; Jacobs, p. 282; and Robinson, pp. 34–5.
33. May, pp. 209–12 and ch. 8 *passim*.
34. Jacobs, p. 338.
35. May, pp. 232–6.
36. Charles Eckert, 'The Carole Lombard in Macy's Window', *Quarterly Review of Film Studies*, 3, 1 (Winter 1978) p. 7.
37. Cecil B. De Mille cited by Eckert, ibid.
38. Garth Jowett, 'Bullets, Beer and the Hays Office: *Public Enemy* (1931)', in John E. O'Connor and Martin A. Jackson, *American History/American Film* (New York: Frederick Ungar, 1979) p. 61.
39. May, pp. 164–5.
40. Jeanne Allen, 'The Film Viewer as Consumer', pp. 484–6.
41. May, pp. 189–90.
42. Ibid., pp. 86–92.
43. Arthur F. McClure (ed.), *The Movies: An American Idiom* (Rutherford: Fairleigh Dickinson UP, 1971) pp. 122–6.
44. Neville March Hunnings, *Film Censors and the Law* (London: George Allen & Unwin, 1967) pp. 153–4.
45. Ibid., p. 154; *Fortune*, 'The Hays Office', in Balio, *The American Film Industry*, 1st edn, p. 304.
46. Raymond Moley, *The Hays Office* (Indianapolis: Bobbs-Merrill, 1945) pp. 58–9.
47. McClure, p. 133.
48. Will Hays cited by May, p. 205.
49. May, p. 205.
50. *Fortune*, 'The Hays Office', pp. 310–11.
51. Guback, in Balio, *The American Film Industry*, rev. edn, p. 470.
52. Murray Ross, *Stars and Strikes* (1941) (New York: AMS Press, 1967) p. 214.

53. Sklar, pp. 83–4.
54. Ibid., p. 84.

7 **The Coming of Sound**

1. Gomery, in Balio, *The American Film Industry*, 1st edn, pp. 193–4.
2. Douglas Gomery, 'Writing the History of the American Film Industry: Warner Brothers and Sound', *Screen*, 17, 1 (Spring 1976) p. 46; Charles Higham, *Warner Brothers* (New York: Charles Scribner's Sons, 1975) pp. 40–5.
3. Gomery, 'Writing the History of the American Film Industry', pp. 45–6.
4. Ibid., p. 47.
5. Ibid., pp. 48–51.
6. Hampton, p. 369.
7. Robinson, p. 18; Alexander Walker, *The Shattered Silents* (London: Elm Tree Books, 1978) p. 5.
8. William K. Everson, *American Silent Film* (New York: Oxford UP, 1978) pp. 290–1.
9. Hall, pp. 71–4.
10. Walker, p. 5; Gomery, 'Writing the History of the American Film Industry', p. 49.
11. Gomery, in Balio, *The American Film Industry*, 1st edn, pp. 200–1.
12. Balio, *United Artists*, p. 75; and Walker, p. 6.
13. Walker, p. 12.
14. Ibid., p. 42.
15. Douglas Gomery, 'The "Warner-Vitaphone Peril": the American Film Industry Reacts to the Innovation of Sound', in Kindem, p. 120.
16. Walker, p. 21.
17. Ibid., pp. 27, 42.
18. Gomery, 'Writing the History of the American Film Industry', p. 52.
19. Gomery, 'Problems in Film History', pp. 318–19.
20. Ibid., pp. 320–1.
21. Ibid., pp. 321–2.
22. Ibid., p. 323.
23. Douglas Gomery, 'Failure and Success: Vocafilm and RCA Photophone Innovate sound', *Film Reader*, 2 (1977) pp. 215–17.
24. Ibid., pp. 217–18.
25. Richard Maltby, 'The Political Economy of Hollywood: The Studio System', in Philip Davies and Brian Neve (eds), *Cinema, Politics and Society in America* (Manchester UP, 1981) pp. 46–8.
26. McLaughlin, p. 285.
27. Hampton, p. 399.
28. Walker, p. 201.
29. Norman Mailer, *The Armies of the Night* (Harmondsworth: Penguin Books, 1968) p. 167.
30. Higham, *Warner Brothers*, p. 89.
31. Hall, pp. 248–9.
32. Thompson, p. 159.

33. Walker, p. 82; John Shepherd, *Tin Pan Alley* (London: Routledge & Kegan Paul, 1982) pp. 84–6.
34. Fred E. Basten, *Glorious Technicolor* (London: Thomas Yoseloff, 1979) pp. 40–1, 46.
35. Wasko, p. 49.

8 Product Differentiation in the 1930s

1. Nick Roddick, *A New Deal in Entertainment* (London: British Film Institute, 1983) p. 24.
2. Ibid.
3. Leo C. Rosten, *Hollywood* (1941) (New York: Arno Press and New York Times, 1970) p. 246.
4. Roddick, p. 8.
5. Ibid., p. 28.
6. Ibid., chs 5 and 6.
7. Ibid., ch. 9.
8. Ibid., pp. 68–9.
9. William K. Everson, *American Silent Film* (New York: Oxford UP, 1978) pp. 317–33.
10. Roy Pickard, *The Hollywood Studios* (London: Frederick Muller, 1978) p. 72; John Baxter, *Hollywood in the Thirties* (London: Tantivy Press, 1968) pp. 33–4.
11. Pickard, p. 92.
12. Howard T. Lewis, *The Motion Picture Industry* (New York: Van Nostrand 1933) (Jerome S. Ozer, 1971) p. 88.
13. Pickard, p. 336.
14. John Baxter, *Hollywood in the Thirties*, p. 33.
15. Pickard, pp. 340–1.
16. Maltby, in Davies and Neve, *Cinema, Politics and Society*, pp. 49–50; Gomery, *The Hollywood Studio System*, pp. 59–60.
17. Gomery, *Hollywood Studio System*, pp. 63–5.
18. Balio, *United Artists*, pp. 78–9; Walker, pp. 43–4.
19. Orville Goldner and George E. Turner, *The Making of King Kong* (London: Tantivy Press, 1975) pp. 101ff.
20. James Naremore, *The Magic World of Orson Welles* (New York: Oxford UP, 1978) p. 26; and Pickard, pp. 393–8, 409–18.
21. Balio, *United Artists*, pp. 65–6 and *passim*.
22. Ibid., *passim*.
23. I. G. Edmonds, *Big U: Universal in the Silent Days* (London: Thomas Yoseloff, 1977) p. 129.
24. Hampton, pp. 321–2.
25. Sklar, pp. 178–9.
26. Gomery, *The Hollywood Studio System*, pp. 150–1.
27. Lewis, pp. 339–43.
28. Stanley, p. 95.
29. Ibid., pp. 95–6; Rosten, pp. 256–8.

30. Edward Buscombe, 'Notes on Columbia Pictures Corporation, 1926–41', *Screen* 16, 3 (Autumn 1975) pp. 75–6.
31. Gomery, *The Hollywood Studio System*, p. 169.
32. Ibid., p. 165.
33. Hampton, pp. 322–3; Pickard, p. 283.
34. Roddick, pp. 253–4.
35. John E. O'Connor, 'A Reaffirmation of American Ideals: *Drums Along the Mohawk*', in O'Connor and Jackson, p. 112.
36. William J. Fadiman, 'The Sources of Movies', in Gordon S. Watkins (ed.), *The Motion Picture Industry*, Annals of the American Academy of Political and Social Science, 254 (1947) pp. 37–40.

9 Depression and the Mature Oligopoly

1. Wasko, p. 70.
2. Ibid., p. 71.
3. Ibid., p. 50, citing *Moody's Industrial Manuals*.
4. Ibid., pp. 49–51; Balio, *The American Film Industry*, rev. edn, p. 256.
5. Balio, *The American Film Industry*, rev. edn, p. 255.
6. Andrew Bergman, *We're in the Money* (New York UP, 1971) p. xx.
7. Ibid., p. xxii.
8. Jacobs, p. 423.
9. Gomery, *The Hollywood Studio System*, p. 110.
10. Balio, *The American Film Industry*, rev. edn, pp. 255–6.
11. Wasko, pp. 75–6.
12. Ibid., p. 92.
13. Sklar, pp. 164–5.
14. Gomery, *The Hollywood Studio System*, pp. 86–7, 93–5.
15. Ibid., p. 57.
16. John C. Strick, 'The Economics of the Motion Picture Industry: a Survey', *Philosophy of the Social Sciences*, 8, 4 (Dec 1978) p. 408.
17. Barry R. Litman, 'The Economics of the Television Market for Theatrical Movies', in Kindem, p. 309.
18. Ibid.
19. Bordwell, Staiger and Thompson, p. 315.
20. Todd McCarthy and Charles Flynn, *Kings of the Bs* (New York: E. P. Dutton, 1975) p. 15.
21. Paul Kerr, 'Out of What Past? Notes on the B Film Noir', *Screen Education*, 32–3 (Autumn–Winter 1979–80) p. 51.
22. Ibid.; McCarthy and Flynn, p. 17.
23. Gomery, *The Hollywood Studio System*, pp. 45, 71–2, 169.
24. Kerr, 'Out of What Past?', p. 63.
25. Ibid., pp. 51–2; and McCarthy and Flynn, p. 22.
26. Nick Grinde, 'Pictures for Peanuts', in R. K. N. Baxter (ed.), *The Penguin Film Review*, 1 (1946) pp. 40–51.
27. Richard Maurice Hurst, *Republic Studios* (London: Scarecrow Press, 1979) pp. 2, 71.
28. Ibid., p. 61.

29. Ibid., pp. 125–8.
30. Bergman, p. xxii.
31. Sklar, p. 169; Gomery, *The Hollywood Studio System*, p. 21, and 'The Popularity of Filmgoing in the US, 1930–1950', in Colin MacCabe (ed.), *High Theory/Low Culture* (Manchester UP, 1986) pp. 76–7.
32. Gomery, *The Hollywood Studio System*, p. 21.
33. Martin Levin, *Hollywood and the Great Fan Magazines* (New York: Arbor House, 1977), pp. 7–8; Kindem, pp. 79, 84; and Gomery, *The Hollywood Studio System*, p. 7.
34. Eckert, pp. 4–5.
35. Ibid., pp. 11–14; Gomery, *The Hollywood Studio System*, p. 46.
36. Eckert, pp. 6–9.
37. Ibid., pp. 14–17.
38. Richard Schickel, *The Disney Version* (London: Michael Joseph, 1986) pp. 163–5.
39. Eckert, pp. 17–18.
40. Ibid., pp. 18–19; Gomery, *The Hollywood Studio System*, pp. 43–5.
41. Shepherd, pp. 96–8.
42. Eckert, p. 20.
43. Sklar, p. 177.
44. Moley, pp. 61–7.
45. Bergman, pp. 4–5.
46. Sklar, pp. 173–4.
47. Balio, *The American Film Industry*, rev. edn, p. 269.
48. Ibid.; Sklar, p. 173.
49. Balio, *The American Film Industry*, rev. edn, p. 270; and Hunnings, p. 158.
50. Hunnings, pp. 158–9.
51. Sklar, p. 175.
52. Bergman, pp. 83–7.
53. See Sklar, pp. 179–81.
54. Bergman, *passim*.
55. Sklar, pp. 185–7; Gomery, *The Hollywood Studio System*, p. 41.
56. The Breen Office, cited by Hugh Fordin, '*On the Town*', in Paul Kerr (ed.), *The Hollywood Film Industry* (London: Routledge & Kegan Paul/British Film Institute, 1986) pp. 69–70.
57. Balio, *The American Film Industry*, rev. edn, p. 271.
58. Sklar, pp. 189–91.
59. Balio, *The American Film Industry*, rev. edn, pp. 257–60; Sklar, p. 168.
60. Huettig, p. 123.
61. Balio, *The American Film Industry*, rev. edn; but see a differing view in Sklar, pp. 168–9.
62. Murray Ross, 'Labor Relations in Hollywood', in Watkins, pp. 60–1; Balio, *The American Film Industry*, rev. edn, pp. 273–9; Sklar, pp. 170–2; and Gomery, *The Hollywood Studio System*, p. 10.

10 War, Prosperity, Divorce and Loss

1. Lewis Jacobs, 'World War II and the American Film', in McClure, pp. 164–7; Balio, *The American Film Industry*, rev. edn, p. 283.
2. Jacobs, 'World War II in the American Film, p. 168; Colin Shindler, *Hollywood Goes to War* (London: Routledge & Kegan Paul, 1979) p. 39.
3. Guback, in Balio, *The American Film Industry*, rev. edn, pp. 469–70.
4. Shindler, p. 18.
5. Moley, pp. 181–4.
6. Balio, *The American Film Industry*, rev. edn, p. 280.
7. Shindler, p. 28.
8. Balio, *The American Film Industry*, rev. edn, pp. 280–1.
9. Dorothy B. Jones, 'The Hollywood War Film: 1942–44', *Hollywood Quarterly*, 1, 1 (Oct 1945) p. 13.
10. Shindler, p. 28.
11. Jowett, *Film*, p. 316.
12. Hurst, pp. 55–6.
13. Shindler, pp. 12–13; Jacobs, 'World War II', p. 162.
14. Shindler, pp. 13, 21.
15. Jacobs, p. 156.
16. Ibid., pp. 175–6.
17. Shindler, p. 96.
18. Leo A. Handel, *Hollywood Looks at its Audience* (1950) (New York: Arno Press, 1976) p. 4.
19. Ibid., pp. 152–3.
20. Charles Higham and Joel Greenberg, *Hollywood in the Forties* (London: Tantivy Press, 1968) p. 14.
21. Margaret Farrand Thorpe, *America at the Movies* (1939) (New York: Arno Press, 1970) pp. 7–8.
22. Shindler, p. 88.
23. Sylvia Harvey, 'Woman's place', in E. Ann Kaplan (ed.), *Women in Film Noir* (London: British Film Institute, 1978) pp. 22–34.
24. Michael Pye and Lynda Myles, *The Movie Brats* (London: Faber & Faber, 1979) pp. 28–31; Sklar, p. 274.
25. Handel, pp. 99–108.
26. Sklar, p. 271.
27. McCarthy and Flynn, p. 35.
28. Margaret Farrand Thorpe, *America at the Movies* (1939) (New York: Arno Press, 1970) pp. 8–10.
29. Ibid., p. 9.
30. Thomas Cripps, *Slow Fade to Black* (London: Oxford UP, 1977) p. 110.
31. Wasko, p. 109.
32. Guback, in Balio, *The American Film Industry*, rev. edn, pp. 470–5, 'Non-Market Factors in the International Distribution of American Films', in Bruce A. Austin (ed.), *Current Research in Film*, vol. 1 (Norwood, NJ: Ablex Publishing, 1985) pp. 116–17, and 'Shaping the Film Business in Postwar Germany', in Kerr, *The Hollywood Film Industry*, p. 252.

33. Guback, 'Hollywood's International Market', in Balio, *The American Film Industry*, rev. edn, p. 475.
34. Balio, *The American Film Industry*, rev. edn, p. 407.
35. Ibid., p. 408.
36. Balio, *The American Film Industry*, 1st edn, p. 226.
37. Pickard, pp. 285–8.
38. Balio, *United Artists, passim*.
39. Gomery, *The Hollywood Studio System*, pp. 153–4, 157.
40. James Naremore, *The Magic World of Orson Welles* (New York: Oxford UP, 1978) pp. 26–7, 104.
41. Kerr, 'Out of What Past?', pp. 53–4.
42. Sklar, p. 170.
43. Kerr, 'Out of What Past?', p. 57, and 'My Name is Joseph H. Lewis', *Screen*, 24, 4–5 (Jul–Oct 1983) p. 50.
44. Kerr, 'My Name is Joseph H. Lewis', pp. 50–2.
45. Kerr, 'Out of What Past?', pp. 53–6.
46. Temporary National Economic Committee, *The Motion Picture Industry – A Pattern of Control* (Washington: US Government, 1941) pp. 77–9.
47. Balio, *The American Film Industry*, rev. edn, pp. 402–3.
48. Ibid.; Ralph Cassady, 'Impact of the Paramount Decision on Motion Picture Distribution and Price Making', *Southern California Law Review*, 31 (1958) pp. 158–60; Simon N. Whitney, 'Antitrust Policies and the Motion Picture Industry', in Kindem, pp. 166–72.
49. Balio, *The American Film Industry*, rev. edn, pp. 403–4, and *United Artists*, pp. 226–8.
50. Ernest Borneman, 'United States Versus Hollywood', in Balio, *The American Film Industry*, rev. edn, pp. 459–60.
51. Ibid., p. 460.
52. Michael Conant, 'The Impact of the *Paramount* Decrees', in Balio, *The American Film Industry*, 1st edn, p. 368.
53. Borneman, in Balio, *The American Film Industry*, rev. edn, p. 462.
54. Conant, in Balio, *The American Film Industry*, 1st edn, p. 356.
55. Ibid., pp. 358–9.
56. Pye and Myles, p. 19.
57. Stanley, pp. 126–7.
58. Higham and Greenberg, p. 15.
59. Conant, in Balio, *The American Film Industry*, 1st edn, p. 357.
60. Ibid., pp. 359–60.
61. Janet Staiger, 'Individualism Versus Collectivism', *Screen*, 24, 4–5 (Jul–Oct 1983) pp. 68–9.
62. Ibid., p. 70.
63. Ibid., pp. 71–3; Conant, in Balio, *The American Film Industry*, 1st edn, p. 350.
64. Conant, in Balio, *The American Film Industry*, 1st edn, p. 349.
65. Staiger, 'Individualism versus Collectivism', p. 72.
66. Wasko, pp. 108–9, 137–42.
67. Conant, in Balio, *The American Film Industry*, 1st edn, p. 353; Terry

B. Sanders, 'The Financing of Independent Feature Films', *Quarterly of Film, Radio and Television*, 9 (1954–5), pp. 381–3.
68. Conant, in Balio, *The American Film Industry*, 1st edn, p. 352.
69. Gary R. Edgerton, *American Film Exhibition and an Analysis of the Motion Picture Industry's Market Structure, 1963–1980* (London: Garland Publishing, 1983) pp. 22–4.
70. Ibid.; and Conant, in Balio, *The American Film Industry*, 1st edn, pp. 347–8.
71. Conant, in Balio, *The American Film Industry*, 1st edn, pp. 364–7; Richard Maltby, 'Political and Stylistic Interactions in the American Cinema of the Consensus, 1930–1970', (unpublished doctoral dissertation: University of Exeter, 1978) pp. 32–4.
72. Conant, in Balio, *The American Film Industry*, 1st edn, p. 369.
73. Ibid., p. 363.
74. Sklar, p. 273.

11 Hollywood in Transition

1. Balio, *United Artists*, pp. 210–4.
2. Wasko, pp. 110–11, 117.
3. Shindler, p. 111.
4. Ibid., pp. 120–1.
5. Ibid., pp. 132–3.
6. Andrew Dowdy, *Films of the Fifties* (New York: William Morrow & Co., 1975) pp. 38–9.
7. Michael Conant, *Antitrust in the Motion Picture Industry* (Berkeley: University of California Press, 1960) pp. 10–11.
8. Frederic Stuart, *The Effects of Television on the Motion Picture and Radio Industries* (New York: Arno Press, 1976) pp. 24–7.
9. Gomery, *The Hollywood Studio System*, pp. 36–7.
10. Gomery, 'The History of the American Film: Methodology, Industry, and Technology' (unpublished paper given to La Mostra Internazionale del Nuovo Cinema, Ancona, Dec 1982) p. 15; Pye and Myles, p. 21.
11. Gomery, 'The History of the American Film', op. cit., pp. 16–19.
12. Richard Dyer MacCann, *Hollywood in Transition*, 2nd edn, (Westport, Conn.: Greenwood Press, 1977) p. 10.
13. Balio, *United Artists*, pp. 224–5.
14. Balio, *The American Film Industry*, rev. edn, p. 433; Stanley, p. 168.
15. Richard Griffith, *The Movie Stars* (Garden City, NY: Doubleday & Co., 1970) p. 421.
16. Kindem, p. 156.
17. Ibid., pp. 152–3.
18. Ibid., pp. 153–4; Basten, pp. 141–6; Dudley Andrew, 'The Post-War Struggle for Colour', in Teresa de Lauretis and Stephen Heath (eds), *The Cinematic Apparatus* (London: Macmillan, 1980) p. 71.
19. Kerr, 'Out of What Past?', p. 62; Basten, p. 146.
20. Kindem, pp. 156–7.
21. Kerr, 'Out of What Past?', p. 62.

22. Kindem, p. 154.
23. Ibid., p. 154–6.
24. Peter Wollen, *Readings and Writings* (London: Verso, 1982) p. 174.
25. Charles Higham, *Hollywood at Sunset* (New York: Saturday Review Press, 1972) pp. 81–9; Stanley, pp. 161–4; Dowdy, pp. 46–51.
26. Stuart, pp. 63–4; Thorold Dickinson, *A Discovery of Cinema* (London: Oxford UP, 1971) pp. 106–7.
27. Higham, *Hollywood at Sunset*, pp. 95–101; Stanley, pp. 164–5.
28. Higham, *Hollywood at Sunset*, pp. 101–3; Stanley, pp. 165–6.
29. Edgerton, *American Film Exhibition*, p. 27.
30. Dowdy, pp. 53–5; Freeman Lincoln, 'The Comeback of the Movies', in Balio, *The American Film Industry*, 1st edn, p. 372.
31. Lincoln, in Balio, *The American Film Industry*, 1st edn, p. 379.
32. Stuart, p. 37.
33. Ibid., p. 56; Sklar, p. 274.
34. McCarthy and Flynn, p. 42.
35. Stuart, pp. 32–9.
36. Austin pp. 63–70.
37. Pye and Myles, pp. 32–5; Dowdy, pp. 149–52; McCarthy and Flynn, pp. 35–6; Richard Staehling, 'From Rock Around the Clock to The Trip: the Truth about Teen Movies', in McCarthy and Flynn, pp. 220–36; Thomas Doherty, 'Teenagers and Teenpics, 1955–1957', in Austin, *Current Research in Film*, vol. 2, pp. 47–61; Kerr, 'My Name is Joseph H. Lewis', p. 58.
38. Dowdy, p. 157.
39. Jowett, *Film*, p. 476.
40. Pye and Myles, p. 35.
41. Gilbert Seldes, *The Great Audience* (New York: Viking Press, 1950) pp. 12, 23–4, 63.
42. Sklar, pp. 293–5; Guback, 'Hollywood's International Market', in Balio, *The American Film Industry*, rev. edn, p. 477.
43. Balio, *The American Film Industry*, rev. edn, p. 405.
44. Sklar, pp. 294–5.
45. Sklar, pp. 295–6.
46. Dowdy, p. 90.
47. Richard S. Randall, 'Censorship: From *The Miracle* to *Deep Throat*', in Balio, *The American Film Industry*, rev. edn, p. 517.
48. Douglas Ayer, Roy E. Bates and Peter J. Herman, 'Self-Censorship in the Movie Industry', in Kindem, p. 224.
49. Dowdy, pp. 115–6.
50. Handel, pp. 99–115 and *passim*; Jowett, *Film*, pp. 476–7.
51. Handel, p. 107.
52. Ibid., pp. 155–6.
53. Dowdy, p. 183; Freeman Lincoln, 'The Comeback of the Movies' in Balio, *The American Film Industry*, 1st edn, p. 382; Gomery, *The Hollywood Studio System*, p. 158.
54. Irving Bernstein, *Hollywood at the Crossroads* (Hollywood: Hollywood AFL Film Council, 1957) pp. 23–4.
55. Stanley, p. 141.

56. Donald Knox, *The Magic Factory* (London: Praeger, 1973) pp. xvi–xvii.

12 The New Order

1. Conant, in Balio, *The American Film Industry*, 1st edn, p. 354.
2. Balio, *United Artists*, pp. 233–9.
3. Steven Bach, *Final Cut* (London: Jonathan Cape, 1985) pp. 47–8.
4. Stanley, pp. 141–2.
5. MacCann, pp. 53–8; Ted Simonski, 'The "Billy Jack" Phenomenon', *Velvet Light Trap*, 13 (Fall 1974) pp. 36–9.
6. Sklar, p. 287.
7. Handel, p. 22.
8. Dowdy, p. 208.
9. Lee Beaupré, 'How to Distribute a Film', in Kerr (ed.), *The Hollywood Film Industry*, pp. 192–3.
10. McLaughlin, pp. 238–60; Dowdy, pp. 206–8.
11. Dowdy, p. 209.
12. Michael Pye, *Moguls* (London: Temple Smith, 1980) pp. 39–44.
13. MacCann, p. 53.
14. Bordwell, Staiger and Thompson, p. 332.
15. Pye, p. 45.
16. Barry King, 'Stardom as an Occupation', in Kerr, pp. 169–70.
17. Pye, pp. 51–65; James Naremore, *The Magic World of Orson Welles* (New York: Oxford UP, 1978) p. 176.
18. Handel, pp. 139–40.
19. Dowdy, p. 173.
20. MacCann, pp. 80–1.
21. Stuart, p. 59.
22. MacCann, pp. 82–3; Guback, in Balio, *The American Film Industry*, rev. edn, p. 478.
23. Bernstein, p. 69.
24. Richard Maltby, *Harmless Entertainment* (London: Scarecrow, 1983) p. 50; Guback, 'Hollywood's International Market' in Balio, *The American Film Industry*, rev. edn, pp. 478, 481; Bernstein, pp. 30–2.
25. Guback, 'Hollywood's International Market' in Balio, *The American Film Industry*, rev. edn, p. 478.
26. Ibid., p. 479.
27. Ibid., p. 485.
28. Thomas H. Guback, 'Film and Cultural Pluralism', *Cineaste* 5, 1 (Winter 1971–2) pp. 5–6.
29. Guback, in Balio, *The American Film Industry*, rev. edn, p. 482.
30. Barry R. Litman, 'Decision-Making in the Film Industry: the Influence of the TV Market', *Journal of Communication*, 32, 3 (Summer 1982) p. 33.
31. The following section was first published as John Izod, 'Walt Disney Innovates the Television Showcase', *The AMES Journal*, 2 (1985) pp. 38–41.

32. Schickel, pp. 308–9.
33. Max E. Youngstein, 'Anyone for Guts and Intelligence?' *Journal of the Screen Producers Guild*, 7, 10 (Dec 1961) pp. 7–9.
34. Schickel, pp. 308–9; Conant, in Balio, p. 355.
35. Schickel, pp. 308–9.
36. Ibid., pp. 312–3.
37. Gary Edgerton and Cathy Pratt, 'The Influence of the Paramount Decision on Network Television in America', *Quarterly Review of Film Studies*, 8, 3 (Summer 1983) pp. 11–12.
38. Erik Barnouw, *A History of Broadcasting in the United States*, vol. 2 (New York: Oxford UP, 1968) pp. 291–2.
39. Schickel, pp. 313–4.
40. MacCann, pp. 13–15.
41. Schickel, p. 314.
42. Ibid., p. 20.
43. Balio, *The American Film Industry*, rev. edn, pp. 433–4.
44. MacCann, pp. 15–16; and Stuart, p. 71.
45. Stuart, p. 71.
46. Balio, *The American Film Industry*, rev. edn, pp. 434–5; Stanley, pp. 149–52.
47. Stuart, p. 75, citing *Sponsor*, 12, 37, (22 Feb 1958), and *Magazine of Wall Street*, 101, 634 (15 Feb 1958).
48. Conant, in Balio, *The American Film Industry*, 1st edn, pp. 368–9; and Beaupré, in Kerr, *The Hollywood Film Industry*, pp. 191–2.
49. Robert D. Lamson, cited by Edgerton, *American Film Exhibition*, p. 30.
50. Balio, *The American Film Industry*, 1st edn, pp. 324–5; and Conant, in Balio, ibid., pp. 363–4.
51. Maltby, *Harmless Entertainment*, p. 72.
52. Dowdy, pp. 217–20.
53. Balio, *The American Film Industry*, rev. edn, p. 435.
54. Ibid., pp. 435–6; Charles Champlin, 'Can TV Save the Films?' in McClure, pp. 370–1.
55. Champlin, in McClure, pp. 370–1.
56. Balio, *The American Film Industry*, rev. edn, p. 437.
57. Champlin, in McClure, p. 374.
58. Balio, *The American Film Industry*, rev. edn, p. 437.
59. Stanley, p. 247.
60. Champlin, in McClure, pp. 372–3.
61. Edgerton and Pratt, pp. 16–17; and Stanley, p. 247.
62. Bach, p. 287.
63. Pye, pp. 56–7.
64. Champlin, in McClure, p. 374.
65. Pye and Myles, p. 41.

13 Conglomerates and Diversification

1. John Baxter, *Hollywood in the Sixties* (London: Tantivy Press, 1972), pp. 8, 45; Sklar, p. 289; and Pye and Myles, pp. 45–6.
2. David Gordon, 'Why the Movie Majors are Major', in Balio, *The American Film Industry*, 1st edn, p. 464; Stanley, pp. 250–1.
3. Edgerton, *American Film Exhibition*, pp. 48–9, 69–70; David J. Londoner, 'The Changing Economics of Entertainment', in Balio, *The American Film Industry*, rev. edn, pp. 605–7.
4. See for example David Gordon, 'The Movie Majors', *Sight and Sound*, 48 (1979) p. 151.
5. A. H. Howe, 'A Banker Looks at the Picture Business – 1971', *Journal of the Producers Guild of America*, 13, 2 (Jun 1971) p. 5.
6. Londoner, in Balio, *The American Film Industry*, rev. edn, p. 607.
7. Howe, pp. 3–6.
8. Jowett, *Film*, p. 481; Edgerton, *American Film Exhibition*, p.71.
9. Balio, *The American Film Industry*, rev. edn, pp. 440–1.
10. Londoner, in Balio, *The American Film Industry*, rev. edn, p. 608.
11. Stanley, pp. 235–6.
12. Jerzy Toeplitz, *Hollywood and After* (London: George Allen & Unwin, 1974) pp. 26–7.
13. Axel Madsen, 'The Changing of the Guard', *Sight and Sound*, 39 (1970) pp. 63–5, 111.
14. Robert Gustafson, 'What's Happening to Our Pix Biz?' in Balio, *The American Film Industry*, rev. edn, pp. 575–6.
15. Bach, pp. 53–6, 410, 416.
16. Myron Meisel, 'Industry: Seventh Annual Grosses Gloss', *Film Comment*, 18, 2 (Mar–Apr 1982) p. 60; Harlan Jacobson, 'Hollywood Lays an Egg', *Film Comment* 18, 3 (May–June 1982) p. 49; Wasko, pp. 157–8, 161–2.
17. Leonard Quart and Albert Auster, *American Film and Society since 1945* (London: Macmillan, 1984) p. 129.
18. Gustafson, in Balio, *The American Film Industry*, rev. edn, p. 570.
19. Ibid., pp. 578–80; James Monaco, 'Who Owns the Media?' *Take One*, 6, 12 (Nov 1978) p. 59; Armand Mattelart, *Multinational Companies and the Control of Culture* (Brighton: Harvester Press, 1979) pp. 196–8; Stanley, pp. 262–3.
20. Douglas Gomery, 'Corporate Control and Ownership in the Contemporary US Film Industry', *Screen*, 25, 4–5 (Jul–Oct 1984) pp. 61–2.
21. Robert Hutchison, *Cable, DBS and the Arts* (London: Policy Studies Institute, 1984) pp. 55–6; Andrew Laskos, 'The Hollywood Majors', in David Pirie (ed.), *Anatomy of the Movies* (London: Windward, 1981) pp. 18–25; Mike Bygrave, 'Hollywood 1985', *Sight and Sound*, 54 (1985) p. 87.
22. Monaco, 'Who Owns the Media?' pp. 58–9, and *American Film Now* (New York: Oxford UP, 1979) p. 35.
23. Gordon, 'The Movie Majors', pp. 152–3; Hy Hollinger, 'Production Control Changes Marked 1981', *Variety*, 13 Jan 1982, p. 50.

24. For information about conglomerate media holdings see Benjamin M. Compaine *et al.*, *Who Owns the Media?*, 2nd edn, (London: Knowledge Industry Publications, 1982).
25. Timothy Hollins, *Beyond Broadcasting* (London: British Film Institute, 1984) p. 181; Hutchison, pp. 22–3; Austin, vol. 2, p. 99; Alan Stanbrook, 'The Wall Street Shuffle', *Stills*, 9 (Nov–Dec 1983) p. 45.
26. Douglas Gomery, 'Vertical Integration, Horizontal Regulation: the Growth of Rubert Murdoch's US Media Empire', *Screen*, 27, 3–4 (May–Aug 1986) pp. 78–86.
27. Jacobson, p. 52; Armand Mattelart, Xavier Delcourt and Michèle Mattelart, *International Image Markets* (London: Comedia, 1984) p. 78.
28. *Variety*, 16 Jan 1985, p. 7.
29. Laskos, in Pirie, pp. 12–13.
30. A. D. Murphy, cited by David Docherty, David Morrison and Michael Tracey, 'Who Goes to the Cinema?' *Sight and Sound*, 55 (1986) p. 82.
31. Jowett, *Film*, p. 482; *Variety*, 9 Jan 1985, pp. 5, 24.
32. Gordon, 'The Movie Majors', pp. 152–3, and in Balio, *The American Film Industry*, 1st edn, pp. 463–4.
33. Mike Bygrave, 'Ned Tanen Talks About the Cost Squeeze on the Major Studios', *Guardian*, 7 Apr 1983, p. 11.
34. Docherty, Morrison and Tracey, p. 83.
35. Litman, 'Decision-Making in the Film Industry', pp. 44–5.
36. Docherty, Morrison and Tracey, pp. 83–4.
37. Bygrave, 'Hollywood 1985', p. 86.
38. Litman, 'Decision-Making in the Film Industry', pp. 44–5.
39. Olen J. Earnest '*Star Wars*: a Case Study of Motion Picture Marketing', in Austin, vol. 1, p. 9.
40. Frank Yablans, cited by Pye and Myles, p. 90.
41. See for instance Seth Cagin and Philip Dray, *Hollywood Films of the Seventies* (New York: Harper & Row, 1984) pp. xiv, 254–5.
42. Bruce Cook, 'Producers and Publishers', *American Film*, 3, 6 (Apr 1978) pp. 22–3.
43. Garth Jowett and James M. Linton, *Movies as Mass Communication* (London: Sage, 1980) pp. 58–60; B. J. Franklin, 'Promotion and Release', in Pirie, p. 97; Monaco, *American Film Now*, pp. 24–7.
44. Gustafson, in Balio, *The American Film Industry*, rev. edn, pp. 582–3; and Guback, 'Theatrical Film', in Compaine, pp. 221–3.
45. Earnest, in Austin, vol. 1 p. 17.
46. Les Keyser, *Hollywood in the Seventies* (London: Tantivy, 1981) p. 27.
47. Litman, 'Decision-Making in the Film Industry', pp. 34–6.
48. Balio, *The American Film Industry*, rev. edn, p. 438; Laskos, in Pirie, p. 16.
49. Monaco, *American Film Now*, pp. 21–2.
50. Pye, pp. 235–6.
51. Jowett and Linton, p. 121.
52. Steve Hanson and Patricia King Hanson, 'Picture Discs', *Stills*, 26 (Apr 1986) pp. 28–30.
53. Richard Combs, '*The Care Bears Movie*', *Monthly Film Bulletin*, 52 (1985) p. 244.

54. Alan Stanbrook, 'Hollywood's Crashing Epics', *Sight and Sound*, 50 (1981), pp. 84–5; David Thompson, 'The Missing Auteur', *Film Comment*, 18, 4 (Jul–Aug 1982) pp. 34–9; David Thomson, 'The Real Crisis in American Films', *American Film*, 6, 8 (Jun 1982) pp. 41–5.
55. Randall, in Balio, *The American Film Industry*, rev. edn, pp. 525, 529–34.
56. Ibid., pp. 526–7.
57. Bruce A. Austin, Mark J. Nicolich and Thomas Simonet, 'MPAA Ratings and the Box Office', *Film Quarterly*, 35, 2 (Winter 1981–2) pp. 28–30.
58. Sklar, pp. 297–300.
59. Jowett, *Film*, p. 452.
60. Monaco, *American Film Now*, pp. 190–3, 208–13.
61. Ibid., pp. 63–4.
62. David Talbot and Barbara Zheutlin, *Creative Differences* (Boston: South End Press, 1978) pp. viii–x, 160–1.
63. *Variety*, 29 May 1985, p. 1.
64. Gary Edgerton, 'The Film Bureau Phenomenon in America', in Austin, vol. 2, pp. 204–24.
65. For a recent example see William Fisher, 'Germany: A Never Ending Story', *Sight and Sound*, 54 (1985) pp. 174–9.
66. Michael Conant, 'The Paramount Decrees Reconsidered', in Balio, *The American Film Industry*, rev. edn, pp. 569–72; Guback, 'Theatrical Film', p. 225; and Edgerton, *American Film Exhibition*, p. 82.
67. Litman, 'The Economics of the Television Market for Theatrical Movies', in Kindem, *The American Movie Industry*, p. 317.
68. Janet Maslin, 'Splitting Jaws with the Happy Booker', *Film Comment*, 11, 4 (Jul–Aug 1975) p. 57; Guback 'Theatrical Film', p. 225; Edgerton, *American Film Exhibition*, pp. 109–11; Beaupré, in Kerr, *The Hollywood Film Industry*, p. 198.
69. Edgerton, *American Film Exhibition*, p. 80.
70. Keyser, p. 18; David Lees and Stan Berkowitz, *The Movie Business* (New York: Random House, 1981) pp. 131–41.
71. Edgerton, *American Film Exhibition*, p. 93.
72. Conant, in Balio, *The American Film Industry*, rev. edn, p. 569; Maslin, p. 57; Guback, 'Theatrical Film', p. 225.
73. Franklin, in Pirie, p. 95; Manjunath Pendakur, 'Canadian Films in the Chicago Theatrical Market, 1978–1981', in Austin, vol. 2, p. 201.
74. Edgerton, *American Film Exhibition*, p. 85, and (citing Phillip Lowe) p. 136.
75. Conant, in Balio, *The American Film Industry*, rev. edn, pp. 561–8.
76. Edgerton, *American Film Exhibition*, pp. 28, 50; Londoner, in Balio, *The American Film Industry*, rev. edn, p. 617; *Screen International*, 3–10 Aug 1985, p. 1.
77. Jowett and Linton, p. 43; and Edgerton, *American Film Exhibition*, pp. 94–5.
78. Edgerton, *American Film Exhibition*, p. 50; Austin, vol. 1, p. 64.
79. Edgerton, *American Film Exhibition*, pp. 50–1.
80. Ibid., pp. 55, 79–80; *Screen International*, 3–10 Aug 1985, p. 1.

81. Pye and Myles, p. 41; and Edgerton, *American Film Exhibition*, pp. 35–6.
82. Edgerton, *American Film Exhibition*, pp. 35–9; Conant, in Balio, *The American Film Industry*, rev. edn, p. 562.
83. Jowett, *Film*, p. 431.
84. Drew Eberson, cited by Edgerton, *American Film Exhibition*, p. 140.
85. Edgerton, *American Film Exhibition*, pp. 141–2.

Bibliography

Books

Austin, Bruce A. (ed.), *Current Research in Film*, vols 1–2 (Norwood, NJ: Ablex Publishing, 1985–6).

Bach, Steven, *Final Cut* (London: Jonathan Cape, 1985).

Balio, Tino (ed.), *The American Film Industry*, 1st edn (London: University of Wisconsin Press, 1976); rev. edn, 1985.

——, *United Artists* (London: University of Wisconsin Press, 1976).

Barnouw, Erik, *The Golden Web* (New York: Oxford UP, 1968).

Basten, Fred E., *Glorious Technicolor* (London: Thomas Yoseloff, 1979).

Baxter, John, *Hollywood in the Sixties* (London: Tantivy Press, 1972).

——, *Hollywood in the Thirties* (London: Tantivy Press, 1968).

Bergman, Andrew, *We're in the Money* (New York UP, 1971).

Bernstein, Irving, *Hollywood at the Crossroads* (Hollywood: Hollywood AFL Film Council, 1957).

Bordwell, David, Staiger, Janet, and Thompson, Kristin, *The Classical Hollywood Cinema* (London: Routledge & Kegan Paul, 1985).

Brownlow, Kevin and Kobal, John, *Hollywood: The Pioneers* (London: Collins, 1979).

Cagin, Seth, and Dray, Philip, *Hollywood Film of the Seventies* (New York: Harper & Row, 1984).

Ceplair, Larry, and Englund, Steven, *The Inquisition in Hollywood* (London: University of California Press, 1983).

Compaine, Benjamin M., Sterling, Christopher H., Guback, Thomas, and Noble, J. Kendrick, Jr., *Who Owns the Media?*, 2nd edn (London: Knowledge Industry Publications, 1982).

Conant, Michael, *Antitrust in the Motion Picture Industry* (Berkeley: University of California Press, 1960).

Cripps, Thomas, *Slow Fade to Black* (London: Oxford UP, 1977).

Davies, Philip, and Neve, Brian (eds), *Cinema, Politics and Society in America* (Manchester UP, 1981).

de Lauretis, Teresa and Heath, Stephen (eds), *The Cinematic Apparatus* (London: Macmillan, 1980).

Dowdy, Andrew, *Films of the Fifties* (New York: William Morrow & Co., 1975).

Edgerton, Gary R., *American Film Exhibition and an Analysis of the Motion Picture Industry's Market Structure, 1963–1980* (London: Garland Publishing, 1983).

Fell, John L., *Film and the Narrative Tradition* (Norman: University of Oklahoma Press, 1974).

—— (ed.), *Film Before Griffith* (London: University of California Press, 1983).

Geduld, Harry M., *The Birth of the Talkies* (London: Indiana UP, 1975).

Gomery, J. Douglas, *The Hollywood Studio System* (London: British Film Institute/Macmillan, 1986).

Gow, Gordon, *Hollywood in the Fifties* (London: A. Zwemmer, 1971).

Guback, Thomas H., *The International Film Industry* (Bloomington: Indiana UP, 1969).

Hall, Ben M., *The Golden Age of the Movie Palace* (New York: Clarkson N. Potter, n.d.). First published as *The Best Remaining Seats* (New York: Clarkson N. Potter, 1961).

Hampton, Benjamin B., *History of the American Film Industry* (1931) 2nd edn (New York: Dover, 1970).

Handel, Leo A., *Hollywood Looks at its Audience* (1950) (New York: Arno Press, 1976).

Higham, Charles, *Hollywood at Sunset* (New York: Saturday Review Press, 1972).

——, *Warner Brothers* (New York: Charles Scribner's Sons, 1975).

—— and Greenberg, Joel, *Hollywood in the Forties* (London: Tantivy Press, 1968).

Huettig, Mae D., *Economic Control of the Motion Picture Industry* (Philadelphia: University of Pennsylvania Press, 1944).

Hunnings, Neville March, *Film Censors and the Law* (London: George Allen & Unwin, 1967).

Hurst, Richard Maurice, *Republic Studios* (London: Scarecrow Press, 1979).

Hutchison, Robert, *Cable, DBS and the Arts* (London: Policy Studies Institute, 1984).

Jacobs, Lewis, *The Rise of the American Film* (1939) (New York: Teachers College Press, 1975).

Jenkins, Reese V., *Images and Enterprise* (London: Johns Hopkins UP, 1975).

Jowett, Garth, *Film: The Democratic Art* (Boston: Little, Brown & Co., 1976).

—— and Linton, James M., *Movies as Mass Communication* (London: Sage Publications, 1980).

Kerr, Paul (ed.), *The Hollywood Film Industry* (London: Routledge & Kegan Paul/British Film Institute, 1986).

Keyser, Les, *Hollywood in the Seventies* (London: Tantivy Press, 1981).

Kindem, Gorham (ed.), *The American Movie Industry* (Carbondale: Southern Illinois UP, 1982).

Klingender, F. D., and Legg, Stuart, *The Money Behind the Screen* (London: Lawrence & Wishart, 1937).

Lees, David, and Berkowitz, Stan, *The Movie Business* (New York: Random House, 1981).

Lewis, Howard Thompson, *The Motion Picture Industry* (New York: Van Nostrand, 1933), (Jerome S. Ozer, 1971).

Lyons, Timothy James, *The Silent Partner* (New York: Arno Press, 1974).

MacCann, Richard Dyer, *Hollywood in Transition*, 2nd edn (Westport, Conn.: Greenwood Press, 1977).

McCarthy, Todd, and Flynn, Charles (eds), *Kings of the Bs* (New York: E. P. Dutton, 1975).

McClure, Arthur (ed.), *The Movies: An American Idiom* (Rutherford: Fairleigh Dickinson UP, 1971).

McLaughlin, Robert, *Broadway and Hollywood* (New York: Arno Press, 1974).

Maltby, Richard, *Harmless Entertainment* (London: Scarecrow, 1983).

Mattelart, Armand, *Multinational Corporations and the Control of Culture* (Brighton: Harvester Press, 1979).

——, Delcourt, Xavier, and Mattelart, Michèle, *International Image Markets* (London: Comedia, 1984).

May, Lary, *Screening Out the Past* (New York: Oxford UP, 1980).

Moley, Raymond, *The Hays Office* (Indianapolis: Bobbs-Merrill, 1945).

Monaco, James, *American Film Now* (New York: Oxford UP, 1979).

Nichols, Bill, *Movies and Methods*, vol. 2 (London: University of California Press, 1985).

O'Connor, John E., and Jackson, Martin A., *American History/American Film* (New York: Frederick Ungar, 1979).

Pickard, Roy, *The Hollywood Studios* (London: Frederick Muller, 1978).

Pirie, David (ed.), *Anatomy of the Movies* (London: Windward, 1981).

Pye, Michael, *Moguls* (London: Temple Smith, 1980).

—— and Myles, Lynda, *The Movie Brats* (London: Faber & Faber, 1979).

Quart, Leonard, and Auster, Albert, *American Film and Society since 1945* (London: Macmillan, 1984).

Robinson, David, *Hollywood in the Twenties* (London: A. Zwemmer, 1968).

Roddick, Nick, *A New Deal in Entertainment* (London: British Film Institute, 1983).

Ross, Lillian, *Picture* (New York: Avon Books, 1969).

Ross, Murray, *Stars and Strikes* (1941) (New York: AMS Press, 1967).

Rosten, Leo C., *Hollywood* (1941) (New York: Arno Press/New York Times, 1970).

Schickel, Richard, *The Disney Version*, rev. edn (London: Michael Joseph, 1986).

Seabury, William Marston, *The Public and the Motion Picture Industry* (New York: Macmillan, 1926).

Shales, Tom (ed.), *The American Film Heritage* (Washington: Acropolis Books, 1973).

Shepherd, John, *Tin Pan Alley* (London: Routledge & Kegan Paul, 1982).

Shindler, Colin, *Hollywood Goes to War* (London: Routledge & Kegan Paul, 1979).

Sklar, Robert, *Movie-Made America* (London: Chappell & Co., 1978).

Slide, Anthony, *Aspects of American Film History prior to 1920* (Metuchen, NJ: Scarecrow Press, 1978).

——, *The Big V* (Metuchen, NJ; Scarecrow Press, 1976).

——, *Early American Cinema* (London: A. Zwemmer, 1970).

Stanley, Robert H., *The Celluloid Empire* (New York: Hastings House, 1978).

Stuart, Frederic, *The Effects of Television on the Motion Picture and Radio Industries* (New York: Arno Press, 1976).

Temporary National Economic Committee, *The Motion Picture Industry* (Washington: United States Government, 1941).

Thomas, Sari (ed.), *Film/Culture* (London: Scarecrow Press, 1982).
Thompson, Kristin, *Exporting Entertainment* (London: British Film Institute, 1985).
Toeplitz, Jerzy, *Hollywood and After* (London: George Allen & Unwin, 1974).
Walker, Alexander, *The Shattered Silents* (London: Elm Tree Books, 1978).
Wasko, Janet, *Movies and Money* (Norwood, NJ: Ablex Publishing, 1982).
Watkins, Gordon S. (ed.), *The Motion Picture Industry, The Annals of the American Academy of Political and Social Science*, vol. 254 (1947).

Articles

Allen, Jeanne Thomas, 'Copyright and Early Theater, Vaudeville and Film Competition', *Journal of the University Film Association*, 31, 2 (Spring 1979) pp. 5–11.
——, 'The Film Viewer as Consumer', *Quarterly Review of Film Studies*, 5, 4 (Fall 1980) pp. 481–99.
Anderson, Robert, 'The Role of the Western Film Genre in Industry Competition, 1907–1911', *Journal of the University Film Association*, 31, 2 (Spring 1979) pp. 19–27.
Austin, Bruce, Nicolich, Mark J., and Simonet, Thomas, 'MPAA Ratings and the Box Office', *Film Quarterly*, 35, 2 (Winter 1981–2) pp. 28–30.
Baxter, Peter, 'On the History and Ideology of Film Lighting', *Screen*, 16, 3 (Autumn 1975) pp. 83–106.
Buscombe, Edward, 'Bread and Circuses', in Patricia Mellencamp and Philip Rosen (eds), *Cinema Histories, Cinema Practices* (Los Angeles: American Film Institute, 1984).
——, 'Notes on Columbia Pictures Corporation, 1926–41', *Screen* 16, 3 (Autumn 1975) pp. 65–82.
Bygrave, Mike, 'Hollywood 1985', *Sight and Sound*, 54, 2 (1985) pp. 84–8.
Campbell, Russell, 'Warner Brothers in the Thirties', *Velvet Light Trap*, 1 (Jun 1971) pp. 2–4.
Cassady, Ralph, 'Impact of the Paramount Decision on Motion Picture Distribution and Price Making', *Southern California Law Review*, 31 (1958) pp. 150–80.
——, 'Monopoly in Motion Picture Production and Distribution: 1908–1915', *Southern California Law Review*, 32 (Summer 1959) pp. 325–90.
Docherty, David, Morrison, David, and Tracey, Michael, 'Who Goes to the Cinema?' *Sight and Sound*, 55 (1986) pp. 81–5.
Eckert, Charles, 'The Carole Lombard in Macy's Window', *Quarterly Review of Film Studies*, 3, 1 (Winter 1978) pp. 1–21.
Edgerton, Gary, and Pratt, Cathy, 'The Influence of the Paramount Decision on Network Television in America', *Quarterly Review of Film Studies*, 8, 3 (Summer 1983) pp. 8–23.
Gomery, J. Douglas, 'Corporate Ownership and Control in the Contemporary US Film Industry', *Screen*, 25, 4–5 (Jul–Oct 1984) pp. 60–9.

——, 'Failure and Success: Vocafilm and RCA Photophone Innovate Sound', *Film Reader*, 2 (1977) pp. 213–21.

——, 'Film and Business History', *Journal of Contemporary History*, 19, 1 (Jan 1984) pp. 89–103.

——, 'Hollywood, the National Recovery Administration, and the Question of Monopoly Power', *Journal of the University Film Association*, 31, 2 (Spring 1979) pp. 47–52.

——, 'The Picture Palace: Economic Sense or Hollywood Nonsense?', *Quarterly Review of Film Studies*, 3, 1 (Winter 1978) pp. 23–36.

——, 'The Popularity of Filmgoing in the US, 1930–1950', in Colin MacCabe (ed.), *High Theory/Low Culture* (Manchester UP, 1986) pp. 71–9.

——, 'Problems in Film History: How Fox Innovated Sound', *Quarterly Review of Film Studies*, 1, 3 (Aug 1976) pp. 315–30.

——, 'Rethinking US Film History: the Depression Decade and Monopoly Control', *Film and History*, 10, 2 (May 1980) pp. 32–8.

——, 'Vertical Integration, Horizontal Regulation: the Growth of Rupert Murdoch's US Media Empire', *Screen*, 27, 3–4 (May–Aug 1986) pp. 78–86.

——, 'Writing the History of the American Film Industry: Warner Brothers and Sound', *Screen*, 17, 1 (Spring, 1976) pp. 40–53.

—— and Staiger, Janet, 'The History of World Cinema: Models for Economic Analysis', *Film Reader*, 4 (1979) pp. 35–44.

Gordon, David, 'The Movie Majors', *Sight and Sound*, 48 (1979) pp. 151–3.

Grinde, Nick, 'Pictures for Peanuts', *The Penguin Film Review*, 1 (1946) pp. 40–51.

Guback, Thomas H., 'Film and Cultural Pluralism', *Cineaste* 5, 1 (Winter 1971–2) pp. 1–7.

Gunning, Tom, 'Weaving a Narrative: Style and Economic Background in Griffith's Biograph Films', *Quarterly Review of Film Studies*, 6, 1 (Winter 1981) pp. 11–25.

Hanson, Steve, and Hanson, Patricia King, 'Turn-of-the-Century Fox', *Stills*, 24 (Feb 1986) pp. 64–7.

Herzog, Charlotte, 'The Archaeology of Cinema Architecture', *Quarterly Review of Film Studies*, 9, 1 (Winter 1984) pp. 11–32.

——, 'Movie Palaces and Exhibition', *Film Reader*, 2 (1977) pp. 185–97.

Howe, A. H., 'A Banker Looks at the Picture Business', *Journal of the Screen Producers' Guild*, 7, 4 (Dec 1965) pp. 9–16. (Reprinted in *JSPG*, 11, 1 (Mar 1969) pp. 15–22.)

——, 'A Banker Looks at the Picture Business – 1971', *Journal of the Producers Guild of America*, 13, 2 (Jun 1971) pp. 3–10.

——, 'Hollywood at the Crossroads', *Journal of the Producers Guild of America*, 12, 1 (Mar 1970) pp. 13–14.

Izod, John, 'Walt Disney Innovates the Television Showcase', *The AMES Journal*, 2 (1985) pp. 38–41.

Jacobson, Harlan, 'Hollywood Lays an Egg', *Film Comment*, 18, 3 (May–Jun 1982) pp. 49–52.

Kerr, Paul, 'My Name if Joseph H. Lewis', *Screen*, 24, 4–5 (Jul–Oct 1983) pp. 48–66.

——, 'Out of What Past? Notes on the B Film Noir', *Screen Education*, 32–3 (Autumn–Winter 1979–80) pp. 45–65.

Litman, Barry R., 'Decision-Making in the Film Industry: the Influence of the TV Market', *Journal of Communication*, 32, 3 (Summer 1982) pp. 33–52.

Maslin, Janet, 'Splitting Jaws with a Happy Booker: a Talk with a Circuit Buyer', *Film Comment*, 11, 4 (Jul–Aug 1975) pp. 57–62.

Monaco, James, 'Who Owns the Media?' *Take One*, 6, 12 (Nov 1978) pp. 24–8, 58–9.

Sanders, Terry B., 'The Financing of Independent Feature Films', *Quarterly of Film, Radio and Television*, 9 (1954–5) pp. 380–9.

Siminoski, Ted, 'The "Billy Jack" Phenomenon', *Velvet Light Trap*, 13 (Fall 1974) pp. 36–9.

Staiger, Janet, 'Individualism versus Collectivism', *Screen*, 24, 4–5 (Jul–Oct 1983) pp. 68–79.

——, '"Tame" Authors and the Corporate Laboratory: Stories, Writers, and Scenarios in Hollywood', *Quarterly Review of Film Studies*, 8, 4 (Fall 1983) pp. 33–45.

Stanbrook, Alan, 'Hollywood's Crashing Epics', *Sight and Sound*, 50 (1981) pp. 84–5.

——, 'The Wall Street Shuffle', *Stills*, 9 (Nov–Dec 1983) pp. 44–6.

Strick, John C., 'The Economics of the Motion Picture Industry: a Survey', *Philosophy of the Social Sciences*, 8, 4 (Dec 1978) pp. 406–17.

Index of Films and Programmes

Index of Names and Subjects

229